Haight-Ashbury
1965-1967

William Schnabel

Copyright © 2016, 17 January 2020 William Schnabel

This book was previously published under the title:
Summer of Love and Haight. 50th Anniversary of the Summer of Love
without the chapter on poster art, or the preface.
Different parts of the original text have been modified.

All rights reserved. No part of this book may be reproduced in any form or by any electronic or mechanical means without permission in writing from the publisher, except in the case of brief passages in reviews and critical articles.

Library of Congress Cataloging–in–Publication Data
Schnabel, William.
Haight-Ashbury 1965-1967
Includes preface, index and bibliography
1. Haight-Ashbury–History–Twentieth century. 2. Summer of Love–San Francisco–1967. 3. Counterculture–History–Sociology–USA. 4. Rock music–San Francisco. 6. Be-In–History–San Francisco. 7. Underground press–San Francisco. 8. Lysergic acid diethylamide–History. 9. Rock posters–History–San Francisco.

ISBN-13: 979-8600328990

Book and cover design by Le Diable Ermite
Composition by Le Diable Ermite

Published in France by:
Le Diable Ermite
16 La Petite Rue
55140 Brixey-aux-Chanoines

https://le-diable-ermite.blog4ever.xyz/

For Fabienne

Table of Contents

Preface 7
San Francisco and the Haight-Ashbury 17
The Love Pageant Rally..23
The Human Be-In 33
The Houseboat Summit 51
The Invisible Circus..77
The Monterey Pop Festival...89
The Diggers...123
The Communication Company 147
The San Francisco Oracle 163
The San Francisco Music Scene 205
Lysergic Acid Diethylamide 261
Poster Art 301
Conclusion 335
Bibliography 343
Index 349

Preface

When I began working on this text in 1966, the year of the monkey, I knew I needed to discuss San Francisco poster art because of its impact on the counterculture. It was not possible to devote an entire chapter to the subject at the time, so I've added that chapter to this edition, making this analysis of the Haight-Ashbury more complete, since poster art was an integral part of the music scene. Only the principal artists that produced posters from 1965 to 1967 were discussed because of the narrow time span. It goes without saying that there were many fine artists producing posters after the summer of 1967, such as those mentioned in *The Art of the Fillmore* by Gayle Lemke and *The Art of Rock* by Paul Grushkin. Those wishing to explore the medium further will find valuable information in those works on such artists as Lee Conklin, Greg Irons, Randy Tuten, David Byrd, David Singer, Norman Orr, Robert Fried, Doyle Phillips, Bob Schnepf, Chris Johnson and many others.

Many have wondered why the Summer of Love drew so much attention and why it has been transformed into a modern myth. There are several reasons for that, and one involves the commercialization of a marketable product. The expression itself came about on 5 April 1967, when the Council for the Summer of Love was announced during a press conference. The words *summer* and *love* evoke strong feelings and imagery in our collective unconscious. Summer is a time of freedom, when the days are longer and warmer. It is often a time of joy when we go to the seaside to soak up the sun's life-giving rays. It is a time of popsicles, watermelons, strawberries and flowers, a happy time when people are on vacation and can relax because they don't have to work or go to school, though Eddie Cochran contradicts that premise in his classic tune "Summertime Blues."

Psychologist Abraham Maslow established a hierarchy of basic human needs: physical survival, safety, self-esteem, self-fulfillment, and *love*. Everyone needs love, but human beings often have a problem expressing this emotion, maybe out of fear of appearing vulnerable. Love is about feeling compassion and empathy when others need help. It is about caring, being generous, kind, forgiving, and understanding. The Bible has a lot to say about love because it comes from God: "Whoever does not love does not know God, because God is love" (I John 4: 8); and "There is no fear in love. But perfect love drives out fear, because fear has to do with punishment. The one who fears is not made perfect in love" (I John 4: 18). There are numerous passages of this kind in the Bible.

Love in Buddhism is a different matter. It is antithetical to attachment and holding on. Buddhism describes love as kindness to all, compassion for oneself and others, and assisting those in need. It is also associated with the joy of living and being able to appreciate the short time we have in this world where nothing is permanent. It is also associated with a feeling of quietude or inner tranquility. Love, then, is a kind of liberation that cannot be selfish. In this sense it is the antipode of the way love is often portrayed by Hollywood.

"Peace and love" was a popular slogan of the flower children. Some believed in it, for others it was a cliché. All you need is love, said some. Maybe, but genuine love was rare in 1967, and it's just as rare or probably rarer today. Most would agree that there is a lack of compassion and empathy in our world; not that greed and selfishness are anything new, for they've been around at least as long as *Homo sapiens* has walked the face of the earth.

The disastrous situation of the world today dramatically underscores our lack of love, not only for the environment, but for other cultures and our own. Respect is an aspect of love, too. Our long list of environmental catastrophes not only demonstrates a lack of responsibility, but also a lack of respect and love. The European colonization of the Americas, when indigenous peoples were enslaved and slaughtered, is a frightening example. The numerous oil spills, use of Agent Orange in Vietnam, the environmental impact of nuclear energy, the Love Canal toxic waste site in Niagara Falls and the proliferation of plastic shopping bags are other examples. In the fifties and sixties some predicted catastrophic consequences if we continued to burn fossil fuels, but petroleum companies failed to listen. Everything is related in some way in this world, and resources are not infinite.

The San Francisco Diggers, who took their name from the English seventeenth century Diggers, had some utilitarian ideas about love. "When comes the time to leave this world someday, what you get to keep is what you gave away," they said. The Diggers were not capitalists because they believed everything should be free. That was a difficult idea for many to accept in the sixties and probably even more so today. But if you stop to think about money and what it does to us, you see that it determines the way we think and act, and that it is an obstacle in our relationships with other people. In a capitalist society, money and what money can buy become more important than our human relationships and even more important than people and the world we live in. "For the love of money is the root of all kinds of evil. By craving it, some have wandered away from the faith and pierced themselves with many sorrows," (I Timothy 6: 10). The text is meant to be self-explanatory. But you can expect some sophists to tell you that money is not the problem at all, that the real problem is greed. But a society based on materialism is a society based on greed, where everything is valued in terms of possession, and that includes human beings that can be bought and sold in a variety of ways. In such a society human worth is determined in terms of wealth and material possessions. Those that possess have value, those that do not have less value or none at all. A feeling of solidarity will not be prevalent in that sort of society, where competition may result in ruthless domination. But when we leave this world, we are forced to recognize the true value of material possessions. The point is that money perverts relationships, and thus it debases love. We need to imagine a world without money.

Before the Summer of Love, there was a feeling of community in the Haight-Ashbury because people knew their neighbors and felt concerned about them. There was no problem with being friendly and generous. It is easier to be friendly and generous when you trust your neighbors and, reciprocally, it is more difficult when anonymity prevails. It is also easier to rip someone off if you don't know who they are. That's what happened when thousands of people were pouring into the Haight-Ashbury. What were they looking for? What did they have to give? For some, it was more about taking and exploiting than about sharing, attitudes which run counter to love. But in a society based on profit, human feelings are at best ignored and at worst manipulated and perverted.

Mammon is worshipped by many, but what is our money really based on? President Nixon, whom the counterculture loved to call Tricky Dick, took the United States off the gold standard in 1971. Since then the country has functioned on a system of *fiat* money, in other words the American dollar is not tied to any precious metal or commodity. *Fiat*, from the Latin word *facere*, is the imperative mood of to make or become. In short, the paper money in your wallet is just paper; it only has "value" because we are told that it does.

The Summer of Love was about wanting to get away from all that, in other words a coercive society based primarily on material values. Young people had heard about the Haight-Ashbury and they fantasized about creating a new kind of society where the materialistic values of the establishment would be abandoned, where you could live for almost nothing, and where you could have a good time smoking dope and dropping acid, going to dance-concerts and where *love* was supposedly for free. For many, those were their motivations for going to San Francisco. They were getting away from something, too, but the going was even more important than the getting away.

Hate is the antithesis of love, and the extreme form of hate is war. The establishment knew a lot about that. By the end of 1967 there were nearly 500,000 American troops in Vietnam, and by 1968 there would be still more. The countercultural movement was, in many ways, a reaction against war and state sponsored violence. The establishment said, "Make war because it's a good thing. Uncle Sam says so." The counterculture disagreed and said, "Make love not war, because war is dangerous for living things." The draft existed in the sixties, so young men were faced with having to take a plane to the other side of the world to supposedly defend their country against the scourge of communism. "Boys, it is just like the Alamo. Somebody should have by God helped those Texans. I'm going to Vietnam," crowed President Johnson. He also said that "If we quit Vietnam tomorrow we'll be fighting in Hawaii and next week we'll have to be fighting in San Francisco." We know how that story ended. The counterculture in the Haight-Ashbury was adamantly opposed to the War in Vietnam, or any other war for that matter, which does not necessarily mean that people were ideologically "commies," though some were living a communal existence.

Consequently, going west to San Francisco, for many, was a rejection of the war, the material-industrial complex, and the whole apparatus built on maintaining the gigantic war machine. The total cost of the war in Vietnam was about $170 billion. The cost in human lives was great, too, with thousands of American soldiers and millions of Vietnamese killed for no good reason.

In May of 1967, "San Francisco (Be Sure to Wear [Some] Flowers in Your Hair)" was released. It was written by "Papa" John Phillips of the Mamas and Papas and sung by Scott McKenzie to promote the Monterey Pop Festival that began in June. The song reached number one on the charts in the United Kingdom and was near the top in the United States. When young people heard it they started packing their bags. It has been called the anthem of the counterculture, though certainly not for everyone. Strangely enough, it could not have been written or sung by a San Francisco band because it was too blatantly commercial.

For the mainstream media, psychedelia was a Godsend. It sold papers (when people still bought newspapers), record albums, White Levi's, bellbottom pants, paisley shirts, rolling papers, psychedelic posters, and a lot more. At that point you could see that the dream was frayed at the edges and that its days were numbered. But if you were fifteen or sixteen, you wanted to believe and you wanted to be part of the dream because it represented hope. It was all so magical, like a hopeful sign heralding a new dawn or millennium. Young people had already heard about the Human Be-In on 12 January 1967, and wanted to check out what was happening in California where the grass had to be greener.

There was a sense of adventure involved, too, and as Jack Kerouac has shown, just travelling across the country could be an adventure, and for many who took the trip, it was the first time.

But the rightwing press, including the San Francisco Chronicle, was resorting to fear-mongering to scare parents with headlines that screamed. It was as if war had been declared against the hippies. Hippie stories appeared on the front page of the Chronicle in May 1967 as a form of propaganda and disinformation. One front page story went so far as to suggest that the hippies of the Haight-Ashbury would evolve into some sort of "Gestapo," and psychiatrists were interviewed to prove that the hippies were crazy. In the same vein of political hysteria, the San Francisco Board of Supervisors, which decides city policies and adopts ordinances and resolutions, declared straight out that the hippies were unwelcome, and a Municipal Transit commissioner insisted that the city change two bus routes to avoid the neighborhood that he compared to Sodom and Gomorrah. Mayor John Shelley didn't particularly like the long-haired bohemians, but his police chief, Thomas J. Cahill, was virulent. "Hippies are no asset to the community. There has been enough glamorization given to hippies. These people do not have the courage to face the reality of life. [...] Nobody should let their young children take part in this hippie thing," he warned. When the young people began arriving, Cahill lost no time in calling governor Reagan in Sacramento, the California National Guard and the California Highway Patrol to have them march through the city rounding up youths, as if they were the Vietcong in disguise. Unfortunately for the Police Chief, Mayor Shelley had to make the request, and he was not willing to transform San Francisco into a police state. Thomas Cahill was a special sort of guy. He was greatly admired by J. Edgar Hoover who had established special files on the underground, and Cahill was the only police chief to serve on President Johnson's Commission on Law Enforcement. Cahill was even considered as a logical candidate for the post of FBI director because he and Hoover hated the same things. For these officials and others in the government, the Summer of Love was described as a subversive invasion that needed to be firmly dealt with to defend traditional American values. That didn't stop tourists from driving through the neighborhood and creating tremendous traffic jams just to get a glimpse of the exotic species with long hair.

Paradoxically, those who went to the Haight-Ashbury in the summer of 1967 missed the *real* Summer of Love, because it had taken place the previous year. But that one was not announced to the media or City Hall.

1

San Francisco and the Haight-Ashbury

It all started millions of years ago. The San Francisco Bay, as we know it today, has not always existed. Some 125,000 years ago, the city itself was merely an island, separated on the west by the Colma Strait and on the east by the waters of the Bay. Millions of years ago, geologists say somewhere between one hundred and two hundred, the rocks underlying the Presidio were formed as the result of tectonic plate movement, one gigantic plate grating and grinding beneath the other. These "plates" are great sheets of rock that cover the surface of our planet. The mountains of the Coastal Ranges, including the Santa Cruz Mountains and the Diablo Range, were thrust upward some four million years ago–a geological wink of an eye–when the plates changed direction. The city of San Francisco is caught between two tectonic plates: the North American and the Pacific Plates. Long before anatomically modern man existed–some 600,000 years ago–mother earth had strong and regular contractions, labor pains brought about by movement of the San Andreas Fault System. Thus it was that she gave birth to the San Francisco Bay that we know and love today.

Thousands of years before the Spanish began colonizing the Pacific Coast in 1769, the land was inhabited by the Native Americans, the Ohlone people, also referred to as the Costanoan. They were sharply attuned to nature and lived in harmony with their sacred environment. This humble people lived off the land, something that not all colonizers were capable of doing. This fundamental principle of survival would later be revered by the Flower Children of the Haight-Ashbury, though few of them would take a leaf out of the Ohlone's book.

Ohlone culture was rich and varied, with hundreds of thousands of natives living in dozens of tribes inhabiting the central and northern coast of California. These tribes lived together peacefully and in harmony for thousands of years–a remarkable accomplishment for the human race. They practiced hunting, fishing, gathering and also harvesting. But contact with the Spanish sounded the death knell for their intelligent and peaceful culture. In *A Cross of Thorns: The Enslavement of California's Indians by the Spanish Missions*, Elias Castillo compares the compounds into which the Ohlone were herded to "death camps," and asserts that probably more than 62,000 Native Americans died in California's Spanish missions. Colonization, proselytization and the expropriation of native lands laid waste to their traditions and decimated the Ohlone people, who would be all but extinct by 1880.

In 1822, the Mexican government took control of California, but as trade flourished in the form of whaling and seafaring traders and merchants, Americans immigrated in ever growing numbers to the prosperous and Edenic region. Then farmers emigrated from the East to California, eager to till the fertile soil and claim it as their own. Assuredly, the land possessed mythical, God given gifts, like those depicted in *Las Sergas de Esplandián* (*The Adventures of Esplandián*) by Garci Rodríguez de Montalvo, from which the region got its name.

Soon, American settlements flourished along the coast in Los Angeles, Santa Barbara and Monterey, with the desire of annexation treading on the heels of development and capital investment. President Polk, an expansionist who dreamed of establishing a continental United States during his presidency, soon committed his administration to acquiring the vast regions of California and the Southwest by whatever means necessary. War was soon declared on May 13, 1846, and fighting stopped when General Winfield Scott's army captured the gates of Mexico City on September 13, 1847. The Treaty of Guadalupe Hidalgo was signed on March 10, 1848.

Shortly before that, on January 24, 1848, a serendipitous discovery would radically change the West—gold was discovered in Coloma by James W. Marshall. Almost immediately word was out, and tens of thousands of prospectors were pouring into the region from all over the world; California's population soared to more than the

60,000 residents required to petition for statehood. As part of the Compromise of 1850, California was admitted to the union as a free state on September 9, 1850, though it sent one pro-slavery and one anti-slavery senator to Congress.

The completion of the transcontinental railroad in 1869 greatly accelerated growth and development. Between 1880 and 1890, San Francisco's population increased from 234,000 to 299,000. California's population continued to grow as well, increasing from 380,000 in 1860 to roughly 3.5 million in 1920. In the 1960s, the population of San Francisco was about 740,000 and declining, due to the continuing exodus of white, middle-class Americans to the suburbs.

The Haight-Ashbury district, which is today internationally known, gets its name from two influential men of the city: Henry Huntly Haight (1825-1878) and Munroe Ashbury (1817-1880). Henry Haight, a pioneer and exchange banker, managed the Banking House of Page, Bacon & Company, which he used to make a fortune during the 1849 gold rush. He was also governor of the state from 1867 to 1871. Munroe Ashbury was a member of the Board of Supervisors and the first Park Commission. Both men played a role in organizing the neighborhood and creating Golden Gate Park. In the nineteenth century, most major cities in Europe and the United States developed public parks for leisure activities, and San Francisco was not to be outdone by New York's Central Park.

Few today would have recognized the Haight-Ashbury at the end of the century, because before the construction of a cable car line in 1883, linking it with the bustling downtown area, the district was a conglomerate of dunes, farms and "ranches." Plots of land up to ten acres were fenced off to raise livestock and fowl to feed the city. There was an amusement park called the Chutes on Haight Street, squeezed in between Clayton and Cole and the Haight Street Grounds. The "Grounds," bordered by Stanyan, Waller, Cole and Frederic Streets, served as an early baseball park, or sand lot, where California League teams such as the Pioneers, Knickerbockers, Colonels, Senators or Athletics squared off before thousands of enthusiastic spectators. Their uniforms were certainly as unique as the equipment they used.

Later, beginning in the 1890s and continuing into the early twentieth century, the Haight-Ashbury was leveled off and transformed into a residential district for reasonably wealthy homeowners. Then, suddenly, on Wednesday, April 18, 1906, at 5:12 a.m., all hell broke loose when a tremendous earthquake shook northern California. It would be documented as one of the greatest natural disasters the country has ever known. Three thousand people died and fires raged for days, destroying more than eighty percent of the city. Thousands of San Franciscans lost their homes and had nowhere to go. Yet the Haight-Ashbury neighborhood was saved from the disaster because of its distance from the downtown, commercial area of the city.

Like the rest of the nation, the district suffered from overcrowding during the Great Depression of the thirties and during World War II. Many of the large Victorian houses were split up into apartments in response to the national housing shortage. The Haight-Ashbury was a declining neighborhood in the fifties, with numerous vacant or dilapidated buildings. When the GIs returned home after the war, San Francisco, like other urban areas across the United States, fell victim to the growing flight to the suburbs. The Servicemen's Readjustment Act, better known as the GI Bill of Rights, allowed sixteen million servicemen to borrow money at low interest rates to start a business or buy a home. Many preferred to raise their families in the suburbs where there was more space and less crime, noise and pollution.

In the sixties, property values declined considerably, due in part to the proposed construction of a freeway through the Panhandle. Fortunately, staunch community activism prevented the freeway from being approved and saved the district and City Hall from a gargantuan political blunder. In the wake of rising property values in North Beach, many students sought cheap rooms or apartments in the Haight where it was easy to get to San Francisco State or the University of San Francisco. Michael Fallon, journalist for the *San Francisco Examiner*, confirmed this in "A New Paradise for Beatniks."

Soon the neighborhood was titivating itself by renovating the Victorian houses. To raise their rent money, some residents organized parties or sold marijuana, a staple of the hippie diet. After the Beatles and the British music invasion, culture accelerated, and the Haight-Ashbury became a hip, carefree community.

2

The Love Pageant Rally

In a way, it can be said that the Love Pageant Rally began with a Coca-Cola bottle flying out of a window, and in 1967, when the incident occurred, the bottles were pretty thick.

Somebody threw the bottle out of a top floor window and it exploded on the pavement near two policemen on the Haight Street beat. The result was all too predictable: four policemen came in through the back door of 1090 Page Street at 2:05 a.m. on Thursday morning. After checking the IDs of the residents, Vince Dalviso was forced to open his closet where he kept his stash of marijuana that the police quickly found. He was arrested and subsequently booked for the possession of narcotics.

Naturally, the tenants of 1090 Page Street were in an uproar over the bust involving illegal entry, and a noisy demonstration down Haight Street and to Park Station was hastily set in motion.

The demonstration went past the Drogstore Café [*sic*] at the busy intersection of Haight and Masonic. Michael Bowen and Allen Cohen of *The San Francisco Oracle* were seated inside, drinking espresso and talking about the neighborhood.

They watched the bristling throng with their makeshift signs, threading their way through the traffic as they proceeded down the street. "What could be done to transform the negative energy of an angry demonstration into a more positive, productive force?" they wondered. Their causerie would spawn the Love Pageant Rally, which in turn would provide the epiphany for the Human Be-In.

1090 Page Street, where the illegal bust took place, is steeped in psychedelic history. The large, elegant Victorian known as the Albin Rooming House, was run by Rodney Albin. The house had been built in 1898 and originally had six bedrooms. Rodney and his brother Peter, who later became bassist for Big Brother and the Holding Company, were accomplished bluegrass musicians and students at San Francisco State University. The tenants of the rooming house, a singular group of freaks and aspiring artists, were mostly students from the same university.

With its large ballroom basement, ornately decorated with fine rosewood paneling, proscenium stage, columns and alcoves, the house was an amazing example of Victorian craftsmanship. Its outside entrance made it an ideal place for throwing parties, and it drew aspiring rock musicians like bees to honey.

Chet Helms organized jam sessions there on Wednesdays, and a number of San Francisco bands such as

The Love Pageant Rally

Big Brother and the Holding Company, Quicksilver Messenger Service and Sopwith Camel emerged from these loosely organized sessions. Jerry Garcia and the Warlocks were no strangers there either, since Jerry knew the Albin brothers from San Carlos, about halfway between San Francisco and San Jose. For a while, "ten-ninety" was one big party of music, dope and friendly vibes.

On October 6, 1966, lysergic acid diethylamide became illegal in California, with other states and countries soon following suit. It was declared a Schedule 1 drug in the United States, which means it was judged devoid of any "accepted medical use in treatment." The United States Drug Enforcement Administration declared that "although the study of LSD and other hallucinogens increased the awareness of how chemicals could affect the mind, its use in psychotherapy largely has been debunked. It produces no aphrodisiac effects [and] does not increase creativity [...]. The powerful hallucinogenic effects of this drug can produce profound adverse reactions." The penalization of LSD would help this declaration to become a self-fulfilling prophecy.

One must assume that those who approved the ban had never read *One Flew over the Cuckoo's Nest*. Francis Crick, who discovered the structure of the DNA molecule with James Watson, was reportedly using small amounts of LSD when the discovery was made in 1953. As far as art and music are concerned, much of what was done in San Francisco between 1965 and the Summer of Love was done on acid.

The psychedelic counterculture saw a symbolic element in the date of the ban on LSD and associated the 666 in the date with the Book of Revelation 13:16, which is the symbol of the Antichrist, also referred to as the "beast."

> And he provides that no one will be able to buy or to sell, except the one who has the mark, either the name of the beast or the number of his name. Here is wisdom. Let him who has understanding calculate the number of the beast, for it is the number of a man. That number is 666.

The "beast" in question is a world power, which though speaking in the name of good, betrays itself with false doctrines. It represents the aggressive, hegemonic traits of the demonic "dragon," rather than the peaceful ideals of the Lamb. Its goal is absolute control and subjugation, rather than the liberating power of God consciousness.

The Haight-Ashbury, as a countercultural movement and neighborhood, came about because of marijuana and LSD. Those drugs were a way of life for a majority of the young people living there. Some perceived these illegal substances as a sacrament which was taken to achieve spiritual enlightenment; for others, the consumption of consciousness expanding materials was primarily recreational.

Well before October 1966, police raids in the Haight were becoming ever more frequent and a considerable amount of hostility resulted from them. Above all, Michael Bowen and Allen Cohen wanted to avoid useless altercations with the local authorities and sought a viable alternative.

That alternative was found in the Love Pageant Rally which took place on October 6, 1966. It was organized to show the hypocrisy of the system and the ruling elite with regards to LSD, to find an alternative to hostile confrontation, and make a sincere effort at instituting real change. Many did not feel they were using illegal substances, but rather that they were celebrating higher consciousness and the beauty of existence.

One of the first things the organizers did was to send invitations to elected officials: Assemblyman Willy Brown, Mayor John Shelley, Police Chief Thomas J. Cahill, *et al:*

> Sir:
>
> Opposition to an unjust law creates futility for citizens who are its victims and increases the hostility between the governed and the governors. In the case of the LSD prohibition, the State has entered directly into the sacrosanct personal psyches of its citizens. Our Love pageant Rally is intended to overcome the paranoia and separation with which the State wishes to divide and silence the increasing revolutionary sense of Californians. Similar rallies will be held in communities such as ours all over the country and in Europe. You are invited to attend and address our rally. Thank you.
>
> Sincerely yours,
>
> Citizens for the Love Pageant Rally of October 6, 1966.

The first issue of *The San Francisco Oracle* was published on September 20, 1966, and it chose for its front page title the "Love Pageant Rally." "A Prophesy of Declaration of Independence" on the last page addressed the issues of outmoded social paradigms, being isolated from one's consciousness, creating "revolutionary communities," the equality of all things and, most importantly, individual rights: freedom to dispose of one's body as one wishes, freedom to express joy and freedom to expand one's consciousness. The individual rights summarized what the concept of freedom meant in the Haight-Ashbury and epitomized a few ideals of the social group called "hippies."

A Prophecy of Declaration of Independence

When in the flow of human events it becomes necessary for the people to cease to recognize the obsolete social patterns which have isolated man from his consciousness and to create with the youthful energies of the world revolutionary communities of harmonious relations to which the two-billion-year-old life process entitles them, a decent respect to the opinions of mankind should declare the causes which impel them to this creation. . . . We hold these experiences to be self-evident, that all is equal, that the creation endows us with certain inalienable rights, that among these are: the freedom of body, the pursuit of joy, and the expansion of consciousness . . . and that to secure these rights, we the citizens of the earth declare our love and compassion for all conflicting hate-carrying men and women of the world.

We declare the identity of flesh and consciousness. All reason and law must respect and protect this holy identity.

The first translation of this prophecy into political action will take place October 6, 1966. (666 . . . The mark of the ascension of the beast.) The date the California law prohibiting the possession of LSD comes into effect. The day of the fear-produced legislation against the expansion of consciousness. At 2:00 p.m. in the Panhandle at Masonic and Oak we will gather and walk to the Park District Station to affirm our identity, community, and innocence from influence of the fear addiction of the general public as symbolized in this law. Copies of the prophecy of our Declaration of Independence, living morning glory plants and mushrooms will be presented at 2:00 p.m. to San Francisco Mayor Shelley at City Hall, Cecil Poole, United States Attorney General for Northern California at the Federal Building, and Capt. Kiely of Golden Gate Park District Station.

Similar demonstrations will be held at the same time in New York, Los Angeles, London, and Amsterdam.

Bring the color gold . . . bring photos of personal saints and gurus and heroes of the underground . . . bring children . . . flowers . . . flutes . . . drums . . . feathers . . . bands . . . beads . . . banners . . . flags . . . incense . . . chimes . . . gongs . . . cymbals . . . symbols . . . joy.

Notwithstanding a few clichés, Allen Cohen's text does express ideas pertinent to the psychedelic counterculture, notably the right of self-determination of human beings over their own bodies. This translated into the right to expand one's consciousness.

As a general rule, formal demands and declarations were becoming more common in the sixties. On 12 March 1964, Malcolm X made a formal declaration with respect to his intentions and the rights of African-Americans, and before that a group of Atlanta students published "An Appeal for Human Rights" in 1960. Martin Luther King's "Beyond Vietnam," a speech given on 4 April 1967, exactly one year before his assassination, affirmed that "a time comes when silence is betrayal." "The Port Huron Statement," published in 1962 by Students for a Democratic Society, called for "universal controlled disarmament," demanded that the Democratic Party support voter registration in the South, and also called for immediate university reform. The Free Speech Movement on the campus of U. C. Berkeley in the fall and winter of 1964 asked the administration to recognize the constitutional right of free speech on campus.

It seemed obvious that the San Francisco authorities, particularly the mayor and police chief, would not take the "prophecy" seriously and would see it as a tongue-in-cheek declaration. Moreover, those that presented Mayor Shelley with store-bought mushrooms and morning glory plants probably did not take it too seriously either.

In any event, on the morning of October 6, the official delegation for the Love Pageant Rally converged on City Hall to symbolically get Shelley stoned, though they could probably have done better by investing in a good bottle of Irish whiskey. The local papers sent their reporters to cover the story because hippies and drugs were always newsworthy.

The Love Pageant Rally was held in the Panhandle, a place which gets its name from the fact that on a street map it looks like the handle of a cooking pan, with Golden Gate Park as the pan. It is a long, narrow park about one block wide and shorter than a mile. In the mid-sixties it was traditionally a gathering place for the psychedelic counterculture.

People had fun in the warm California sun that day at the "first public outdoor rock concert," and there was nothing extravagant enough to scare even the canniest and most paranoid broods of City Hall.

The Rally brought together a sizeable crowd; certainly many more than were expected–conceivably as many as eight hundred at a given time, though the real number has been largely exaggerated. The Grateful Dead, Big Brother and the Holding Company and perhaps the Joe Henderson Quartet provided free music during the unauthorized rally, or demonstration of love. There was a sampling of your run-of-the-mill freaks, but there were also children and parents, reporters for the local papers and straights, too.

Ken Kesey's bus "Further" was there and it was rumored that Kesey himself made a brief appearance. He was on the run from the FBI, but had boldly appeared at the recent San Francisco State Acid Test that was held from September 30 to October 2, and before that he had visited a creative writing class at Stanford University. Kesey admitted that he was back in town "to put some salt in the wounds of J. Edgar Hoover." Narcotics agents were looking for Kesey and Chief Cahill's plainclothes officers were keeping an eye on things, too, taking notes and remembering faces. Bobby Beausoleil, who would later be associated with Charles Manson, was there in a top hat.

Christian Marquand, a well known French film actor, director and screenwriter, who appeared in such French classics as Jean Cocteau's *Beauty and the Beast* (1946) and Roger Vadim's *And God Created Woman* (1956) alongside Brigitte Bardot, went to the 666 happening with poet Michael McClure in search of a hippie girl to star in his film *Candy*, undoubtedly one of the worst films ever about the sixties.

They drove out to the park in a chauffeur driven limousine and were strolling along in the crowd when suddenly Marquand saw what he was looking for: a bright-eyed child of the love generation with flowers in her hair. Christian walked boldly up to his prospective Candy and asked her if she would like to be in movies. The wide-eyed flower child gave him the once over before telling him to go fuck himself, then vanished into the crowd (Anthony 134).

Richard Alpert, Timothy Leary's former research associate at Harvard, was in the Panhandle that day, too, and Michael Bowen called out to him as he walked by. They both agreed with Allen Cohen that the Love Pageant was a joyous event and a great success. Cohen asked Alpert what they should call it. Alpert hesitated, but knew it was more than just a rally. It was humans just being, being together. It was a "Human Be-In."

They all agreed that they should do it again, only bigger and better the next time. The Love Pageant Rally on October 6, 1966, would be the springboard for the Human Be-In on January 14, 1967, where many more tribes would gather.

3

The Human Be-In

As legend would have it, on the evening of the Love Pageant Rally, Michael Bowen and Allen Cohen got together to discuss its consequences. Michael's flat was at the corner of Haight Street and Masonic Avenue, above one of the shops there. In the back of his apartment was a small meditation room with one window and mattresses on the floor. It was meant to be a special room, special because of the vibrations, the smell of incense, the posters of Buddha and the Hindu deity Shiva with his inner eye that allows perception beyond the perceivable.

Michael Bowen was somehow special, too, in the Haight-Ashbury neighborhood. He had gained considerable notoriety by being arrested at Millbrook in 1965 when G. Gordon Liddy made his infamous raid. Bowen's apartment was a gathering place in the heart of the Haight and visitors included Allen Ginsberg, Timothy Leary, Richard Alpert,

Gary Snyder, Jerry Rubin and many others.

A Buddhist by conviction and reverence for Siddhartha Gautama, Bowen was interested in many aspects of Eastern religion, particularly in the third eye in the middle of the forehead which refers to the sixth chakra, *Ajna*, usually associated with clairvoyance, enlightenment and supernormal vibrations. It is called *urna* in Buddhism, the Eye of Consciousness and the Eye of the World. But this mystically esoteric third eye is not only found in Buddhism; the third eye is in fact a universal symbol existing in many cultures throughout the world.

The oldest reference to it seems to be in the Rig Veda (1500 - 1200 B.C.). Egypt, too, had its all-seeing eye, the Eye of Horus, or Eye of Ra. In the Middle East it is known as the Hamsa, Khamsa, or Hamesh. Greece and Turkey have the Nazar, and in ancient Ecuador, the Black Pyramid has an eye at its apex.

Michael Bowen took off his Birkenstocks and glided into the room with a telephone, plugged it in and called his guru in Cuernavaca, Mexico. They reportedly spoke about what would come to be known as the Human Be-In (Anthony 138).

The guru in question was a mysterious man by the name of John Starr Cooke. Apart from being a spiritual leader, Cooke was alleged to be an important scientology operative supposedly close to the founder of the organization, L. Ron Hubbard, also a bestselling writer of dime store science fiction novels such as *Battlefield Earth*, *To the Stars* and *Final Blackout*. According to informed sources, Cooke was the first Scientology "clear," or a person who becomes free of traumas and destructive emotions. However, John McMasters was the person the Scientology organization referred to in this role, though he and Hubbard soon parted ways.

Cooke's sister was married to Roger Kent, a prominent figure in the California Democratic Party. His brother Sherman Kent was chief of the CIA's Office of National Estimates (ONE), a position he held for fifteen years, serving under four different directors including Allen Dulles. People who knew the mysterious Cooke said he had very close ties to the CIA. If he knew Sherman Kent, that would be an obvious truism.

Cooke lived for many years in Cuernavaca, and from his headquarters there he dispatched members of the Psychedelic Rangers to evangelize the world with LSD. Cooke undoubtedly first learned about the drug from CIA operatives that he knew. He also knew extremely wealthy and influential people such as Andrija Puharich, who conducted drug experiences for the military in the fifties, and Bernie Cornfeld, director of the Swiss-based Investor Overseas Service (Keith 103, Lee 157-59).

At 10 a.m. at 1542 Haight Street in San Francisco, on Thursday, January 12, 1967, a somewhat formal press conference, complete with fresh marijuana cookies, was organized at the Print Mint to announce an extraordinary happening, maybe *the* happening of all time.

The Print Mint was chosen for the exceptional hippie announcement because it was in the heart of the Haight and because it was one of the best sources for psychedelic information and creativity. The shop at 1542 Haight Street began by selling psychedelic posters, and later it branched out into publishing, printing and distribution. It was owned by Don and Alice Schenker. Their first shop was in Berkeley, on Telegraph Avenue, a stone's throw from Sather Gate and the U. C. Berkeley campus. With the explosion of psychedelic art in San Francisco and the avant-garde works of artists such as Stanley Mouse, Victor Moscoso, Alton Kelley and Rick Griffin, whose drawings announced the concerts at the Avalon Ballroom, the Fillmore Auditorium and Winterland, there was a tremendous demand for original posters. In 1967, Wes Wilson's graphic works were selling at the incredible rate of about 60,000 copies a month. Along with posters, The Print Mint also dealt in underground comix. When Don Schenker found the time, he wrote poetry.

Michael Bowen, Gary Snyder, Allen Cohen and Jay Thelin attended the press conference to answer questions about the happening heralded as a Gathering of the Tribes, which was scheduled for 14 January 1967, at the Polo Field in Golden Gate Park.

The basic idea was to bring the politicos from Berkeley and the hippies from the Haight together in an effort to create unity and enhance interaction; hopefully that would give them more influence on a local and national level. There was also a feeling that the spirit of man needed to be renewed and that a rejuvenation of the spirit was possible at such a gathering.

The Polo Field, a multipurpose sporting field where polo was almost never played, was chosen as a result of a conversation between Michael Bowen and "John the Ghost," a pot dealer on Haight-Street. The San Francisco police and the FBI were trying to arrest John, a young man of Native American and Mexican extraction, but he managed to slip away by jumping out of his apartment window, then disguising himself as a gardener to calmly walk away from the scene. He advised Bowen to use the Polo Field because he knew the place so well.

The date for the Be-In was arrived at by consulting two astrologers: Arthur Gavin and Ambrose Hollingsworth. Arthur Gavin was an astrologer, sexologist and writer. He was in fact the grandson of President Chester A. Arthur (1829-1886). Gavin was well known for his book on sexuality and astrology, *The Circle of Sex*, first published in 1962 with a revised edition printed in 1966. When he was approached to choose a date for the Be-In, he announced January 14 as the best day for people to get together and communicate in a positive way to promote the general good (Anthony 159). Allen Cohen, on the other hand, states that Ambrose Hollingsworth chose the date of the Human Be-In (*Oracle* xxxv-xxxvi). Charles Perry also cites Hollingsworth as the astrologer who chose the day (Perry 141). Since both astrologers knew about the event, it is likely they both consulted the stars to determine the most propitious date.

Arthur Gavin, who adopted that name in the early thirties when he lived in Pismo Beach, California, was living in the nearby Fillmore district, a predominately Black neighborhood where rent was cheap. He wrote a couple of pieces for the *Oracle* as a consulting astrologer: "Evolution and cosmic Consciousness" in issue number nine, August 1967, and "Interview: The Aquarian Age," in issue number six, February 1966. There is a photograph of him in *I Want to Take You Higher: The Psychedelic Era 1965-1969*, in which the gray-haired, bearded Gavin is seated in an armchair, an astrological wheel behind him on the wall and several young people seated nearby.

Ambrose Hollingsworth was in his thirties at the time of the Be-In. He was confined to a wheelchair as the result of a tragic automobile accident. He reportedly belonged to The Brotherhood of Light, an occult group, and began his own esoteric cult called The Six Day School.

Gayla, whose real name was Rosalind Sharpe Wall, was apparently not consulted for the Be-In, but she was the other astrologer on the *Oracle* staff, and the only one who claimed to be psychic. She met John Cooke and worked with him on a new Tarot Deck called "T: The New Tarot for the Aquarian Age."

The date of the Be-In was supposed to indicate the time in which the current population of the world was the same as the total number of dead people in the world.

Of course you could not just have a Human Be-In because the use of an area in Golden Gate Park had to be requested from the Recreation and Parks Department. Peter Ash processed the piles of requests that came through his office in the McLaren Lodge. Because Ash liked the counterculture of the Haight-Ashbury, he granted approval even though the unofficial policy was to reserve the use of park areas exclusively for school and church groups.

A group of posters were made for the Be-In and probably the most publicized ones were those by Rick Griffin and Michael Bowen. Griffin's poster was widely circulated. At the top, in bold letters is the word "pow-wow," a Narragansett or Massachusett term which refers to an American Indian medicine man, or shaman, and various American Indian ceremonies, social gatherings, get-togethers and meetings. Below the word "pow-wow" was written "A Gathering of the Tribes for a Human Be-In." A Native American on a horse occupies the center with an incongruous electric guitar in one hand and a blanket in the other. A giant claw above the Indian clutches two lightning bolts. The hierarchy of the gathering was well depicted by the columns of stars, celebrities and heroes on either side of the Indian. Timothy Leary and Allen Ginsberg headed the lists, followed by Richard Alpert, Lawrence Ferlinghetti, Dick Gregory, Gary Snyder, Lenore Kandel, Michael McClure, Jerry Rubin, Robert Baker and the rock bands. The textual elements indicating the date, place and time were on the bottom of the poster.

Another well known poster was the composite work by Michael Bowen, Casey Sonnabend and Stanley Mouse, depicting a Hindu holy man or *sadhu*.

The *sadhu* ascetic is an intriguing character. His life is devoted to achieving total liberation from the endless cycle of birth and rebirth, or *moksa*. Sadhu comes from Sanskrit and means "good man" and the root *sadh* signifies "to reach one's goal," "to gain power over" or "to make straight." *Sadhana*, or "spiritual practice," has the same root. It is a very difficult path to undertake because it means severing all earthly ties and abandoning all earthly attachments to achieve spiritual liberation. Bowen's choice of the *sadhu* motif is interesting because it connoted the desire to place the Be-In on a spiritual plane, and the psychedelic counterculture was interested in anything spiritual. Above the holy man are the time and date of the gathering and at the bottom the list of celebrities. Timothy Leary and Allen Ginsberg got top billing again. On either side of the *sadhu* are the words "Free," to assure everyone that it was not a commercial venture.

Michael Bowen created at least one other poster that is different from the others. At the center is a kind of mandala with the faces of Native Americans: one at each corner of the mandala and one Indian in the center with a bandana and long hair. The wearing of bandanas by hippies originated from this tradition by the first Americans. Above the mandala is the title of the poster: "Pow-Wow, A Gathering of the Tribes for a Human Be-In," with the day, time and place at the bottom. On each side of the mandala are the names of the psychedelic superstars melded with the things to bring: banners, drums, feathers, candles, flutes, animals and cymbals. Timothy Leary did not get top billing on this poster; that honor was granted to the poets Allen Ginsberg and Lawrence Ferlinghetti.

As luck would have it, Saturday, January 14, 1967, was a remarkably beautiful day in San Francisco, and that helped to create the harmonious vibrations that the organizers and participants were hoping for.

Gary Snyder heralded the opening of the Be-In by blowing a white-beaded conch shell, the sacred symbol of Vishnu, the formless Hindu god called the "Preserver" and the "Protector." In Hindu ritual today, the conch shell is used as a trumpet and formerly it was used in war. In East Indian culture these conches, or *shankha*, are ornately carved with the image of Vishnu, often with silver incrustations. Sometimes a mouthpiece is added. When one blows on the *shankha*, the sound is said to represent the sacred mantra "om." Thus blowing on the conch is capable of awakening those who hear it from ignorance and *maya*, the illusion that keeps humanity in ignorance.

But before the Human Be-In began, Ginsberg, Snyder and others performed a *pradakshina* around the Polo Field. *Parikrama*, also called *pradakshina*, refers to the circling on foot of sacred Hindu temples or places. Literally, *parikrama* means "the path surrounding something," and *pradakshina* means to the right. Hindu temples usually have circumbulatory pathways surrounding them, which worshippers use by moving in a clockwise direction. The purpose of the ambulatory ritual is to purify the space by purging any form of sin. For some it is a guarantee of keeping demons and those with evil intentions away. Devil worshippers apparently sought to disrupt the Be-In by impaling raw meat on the surrounding fence (Perry 124-25).

Although the Be-In was scheduled to begin at 1 p.m., there were large crowds present several hours in advance. For many, this was a show not to be missed, and free to boot, so it was important to get there early.

After the conch trumpeting, Ginsberg led a mantra and invited people to participate. However, by setting up a stage, the organizers created spectators that preferred to watch rather than become active participants. A few people did, albeit timidly, follow the poet in the *Hari om namah shivaya* mantra, which is popular in Hindu religion, and the most important mantra in Shaivism.

Usually chanted in praise of Shiva, it is believed to be an effective healing mantra calling to one's higher self, asking Lord Shiva to assist in the destruction of the ego and a transcendent rebirth. Ginsberg also read his poem "On the Highway toward Saint Louis in the Month of February."

"Welcome to the first manifestation of the Brave New World," said a voice from the stage at the beginning of the Be-In. Was it "Buddha" of the Haight-Ashbury, the hippie who passed out Alice B. Toklas cookies to the panel guests at the January 12 press conference? It was surprising to hear something so incongruous at a happening that was meant to be spiritual.

Aldous Huxley's *Brave New World* is a nightmarish dystopia in which people are enslaved and happy to be so. The entire world has become one totalitarian state run by omnipotent World Controllers. The castes of people are conditioned from birth, both biologically and psychologically, and the inhabitants consume soma, the legal drug that clouds consciousness and prevents anyone from wanting to change anything. Religion in the Brave New World has become a parody of union with God.

Lenore Kandel, author of *The Love Book*, spoke about the subject she knew best. "The Buddha will reach us all through Love," she began. "Not through doctrine, not through teachings, but through Love. And as I'm looking at all of you, all of us, I feel that Maitreya is not this time going to be born in one physical body, but born out of all of us. It's happening perhaps today."

With the milling about, the brouhaha of thousands of people and the inadequate public address system, it is certain that few understood what Kandel was saying, that her homily was an invitation for the rebirth of the Bodhisattva: "This is an invitation for Maitreya, that he come. To invoke the divinity in man, with the mutual gift of love."

Lenore Kandel was one of the "shining lights" of the Haight-Ashbury. She had been immortalized by the beat writer Jack Kerouac in his work *Big Sur* in which she was described as a "big Rumanian monster beauty." Kandel was an active member of the Diggers and a student of Zen. She gained unwanted notoriety when *The Love Book* (1966), a book of erotic poems, was seized by the police as being pornographic, and a long, tiresome court case ensued. For many, her work bridged the gap between the Beats and the hippie counterculture. *The Love Book* exemplified a generation that sought to talk unabashedly about erotic love, but San Francisco authorities used it as a pretext to harass the hippies in the Haight.

Timothy Leary, often referred to as the High Priest of psychedelia, looked every bit the part in his pearly East Indian pajamas, beads, and with a flower tucked ingenuously behind his ear. Leary, who knew virtually everyone in the counterculture, was in San Francisco to promote his League for Spiritual Discovery and perform his "Death of the Mind" shows.

The League for Spiritual Discovery, founded in 1966, the year LSD was outlawed, advocated the pursuit of spiritual enlightenment and the use of psychedelics as a sacrament. There were twelve "Apostles" in the League, all knowledgeable in psychoactive substances: Sidney Cohen, Allen Ginsberg, Albert Hofmann, Alfred Matthew Hubbard,

Aldous Huxley, Ken Kesey, Timothy Leary, Humphry Osmond, Richard Evan Schultes, Alexander "Sasha" Shulgin, Owsley Stanley, and R. Gordon Wasson.

Leary tantalized the crowd with his slogans and paradoxes: "turn on, tune in, drop out" and "the only way out is in." But the former Harvard professor turned guru received flack about his slogan for psychedelia, since many understood it to mean "get stoned and abandon all constructive activity" in society. Afterwards, he felt obliged to put a different spin on it. By "turning on," as explained in *Flashbacks*, he meant being open to different levels of consciousness. "Tuning in" was getting in touch with the world around you and expressing what you feel. "Dropping out" meant being self-reliant, something that is usually thought to be a typically American character trait.

At the San Francisco Be-In he did emphasize "drop out" and was prompt to give examples: "drop out of high school, drop out of college, drop out of graduate school, drop out of junior executive, drop out of senior executive." Much later, Leary said he didn't want to be responsible for the day-to-day quotes, "because we were out there on the front lines, making it up as we went along." Assuredly, there was a considerable amount of improvisation in what the counterculture did and said, and not everything was meant to be taken literally.

Jerry Rubin was the representative of the Berkeley radical community. As a leader of the Berkeley Vietnam Day Committee, he had the qualifications. But Rubin, who had recently turned on to acid, seemed out of place and awkward, and his diatribe about the Vietnam War was largely ignored. "I'm happy to be here," he began rather timidly. "This is a beautiful day. I wish today that all of America could be here. I just came from the Old World, to here, to the New World. The Old World are places like jail, structures where a person cannot feel like a human being."

Michael McClure, well known poet of the Haight, played his autoharp as he sang "The God I Worship is a Lion." Other poets, including Allen Ginsberg, Gary Snyder, Lawrence Ferlinghetti and Lew Welch, also entertained by reading or chanting. The Reverend Suzuki Roshi, from the Zen Temple in San Francisco, meditated on the stage the entire afternoon, even while the rock bands were playing.

The people present at the Be-In wanted to dance, listen to music and just enjoy themselves. Most did not show much interest in what the psychedelic superstars on the stage had to say, or the hippie gurus that Todd Gitlin referred to as "jealous-eyed world-savers" (208).

Unfortunately, the bands were not at their best, but neither were the impromptu installations. Not all the instruments were correctly tuned and some of the singers sang off key, but the crowd didn't seem to notice and were so stoned they couldn't have cared less. Big Brother and the Holding Company was on the bill, but definitely did not play at the Be-In. The Grateful Dead and Quicksilver Messenger Service did not fail to appear, though Quicksilver's set was interrupted for about a half an hour when someone supposedly cut the electric cable. Jefferson Airplane performed, and the Loading Zone and Sir Douglas Quintet were also there. Some members of Country Joe and the Fish performed with Pat Kilroy; other bands were apparently too wiped out on acid to perform.

Augustus Owsley Stanley III arrived early at the Polo Field with a giant size mayonnaise jar filled with tablets of his latest batch of LSD called White Lightning. Long before the sun sank in the West, the jar was completely empty. Owsley had also donated dozens of turkeys for the Be-In, and the Diggers made turkey sandwiches with crushed LSD for the dressing to be sure that the crowd was dosed.

The confluence of the tribes was in constant flux in the periphery. The crowd squeezed as near as it could get to the stage to have a better view of the celebrities, so it was virtually impossible to move about at times. At the height of the Be-In, there were probably between 20,000 and 25,000 people, and many were surprised to see so many "hip" individuals in one place.

The gathering of the tribes was far from being made up exclusively of freaks or hippies who probably accounted for about 25% to 30% of the entire crowd. It was not unusual to see men dressed in white shirt and tie and most people had short hair. There were also nude children playing and older couples enjoying the first-of-a-kind experience. The Hell's Angels were taking care of lost children. They brought a station wagon loaded with beer and other things and seemed to take their babysitting as seriously as their beer drinking. The suburbs had definitely gotten the word and came to the city to see the show. The hippie population was not the only group targeted by the underground publicity campaign, since some sixty thousand copies of *The San Francisco Oracle* were published and sold to publicize the event.

The January 1967 issue of the paper, with the cover of

the sadhu, struck the imagination of the underground in California and throughout the world. Copies of the paper were dispatched to China, Soviet Russia and other foreign countries. In the age of Marshall McLuhan, media shaman of the sixties, extending oneself and one's ideas via the press could have spectacular results. Announcements also appeared around the Bay Area in various shops and coffee houses. The *Berkeley Barb* advertised the Be-In with a banner headline on the front page.

But the Be-In was organized not only for the hippies, but also for the media. In the words of one press release:

> For ten years, a new nation has grown inside the robot flesh of the old. Before your eyes a new free vital soul is reconnecting the living centers of the American body. Berkeley political activists and the love generation of the Haight-Ashbury will join together . . . to powwow, celebrate, and prophesy the epoch of liberation, love, peace, compassion, and unity of mankind. Hang your fear at the door and join the future. If you do not believe, please wipe your eyes and see.

One of the remarkable things about the Be-In was that it was not organized as a protest rally, like a sit-in, where the demonstrators occupy a specific area to militate against injustice. It was essentially, as its Old English root *beon* signifies, about existing, coming to be in the eternal present of existence.

It was remarkable, at least by today's standards, that thousands of people, mostly young, could come together and share what they had–food, grass, wine, brownies–so peacefully. The two mounted policemen kept a respectful distance, though there were several plainclothes policemen circulating in the crowd and probably a few from the intelligence community. The CIA had always been deeply interested in the group effects of lysergic acid diethylamide, and would want to monitor an assembly that had been so well publicized.

Michael McClure was probably right in calling the Be-In "a blossom," "a flower," complete with worms. It was the result of the unique phenomenon which had begun in the Haight-Ashbury, an "epochal event" for many who were convinced that acid was a key to world peace and harmony. But many radicals such as Max Scheer, editor of the *Berkeley Barb*, were worried about trying to plan anything with the politically apathetic hippies. They believed nothing really came of the Be-In that they felt was haphazardly thrown together. Just one more "blown opportunity." Doubt and suspicion accompanied any potential collaboration with the hippies, and the Be-In was no exception.

Ramparts, the most widely read radical magazine, attacked the hippie mentality head on, though radicals tried to coax them into effective action. At the same time, elements of the New Left were adopting the lifestyle of the psychedelic counterculture, or at least some aspects of it. SDS was experimenting with psychedelics and communal living. At the end of the decade, the Weathermen would announce that "revolutionaries are freaks and freaks are revolutionaries."

But their attitudes with regards to change were antipodal. The hippies as a social group wanted to change the world by expanded consciousness and by abandoning their egos. Some of Timothy Leary's associates, such as Richard Alpert, believed that in a few years the psychedelic counterculture would be able to get whoever it wanted elected to the White House. But that was just one more pipe dream.

The politicos wanted to change the world by getting involved, protesting, organizing, taking direct action, and they were not opposed to using force or violence if necessary. For some, the violent overthrow of the American government was considered a viable option if everything else failed.

Despite all the hoopla, one had to admit that the primary goal of the Human Be-In was a failure: the gathering of the tribes did not unify the radicals and the freaks. This was clearly demonstrated by the lack of attention paid to Jerry Rubin. Those who attended the happening wanted to have fun, smoke dope and listen to rock music. But in all fairness to Rubin, one must add that Timothy Leary and other speakers were also largely ignored.

Something that baffled the straight community was the fact that the Polo Field was cleaned up after the Be-In. Somebody with a microphone simply said it would be nice if the garbage was picked up. Groups of people complied in good humor and left the field clean.

After January 14, 1967, the assault on the Haight-Ashbury was manifest. Television and the mainstream media converged on the once peaceful neighborhood and brought it into the living rooms of middle class Americans. Their focus was limited and biased as they concentrated on spectacular stories of sex, drugs and rock 'n' roll. This pretty much determined what the Haight would be like in the very near future. Linda Gravenites, who lived with the Grateful Dead at 710 Ashbury, remarked that the Be-In was a watershed, marking that moment in time when the Haight lost its natural spontaneity and generosity and became a caricature of hippiedom. Before the Be-In, the residents were putting something into the community, after the Be-In, newcomers wanted something out of the community, and many of them were misfits, dropouts or criminals.

Emmett Grogan and other Diggers were extremely cynical about the Be-In. For them, it was merely a case of the HIP merchants placating the Berkeley radicals for business.

Ronald Reagan, the newly elected right-wing governor of California, saw hippies as degenerate and a danger to American values. President Lyndon Johnson felt the same way, as did the next mayor of the city, Joseph Alioto. Those were the people that had the ability to decide the fate of the neighborhood.

4

The Houseboat Summit

Sausalito is a small tourist village just across the Golden Gate Bridge from San Francisco. Its name is of Spanish origin, derived from "sauzalito," which means a "small willow grove." The village is famous for its houseboats, and in the seventies the Weather Underground hid out there when they were being pursued by the FBI. Because it is picturesque, it has been used in a number of films including Orson Welles' *The Lady from Shanghai*, starring Rita Hayworth and Orson Welles; *Dear Brigitte*, starring James Stewart and Glynis Johns; and Woody Allen's *Play It Again, Sam*.

Sausalito was the site of a unique countercultural colloquy, referred to as the "Houseboat Summit," on 5 February 1967, a few weeks after the Human Be-In. The houseboat in question was the S.S. *Vallejo*, which was put into service in 1879 by a certain Henry Villard. Over the years it had been converted into an art studio and then a houseboat. Alan Watts bought a share of it in 1961, using it as his residence and gathering place for The Society of Comparative Philosophy.

The Houseboat Summit was by far the most mediatized event the *Vallejo* had ever witnessed. It involved Alan Watts, acting as host, and three other luminaries of the counterculture: Timothy Leary, Allen Ginsberg and Gary Snyder. The event was recorded on tape and a transcription was published in *The San Francisco Oracle*.

Alan Watts was born in Chislehurst, Kent, today a part of London, on 6 January 1915, five months after the start of World War I. Intrigued by the exotic Chinese paintings given to his mother by missionaries, the young boy, who spent much of his free time identifying butterflies and flowers, sought to learn more about the place they came from, and thus developed an interest in Asian culture. The mysterious, exotic landscapes greatly influenced his perception of nature, and also his idea of man in nature, a vision which later found expression in his philosophy, lectures and writings.

Watts joined the London Buddhist Lodge, whose goal was to encourage the study and practice of Buddhism, and served as its secretary when he was just sixteen years old. As a member of this organization run by Christmas Humphreys, he came into contact with important religious thinkers of his time such as Sarvepalli Radhakrishnan, an Indian philosopher and statesman; Nicholas Roerich, a Russian painter, archaeologist and theosophist; and Alice Ann Bailey, author of more than twenty books on theosophy and esoterism. In 1936, he met D.T. Suzuki, the renowned Zen Buddhist scholar. It is safe to say they all had an impact on his perception of life and the development of his personal philosophy.

In 1938, Watts married the American heiress Eleanor Everett, whom Watts had met in London while she was studying music. Her mother, Ruth Everett, was friends with a group of Zen Buddhists in New York and was more than happy to share her thoughts on religion with Alan. That same year, Watts and his wife went to live in the United States where Alan became a naturalized American citizen in 1943. He promptly enrolled in the Seabury-Western theological Seminary in Illinois where he received a master's degree in theology.

Watts had become an Episcopal priest in 1945, but he left the ministry in 1950 because he was unable to reconcile Buddhism with Episcopal doctrines. From then on, he abandoned the Episcopal faith and devoted himself to Asian religions, philosophy and culture. The year before, his marriage with Eleanor Everett came to an end, and he wedded Dorothy DeWitt. They moved to San Francisco where Alan was going to teach Asian philosophy and religion. The couple raised five children.

From 1951 to 1957, Watts taught at the American Academy of Asian Studies, whose goal was to "publish and make known the principles of Buddhism and to encourage the study and practice of those principles." He also served as administrator at the Academy for a number of years where he studied Chinese ideograms and calligraphy.

From 1953 to 1962, Watts donated his time to give

weekly broadcasts on Eastern religion and philosophy on radio KPFA in Berkeley. These broadcasts were very popular and helped to establish him as a knowledgeable and entertaining public speaker. Many of his enlightening talks are still broadcast today on different radio stations across the United States.

KQED was a public sponsored television station in San Francisco that began broadcasting on 5 April 1954. Alan gave a weekly program there called "Eastern Wisdom and Modern Life" for two complete seasons in 1959 and 1960.

Apart from teaching and broadcasting, he gave numerous academic conferences across the country as a freelance lecturer, though he did not consider himself an academic lecturer, but rather a "philosophical entertainer."

Alan Watts married his third wife, Mary Jane Yates King, in 1964. They lived in Sausalito on their houseboat, or in their cabin on Mount Tamalpais, the highest peak in Marin and a natural wonderland.

Watts admitted having taken LSD as early as 1958, and before that he had taken mescaline and smoked marijuana. As regards psychedelics, he said: "Psychedelic experience is only a glimpse of genuine mystical insight, but a glimpse which can be matured and deepened by the various ways of meditation in which drugs are no longer necessary or useful. If you get the message, hang up the phone."

He had always been a fairly heavy drinker and in later life was not successful in dealing with this problem that seriously affected his health. This dilemma was probably compounded by the hectic, stressful life he was forced to live in order to provide for his seven children and ex-wives.

Watts wrote twenty-seven books, among which are *The Way of Zen* (1957), *Beat Zen, Square Zen and Zen* (1959), *The Joyous Cosmology* (1962), *The Two Hands of God* (1963), and *The Book on the Taboo against Knowing Who You Are* (1966). The author's contribution to philosophy and the understanding of Buddhism was enormous. His writings and lectures helped to popularize Eastern philosophy and religion throughout the United States, and particularly in the San Francisco Bay Area where he had a large following.

Alan Watts died peacefully in his sleep on November 16, 1973. He was reportedly being treated for a heart condition at the time of his death.

Timothy Leary, often referred to as High Priest of the psychedelic counterculture, was born on October 22, 1920, in Springfield, Massachusetts. He received a Ph.D. in psychology at the University of California in Berkeley in 1950. He stayed on at "Cal" as an assistant professor until 1955. Before accepting a post as lecturer in clinical psychology at Harvard in 1959, Leary held the position of Director of Psychological Research at the Kaiser Foundation Hospital in Oakland, California.

Leary's first use of hallucinogenic drugs involved the consumption of psilocybin mushrooms in Cuernavaca, Mexico, on August 9, 1960. He first used LSD in December 1961. In collaboration with Richard Alpert and Ralph Metzner, behavioral studies were conducted at Concord Prison, a maximum-security penitentiary in Concord, Massachusetts, from 1961 to 1963. Prison inmates were given doses of psilocybin taken from hallucinogenic mushrooms. Ideally, the objective was to change antisocial behavior, believed to be the cause of their imprisonment. Recidivism rates were evaluated to determine if the drug and psychotherapy could change the prisoners for the better.

On April 30, 1963, Harvard terminated Leary's salary for being absent without permission, though this was a pretext more than anything. Parents complained about the way the mind altering drugs were changing their children's behavior. *The Harvard Crimson* and other papers jumped into the fray by printing stories that lambasted drug research on campus.

After Harvard, Leary moved to Millbrook, New York, making the luxurious mansion near Poughkeepsie a center for psychedelic research and hearth for his family. He met the attractive Rosemary Woodruff, his future wife, at an art exhibition in New York City in 1965. Many called them the John and Jackie Kennedy of the counterculture. But the skulking G. Gordon Liddy put the kibosh on Leary's plans to make the Millbrook estate a temple for the expansion of consciousness with illegal raids and continuous harassment. Liddy's immediate goal was to make a name for himself by arresting the High Priest of LSD, and to that extent he succeeded, though he would make a much bigger name for himself during the national scandal known as Watergate.

The Psychedelic Experience (1964), coauthored with Richard Alpert and Ralph Metzner, gained notoriety within days of publication by declaring that psychedelic drugs enlarged consciousness. Leary, a prolific writer, drew attention to himself and to the psychedelic movement with such books as *The Politics of Ecstasy* (1968) and *Start Your Own Religion* (1967).

Always eager to be in the media spotlight, he was a candidate for governor of the state of California against Ronald Reagan in 1970, but his arrest, conviction and imprisonment at San Louis Obispo for possession of marijuana put an end to his political ambitions, though in reality his candidature was a media spoof. After the revolutionary Weather Underground helped him to get out of the state and the country, he joined Black Panther Eldrige Cleaver in Algeria. On January 17, 1973, "the most dangerous man in America," according to Richard Nixon, was immediately arrested by United States authorities upon arriving at the Kabul International Airport. On October 24, 1974, he was thoroughly interrogated by the FBI in Sacramento, California (Greenfield 508). The radical *Berkeley Barb* printed a story in its December 13-19, 1974, issue entitled "It's Official–Leary is Singing!" Notwithstanding Leary's "cooperation," his evidence apparently did not lead to any arrests or convictions. Richard Metzger defended Leary by saying he was giving the federal officials the runaround (Higgs 212). But as a result of his testimony, his wife Rosemary was forced to go underground for twenty-three long years.

California Governor Jerry Brown granted Leary a pardon from Folsom Prison, and he was released on 21 April 1976. After that, the former High Priest changed his tune, eschewed his old shibboleths and began to behave in a politically correct manner. He went on tour with the man who arrested him, G. Gordon Liddy, and together they debated the current issues of the day: politics, drugs, radicals, welfare and so on. *Return Engagement*, title of the documentary film of their strange tour, was produced in 1983 by David Blocker, Barbara Leary and Carolyn Pfeiffer. "Return Engagement" is an expression used when referring to theatrical productions. Certainly the debates were meant to be entertaining, and many found them informative as well, though Leary lost a lot of sympathy from the counterculture for teaming up with Liddy.

After his release from Folsom prison, Leary stopped promoting "religion" and moved on to other areas such as the colonization of outer space, computers and video games. "The PC is the LSD of the 1990s," he chirped. His new mantra was "turn on, boot up, jack in," which must have gotten at least a smirk from Steve Jobs and Bill Gates. Leary updated his website like an assiduous geek, remaining intellectually active up to the very end.

Timothy Leary died at his home in Beverly Hills, California, on May 31, 1996, from prostate cancer. His remains were cremated. Some of his ashes were launched into orbit on April 21, 1997, where they circled the earth for six years before replunging into the atmosphere.

Allen Ginsberg was one of America's most important poetic voices in the second half of the twentieth century. Born on June 3, 1926, in Newark, New Jersey, he gained prominence with the beat movement and hobnobbed with the likes of Jack Kerouac and William Burroughs. Ginsberg left New York for San Francisco in 1954 where he met Peter Orlovsky, his future companion. Ginsberg is probably best known for his poem "Howl," published in 1956 by City Lights Books, the North Beach publisher and book shop, created in 1953 by Lawrence Ferlinghetti and Peter Martin.

"Howl" was involved in a well publicized pornography trial in August and September of 1957, during which a host of well known writers and professors defended the work's merits. Judge Clayton W. Horn disappointed conservatives by ruling that *Howl and Other Poems* was not in fact obscene since it had "redeeming social importance," and was thus guaranteed liberty of expression by the First Amendment of the Constitution. By and large, the various obscenity trials of the fifties and sixties were government ploys used to persecute and harass the counterculture.

Allen Ginsberg took psychedelic drugs and smoked grass frequently. He candidly confessed that his best poetry was written under the influence of drugs such as peyote, amphetamines and LSD. He officially became a Buddhist in 1972 when he took the Refuge and Bodhisattva vows. In 1974, together with Anne Waldman, he founded The Jack Kerouac School of Disembodied Poetics of the Naropa Institute, to teach creative writing.

Ginsberg received the National Book Award in 1974 for *The Fall of America: Poems of these States 1965-1971*. He died at the age of seventy on April 5, 1997, in the East Village of several health problems.

Gary Snyder is also one of the most influential American poets of the second half of the twentieth century. He was born in San Francisco, but grew up on farms in Oregon and Washington. From an early age he showed an interest in nature and a desire to conserve it.

In 1952, he relocated to the San Francisco Bay Area, ostensibly to study Oriental languages at U. C. Berkeley. He read his poem "The Berry Feast" at the Six Gallery, 3119

Fillmore Street in San Francisco, on Friday, October 7, 1955. The Six Gallery reading, at which Allen Ginsberg, Michael McClure, Philip Lamantia and Philip Whalen also read poems, helped to establish Snyder as an important voice in American poetry.

Beat novelist Jack Kerouac immortalized Gary Snyder as Japhy Ryder in his classic work *The Dharma Bums* (1958), as a way of thanking Snyder for introducing him to Buddhism.

Snyder went to Japan in 1956 to study Zen, having received a scholarship from The First Zen Institute of America in New York City.

In 1974, he won the prestigious Pulitzer Prize for poetry for *Turtle Island*, his masterwork, which deals with the themes of the self, the environment and man's place in nature. The poems take on mythical proportions when Snyder evokes man's archeological history and the sanctity of the American wilderness, central themes of the hippie counterculture.

Gary Snyder has won numerous other prizes for his works including the Levinson Prize, the American Poetry Society Shelley Memorial Award in 1986 and the Bollingen Prize for Poetry in 1997. He was inducted into the American Academy of arts and Letters in 1987.

The first thing that comes to mind when considering the Houseboat Summit is that the religious tone was established from the start by the backgrounds of the four speakers. Watts, Snyder and Ginsberg had all studied Buddhism and were practicing Buddhists. Leary, for his part, did not believe in monotheism because he thought it created a "Hive

Authority," depriving people of any real choices. To put things more succinctly and in the jargon of the time, "monotheism was simply not where it's at."

Leary's concept of religion was both explicit and abstruse. In *The Seven Tongues of God* he said drugs were the religion of the future. By "drugs" he meant essentially LSD and other hallucinogenic substances. He also felt people had the right to grow their own marijuana and use it.

Without officially proclaiming such, the four speakers established themselves as *de facto* oracles of the psychedelic counterculture. To their minds the psychedelic movement was a religious movement that needed a clear and active spiritual orientation. The Human Be-In seemed to prove the belief that the psychedelic counterculture was burgeoning into a national movement of significance, and like all vast social movements, required astute guidance. A feeling of euphoria and optimism was surging through the Haight-Ashbury and other hip niches across the land, and many wondered where it would all lead.

Alan Watts, acting as moderator, set the impromptu agenda in a single phrase: it must be decided "whether to drop out or take over." The Houseboat Summit was sponsored by *The San Francisco Oracle,* "far-outer than any far-out," according to Alan Watts, who presented Allen Ginsberg as "poet and rabbinic *sadhu*" and Gary Snyder as poet and Zen monk. When he introduced Timothy Leary, he broke out laughing, and there seemed to be an undertone of irony in his laughter.

An early remark by Watts about the peace movement was made to reassure the audience that the panelists were not political radicals from the other side of the Bay.

The word "summit" in itself was somewhat ironic since it refers to a summit conference: a conference of the highest-ranking officials of a government or governments. The term helps to understand the underlying attitude of the four representatives of the counterculture.

Overall, Gary Snyder and Timothy Leary dominated the discussions. Snyder was somewhat aggressive in his attacks against the former Harvard professor. Ginsberg played a passive role in general, and Watts made comments, fulfilling his function as host and moderator. From time to time they seemed to get sidetracked with obscure religious details, perhaps in an effort to underscore their scholarship.

At thirty-seven, Snyder was the youngest of the group, Watts the oldest at fifty-two, Leary was forty-six and Ginsberg forty-one. They were clearly not baby boomers of the love generation. Watts, of course, was of British origin, though he had been living in the United States for some time and had developed what might be described as a feeling of rancor towards the establishment.

An implicit comparison was made between political pacifists and religiously oriented hippies. The pacifists were described as being violent; they desired to move large crowds through anger and moral outrage. Leary made it clear that he wanted no part of mass movements, meaning by that mass political movements, because politics were for power-trippers. These politicos should "drop out" and "turn on," he said, though saying that seemed rather paradoxical in that he advocated a series of Be-Ins, which would necessarily be mass social and cultural movements.

The political radicals were seen as antithetical to the psychedelic movement, the latter being motivated by a religious quest. Leary could hold no brief for "men with menopausal minds," as he disparagingly referred to the radicals. By "menopausal minds" he meant thinking that is sterile and archaic. He believed the psychedelic movement had taken the right course in the arduous navigation of consciousness expansion. Numerous abstract words such as "beauty" and "harmony" were not explained, nor were specific examples cited, thus making it difficult to determine what they really meant in a social context. The semantic ambiguity tended to be the rule rather than the exception throughout the conference, giving a general impression of incoherency, sophistry and irrelevance. It is difficult to comprehend how the accouterments–flowers, beads, chanting, or bellbottoms–could change society in a meaningful way. All four speakers did agree, however, that change was a goal of the new society they were hoping to create.

Forcing a vision on the world was seen as negative and autocratic. If you did that because you believed something was good, then you allowed a parody to be set up. That fostered the "bureaucratic democracy," affirmed Watts, in which everyone was "equally inferior." The remark was directed primarily at the political radicals, but it could be argued that much the same thing was occurring within the psychedelic movement.

Throughout the endless discussions, Leary interjected his pet slogan: "turn on, tune in, drop out." Yet as Ginsberg rightly pointed out, the politicos in Berkeley and elsewhere did not really know what that meant. Moreover, if you put that slogan into practice, you would have a lot of crazy freaks stoned on acid, or speed, doing anything. For the media, too, the mainstream and radical underground press, the slogan didn't mean anything. The question was raised: could this inevitably lead to "fascism?" "Radicals" were described at this point as people craving a leader and an organization. This in turn raised another issue. How could you change something without some form of organization and active, organized people? How could you change something if you didn't know what you wanted to replace it with?

One of the many provocative statements concerned leadership. Alan Watts boldly declared that the underground had no leadership. Ginsberg cited the example of the Human Be-In in San Francisco. Alan Watts supported this supposition by affirming that there was "nobody in charge as a ruler." One would hope there were no "rulers" in the underground, but what about lesser levels of authority within the loosely structured apparat?

If you had attended the Be-In at the Polo Field, this declaration sounded false. It is true there was no Bill Graham running around with a clipboard in his hand and shouting orders, but by putting people up on a platform in front of a microphone, an audience was created that looked at the performers to see what they were going to say and do next. Those on the stage were in charge of communication; they were entertaining.

Watts added that there was no "bossism" in the counterculture, then he went into a rambling dissertation about God as boss, which was opposed to the Chinese, "organic" view of the world. If you were referring to some Oriental philosophers such as Lao-tse or to Taoism and Buddhism, that was probably true, but it was not true for Chairman Mao, one of the greatest mass murderers in the history of mankind. Chung-ying Chen claimed he killed forty-five million people by beating, working or starving them to death.

But with regards to the counterculture of the sixties, Leary, Watts, Snyder and Ginsberg were leaders. They were admired, revered and looked to for a sense of direction. Of course they didn't *proclaim* themselves leaders–nobody could proclaim himself leader of the counterculture, because the counterculture spurned leaders. Yet as far as the mass media and the hippies were concerned, they functioned as leaders: they created the general orientation of the psychedelic movement.

In fact, the whole idea of "dropping out" was open to debate. Ginsberg noted that Leary had not, in fact, dropped out. He did not even drop out of Harvard, he was kicked out. The university rescinded his contract and his salary, forcing him to leave.

Ginsberg also noted that Leary was still tied to the establishment because of his multiple monetary transactions. He was functioning within the capitalist system, and doing fairly well at it one might add. Dropping out in its purest sense was not as easy as it might have seemed. Perhaps the real question was what were you dropping out of? Leary was quick to add, as an afterthought, that he was dropping out step by step. But this could be questioned, too. How far were you dropping out when what you were dropping into was part of the established system? Some, as Snyder remarked, were dropping in, or falling into the counterculture.

Leary used the image of television to criticize the "robot establishment," but then again, Leary, more than many, was particularly adept at making use of television and the media that were an integral part of the system, and they were used to advance his personal agenda, so there was an inherent contradiction in what he was saying. It could be argued, too, that Millbrook, for all its wildness and iconoclasm, was in many ways a "fake, prop, television set" social group. In other words, that it was essentially a sham.

One of the inescapable problems was that the "cellular animals and tribal groups," to use Leary's expression, needed to survive, too. Where was the food, the psychedelic accouterments, the education, the medical care or the money to pay the rent going to come from once you had dropped out? If education was an "addictive process" that we must drop out of, according to Watts and Leary, who was going to do the educating? Ginsberg wondered where students would become competent engineers, astronomers or surgeons. Admittedly, those were things that could not be learned from a hippie guru lacking specialized training and experience. Snyder said there would be an increase in "subculture institutions" and left it at that.

Leary advocated putting all the technology underground, not in a figurative sense, but literally. Even if such a thing were feasible, one ponders the consequences of such a project, particularly for the employees forced to work in conditions evocative of those that the factory workers in

Metropolis or the epsilons in *Brave New World* were forced to work in. Leary's answer was that they were "hung up that way," so that was their problem.

Again, the question of dropping out or taking over was raised. Leary mitigated his earlier notions on the subject by saying that people had to decide for themselves how and when they would do it. Watts suggested that, as was the case in the past, those who dropped out would constitute an "elite minority," "the sages in the mountains" he called them, which sounded like a rather romantic example of self-glorification. Despite their haggling, however, the sages were forced to agree that a one hundred per cent dropout rate would be "ridiculous."

Watts envisioned a vast leisure society in which the unemployed, put out of work by the machines, would be paid by society to buy the products of the machines. Yet he failed to explain how this system would be financed or what the consequences might be worldwide.

As people continued turning on and dropping out, they would become more and more advanced, a more highly conscious species that was healthier and happier than the "ants" and the "bees." This new species of *Homo sapiens* would be the manifestation of the New Age tribal culture—the enlightened ones who had left the beehive and the anthill. The children of the ants would be authentic "tribal people," perceived as an ideal form of community. The mentality of the children would be completely changed, probably in about three generations. Snyder failed to say how this would be done because he didn't know. Looking at the world today, as we know it, we see that it was not done, nor is it easy to imagine how it could be, since that would imply changing and controlling the entire system, not only on a national level, but globally, too.

The sages also believed, or liked to believe, that the institution of the family would change and, as a result, the entire economy of the United States would be transformed for the better. People would voluntarily have fewer children and voluntarily consume less. But this change involved a big "if." For this to occur, people's goals and interests would have to change.

Generally speaking, parents did have fewer children in the decades following the sixties, but the reasons for this were more economic than anything else. It simply became too expensive to adequately provide for large families. However, we see today that the nuclear family is still with us, that communal living has not replaced it, nor is it likely that it will in the present system.

The utopia envisioned by the four panelists would involve the creation of a limited and centralized industrial center situated around Chicago, while the rest of the country would be one huge "buffalo pasture," to use Snyder's metaphor. Clearly, Snyder, and Leary too, were nostalgic for the pastoral existence of the eighteenth century, before westward expansion and Manifest Destiny were institutionalized. People wouldn't be allowed to drive cars in the pastoral utopia, implying an effective means of enforcement to make sure they didn't. But as Snyder added, people wouldn't want to. In a society that is firmly based on the automobile and economically dependent on the automobile, these ideas come off as hokum.

There was obviously a good deal of playful and facetious logic in postulating that the future utopia would mirror their countercultural fantasies. During the course of the conference, it was often difficult to determine which declarations were to be taken seriously and which were merely whimsical fantasies, since a great deal of the discourse was punctuated by laughter. Perhaps the sages were just having fun, a little like George Hanson in the film *Easy Rider*, when he delivered his stoned, mind-blowing "fable" about Venusians living among us.

By citing A. L. Kroeber's *Handbook of the California Indians*, Snyder changed the orientation of the discussion, placing it in a back-to-nature framework. The Native Americans, in their simplicity, were a model to be emulated. The only way for the human race to achieve lasting harmony, said the panelists, was by living a simple, tribal existence. This, of course, was a prominent theme of the sixties counterculture. In 1968, Stewart Brand created the *Whole Earth Catalog*, the goal of which was to give "power to the individual to conduct his own education, find his own inspiration, shape his own environment."

Being paid not to work was also a popular fantasy of the decade, but there was nothing to substantiate the myth that the country as a whole was moving towards that type of society. Many of the communes that were created in the sixties were short-lived failures, but there were also some success stories and, as Timothy Miller has pointed out, communitarianism is still very much alive today and hundreds of communes founded in the sixties and seventies still exist.

Recognizing the desperate need for clarity, Timothy Leary suggested that the speakers be more practical. As practical step number one, he suggested that meditation centers be set up in major American cities across the nation and that San Francisco's Human Be-In be used as a prototype for future manifestations of that sort.

Maha-lila, a clan or communal structure, was seen as a viable way of replacing the nuclear family, the classic self-contained unit consisting of mother, father and children. The Summit panelists noted that that would entail radical economic consequences for the country. With the establishment of group marriage, for example, they assumed that the economy would be "licked," and that the tribal culture would be strengthened as a result: "Capitalism is doomed and civilization goes out." That remark brought on roars of laughter from the speakers. Both Alan Ginsberg and Timothy Leary expressed the same ideas before and after the Houseboat Summit.

It was generally agreed in the psychedelic counterculture that communal living was a better, more socially enriching way to live, though radically opposed to the American way of life and the American dream. Leary advocated communitarianism because communes afforded an ostensible way of dropping out and a convenient way of turning on.

The commune symbolized a grandiose primal mythos for the counterculture–the mythos of primordial man, *Homo perfectus*–and an Edenic prelude to living. The pilgrims of the sixties would build a new society, a better society, just as John Winthrop and the seventeenth century Puritans believed they would build a New Jerusalem. The history of nineteenth century communities confirms their importance in American culture, the most well known of which were New Harmony (1825-1829), Brook Farm (1841-1846), Fruitlands (1843-1844) and Oneida (1848-1881).

The Summit maintained that the hippie communards epitomized the new and expanded human consciousness, that they possessed the freedom to shape their destinies as they thought fit, "to do their own thing in their own time," as some would say. In their view, the communards were the enlightened ones, the rest of society, vilified as the "ants" and the "bees," drudged continuously in darkness. It is within this special context that the return to nature was envisioned as progressive and enlightened, a higher form of existence that could be achieved only by rejecting the established order. The fact that many communards emigrated from densely populated urban areas was no coincidence, and translated a desire to leave a mechanical, repetitive and sterile existence. The pilgrimage was ever present in contemporary American society as young people left metropolitan areas in a mass urban exodus.

The Edenic mythos was associated, to some extent, with the concept of the Noble Savage, the belief that man is innately good, but that he becomes tainted by the corrupt, materialistic nature of society, as expressed by the Third Earl of Shaftesbury, and by John Dryden in *The Conquest of Granada*. *Le bon sauvage* is the French equivalent, but Jean-Jacques Rousseau never used the expression as such, though he did believe that man is naturally good and that he demands justice and order. Closer to home, Thomas

Jefferson said, "When we get piled upon one another in large cities, as in Europe, we shall become as corrupt as Europe." The Noble Savage metaphor was typified by the extensive use of the Native American icon by the counterculture in texts and graphics. The immediate problem, of course, involved finding the land to start a rural commune.

An analysis of sixties communes shows they were anything but idyllic. Apart from the financial difficulties incumbent on this type of life, the all-too-human impieties of selfishness, sexism and jealousy were not alien to "Eden." Straight America did not have a monopoly on iniquity, jealousy or egoism, which some say is in our genetic makeup and our anthropological psychology.

Naturally, there was not just one single type of commune. Between Drop City in Trinidad, Colorado, Morning Star Ranch in Sonoma County, California, the Hog Farm in Tujunga and New Vrindaban in West Virginia, the differences could be enormous. If most communes were not successful, it was often because many repeated the domestic paradigms, role patterns and psychological game playing that communards ostensibly sought to get away from. Women were often expected to work in the kitchen or take care of the children, while the men did the chores outside or engaged in leisurely conversation. Competition to dominate sometimes led to violence. That being said, one needs to remember that there were literally thousands of communes and that they all had their distinctive characteristics.

In many instances, communes were little more than way stations for antisocial individuals, or at worst, criminals, alcoholics and hardcore drug addicts, looking for an easy ride and ready to take advantage of others. Charles Manson is a case in point. He did try to take over the Hog Farm, but they managed to get rid of him before he could do much mischief.

As far as the tribal culture is concerned, Gary Snyder proposed mutual intercourse within the group. Timothy Leary, on the other hand, was opposed to group marriage.

To promote real change, the Houseboat Summit advocated the creation of tribal cultures and meditation centers. It was also in favor of group marriages, or rather extended families and extended cooperation structures, and the organization of periodical gatherings.

The important question of legal protection was also raised. It was strongly suggested that communes indicate in writing their tribal codes, sacraments, rituals, how they planned to worship, and so on, in order to protect themselves. It was firmly believed that a Supreme Court ruling would help to consolidate tribal cultures. Leary suggested that *The San Francisco Oracle* run an information page on how to form one's own religion. Religion, it was agreed, needed to play a major role in the internal structure of the communes since it would help to develop a feeling of cohesion and solidarity.

Another point that was raised concerned initiating a series of Be-Ins, starting in Europe strangely enough, in mid-summer 1967. They should be continued without tight organization or leadership. Timothy Leary, master of specious gambits, was begging the question again. Who would be setting the agendas? Who would be occupying the stage and addressing the audience? If one were to believe the former professor from Harvard, "two billion years of cellular equipment" would assume the natural role of leader. Leary's discourse at the Houseboat Summit gives one the feeling that he equated change with personal power and aggrandizement. When he said, "Ten men [...] can change this planet within a year," one was not sure if the acid was doing the talking or if he genuinely believed this. He obviously underestimated the establishment and the power elite.

Gary Snyder was also guilty of mystification and loose thinking. Snyder said that people were not interested in things, but rather states of mind. And when he said that the idea was bigger than the Reformation, he seemed to be attributing his own motivations to the hippie masses. Granted, a minority, a fringe minority was interested in higher states of consciousness, but it was limited in scope. For many, psychotropes were purely recreational. Moreover, with the ban on hallucinogenic drugs, it would be harder and harder to turn on. Few, it must be acknowledged, had the discipline, or the desire, to alter their state of mind through meditation or Zen.

The Houseboat Summit could be described as an exercise in vocal histrionics. But histrionics don't add to understanding, they create unnecessary fronts. Leary and Watts seemed obsessed with the notion of organization and leadership, but without organization it would be difficult to establish and maintain meditation centers across the country; and leadership per se is not necessarily bad. Martin Luther King and Henri Grouès in France, known as "l'abbé Pierre," were charismatic leaders that acted with modesty.

The Human Be-In was organized by a group of people

who decided who would do what; it was not a spontaneous happening at the Polo Field. The leaders and organizers were up on the platform. The methods of an open forum were not put into practice there, although it would have been interesting to see what could have happened in that type of group situation.

The Houseboat Summit, an expression used ironically by many, could have served a greater purpose if a well defined agenda had been established from the start. Many felt the Be-In was poorly organized as well. In fact, the counterculture seemed to be hung up on organization. Improvisation has its purpose, but during a conference, or when establishing active groups, it is not always the most effective way of communicating or getting things done. Moreover, the counterculture was easily subverted because of its lack of organization. It seems that much of what was said at the Summit was expressed tongue-in-cheek. This undermined the discussions and the credibility of the speakers, though they seemed to be unaware of the fact or simply did not care.

5

The Invisible Circus

The Artists Liberation Front (ALF) was a Bay Area artists' organization that was politically involved on the local, state and federal level. One of their goals was to organize various artistic and cultural activities and blow the whistle on government incompetence and corruption.

Emmett Grogan and Peter Cohon, also known as Coyote, were hashing over the insoluble problems of the world, wondering what they could do to "liberate" people. They knew they wanted to organize some sort of liberating event, or happening, or whatever you wanted to call it, but were not exactly sure what to organize.

Grogan said he had been to the Be-In, but he was annoyed by it. He didn't call it a "gathering of the tribes," but rather a "gathering of the suburbs" that was organized for whites. The organization was make-shift, thrown together to profit the Haight Independent Proprietors (HIP) and promote a few "psychedelic superstars" (Grogan 314). Grogan, one of the movers and shakers in the Diggers, had a burning desire to show them up, so he swung into action by contacting his friends in the Haight.

One of the stumbling blocks was to find a location that could enable ALF to express itself freely, to "perform" without the slightest restriction. It didn't take them long to decide that Glide Memorial Church was their best bet. Its congregation, an assortment of hookers, gays and lesbians, was indicative of the church parish situated in San Francisco's Tenderloin district. The church's *raison d'être* was to alleviate social problems and improve the lives of its parishioners.

Much has been said and written about the Tenderloin district of San Francisco. Its name alludes to the "soft underbelly" of the city, and is an analogy to a tenderloin steak, which in turn is a direct allusion to corruption and graft. There are different versions of how it got its name. One version says police working this beat received "hazard pay," or bonuses due to the violent crime rate there. In any event, they had found a way to line their pockets. According to another, New York Police Captain Alex S. Williams made so much money on bribes that he could afford to eat tenderloin steak, a more expensive cut of meat than his salary would normally permit him to eat.

The Tenderloin was a haven for jazz musicians in the late fifties and early sixties; Thelonious Monk, Miles Davis, Dave Brubeck, Jerry Mulligan and others recorded live there for Fantasy Records, often at The Black Hawk, at the corner of Hyde and Turk Streets. Apart from the jazz clubs, there was regular work for musicians in strip joints and theatres.

The district was the setting for Dashiell Hammett's *The Maltese Falcon*, well known for its film adaptation directed by John Huston, with a pleiad of actors that included Humphrey Bogart, Peter Lorre and Mary Astor.

The Tenderloin has been a violent crime neighborhood for some time, because of rampant poverty, hard drugs and alcoholism. This still seems to be pretty much the case today. It's not the kind of neighborhood that you would normally want to raise your children in. But this is where Glide Memorial Church stands, with its elegant, majestic tower. Cecil Williams did a lot to reinvigorate the church in 1963.

ALF and the Diggers approached the church for their event, saying they needed a place for a "carnival of the performing arts," a kind of "happening." The ministers, who liked to be helpful, agreed, without knowing what kind of "carnival" was in store for them. The organizers, the Diggers and members of ALF, were careful not to say too much in order to keep the ministers in the dark, but they were laughing inside as they led them down the garden path, something the Diggers were old hands at.

A desultory meeting that was organized in the basement of the church drew a fairly large number of artists and activists including Richard Brautigan, Lenore Kandel, Quaker Fish, Claude Hayward, Chester Anderson, Peter Coyote, Eileen Ewing (Sam), Peter Berg (the Hun), Judy Goldhaft, Brooks Butcher, Flame, Emmett Grogan, Siena Riffia (Natural Suzanne), Kent Minault, Robert La Morticella, Nina Blasenheim, Phyllis Wilner and others.

The group was wondering what unlikely events it could

organize. The suggestions that followed were often strange, sometimes even very strange. But then again, in light of the people who were gathered together that evening, maybe they were not *that* strange. Rooms and areas were assigned to groups and individuals to create a "scene" in which people could act out their most secret fantasies, and plunge into the deepest depths of their libidos.

The Invisible Circus was aimed primarily at the psychedelic community–people outside of it, apart from the media, would not hear about it. It would be the Diggers' way of thumbing their noses at the Be-In and those who had organized it. The Invisible Circus would show them what a *real* Be-In was like. It definitely would not be a bunch of wannabee hippies from San Mateo gaping at the charlatans on the stage and bamboozling an ingenuous audience with psychedelic snake oil, they said to themselves. The Diggers and ALF wanted their Circus to be a participatory happening in which people would let it all hang out in one wild freak out. Not in some symbolic Eden, either, but in the loins of skid row. Who knows, you might even get rolled there!

The happening, event, total environment community, or whatever it was, was officially called The Invisible Circus– the Right of Spring [*sic*], or by word of mouth it was advertised in conventional Digger idiom as "It's Yours" or "It's Here."

Emmett Grogan seemed particularly motivated by the event and used all his energy to prepare what he hoped would be an unforgettable experience. Many years later, the Methodist clergymen would have nervous spasms and get goose bumps just thinking about it. Glide Memorial had generously donated its spacious facilities for other countercultural events such as an ALF street fair and a Christmas Happening, and they were led to believe that it would be more or less the same kind of thing. And yet, from its inception, it seems, an excessive, uncontrollable, irreligious rite was dictated by the unconscious motivations of the organizers, some prankish *daimonion*. Monsters from the id would soon be cavorting in every nook and cranny of Glide Memorial.

One poster for the event was designed by Dave Hodges and a thousand postcard sized handbills were printed and distributed. An old-fashioned circus wagon was chosen as the motif for the handbill. Above the wagon, in large capital letters, was the title of the happening: THE INVISIBLE CIRCUS. What appears to be a blue dove in the middle is flanked by two voracious, spotted monsters. In the center, a blue and red tiger is poised to attack. The rest of the poster gives the textual information. On the left-hand side reads: A 72 HR ENVIRONMENTAL COMMUNITY HAPPENING, and on the right the sponsors were listed: the Diggers, ALF and the Glide Foundation. The address, date and starting time were included below the wagon. Hodges' handbill, though intriguing, is somewhat misleading in that he uses an image from a traditional circus, whereas the Diggers' concept of circus was totally figurative.

Victor Moscoso, who gained international attention as a poster artist for the Family Dog, also designed a black and white poster for the event, but his work is much more disturbing. To the right, a dark corridor seems to extend into infinity. The foreground is occupied by a strange creature with an eerie, triangular head sitting on a small bench, wearing what appears to be a simple shift or hospital gown, with one shoulder bare. The style is somewhat gothic, even surrealistic, and the motifs are grotesque, bizarre and phenomenal. A general feeling of mystery and incongruity pervades the poster. At the top reads: The Invisible Circus, a 72 hour community – presented by Artists Liberation Front – Diggers – Glide Foundation [*sic*]. Moscoso's poster was in black and white.

The event was not advertised as a "happening" because the semantics were too vague. It was, however, designed to evoke spontaneous reactions on the part of the "acolytes." The word seems appropriate because it was some kind of ritual, however sacrilegious it might prove to be for those directly related to the church.

Used in its peculiar context the word "circus" evoked a higher level of consciousness and a transcendence of reality, where anything and everything was possible, where human consciousness could be surpassed. On a very puerile level, the Diggers wanted to stick their tongues out at the absurd, grotesque and sacrilegious circus of life that we all play a part in. Maybe sneak up behind your own ego and say "boo!" to see if it jumps.

It had to be huge, bigger than life, with its own information center, the John Dillinger Computer, edited by none other than Richard Brautigan, author of *Watermelon Sugar*. Stanley George Miller, also known as Stanley Mouse, was recruited to do artwork for T-shirts. Big Brother and the Holding Company was supposed to perform "Amazing Grace," but never showed up.

When the saintly church officials finally realized what the Invisible Circus was all about, that it was going to be a razzle-dazzle freak-out, they started to get cold feet, but they felt it was too late to call off the show.

Apart from the handbills by Hodges and the Moscoso poster, advertising was essentially by word of mouth. But in the Haight-Ashbury in 1967, that was enough to draw several thousand acid heads. The McLuanesque invocation was for 9 p.m. on Friday, February 24, 1967. The celebrants were asked to bring sleeping bags so they could crash in the church at the end of their (first) trip.

Entry into Glide Memorial was somewhat like crossing the river Styx because you had to wade through a hall, knee-deep in shredded plastic that Emmet Grogan had scrounged from a nearby factory. People stumbled, fell and floundered like fish out of water.

The second step in the rite of passage involved passing through the low-ceilinged recreation room where promiscuous hands reached out from every direction, rock music blasted your ears to deafness and boiler heat strangled you.

The cafeteria, stripped to austerity and designated as a relaxation center, was where people served themselves to a refreshing Dixie Cup of Tang laced with Owsley LSD.

Once inside the elevator, if you managed to squeeze inside, the ascent would take you to the church and the chance of a new, Icarian view of self.

Amidst a riotous cacophony of drums, flutes and an ear-shattering pipe organ, the swelling throng streamed through a maze of rooms where different encounters tested one's threshold of tolerance. Lenore Kandel deciphered the lines and shapes of people's feet, while in other rooms you could learn tie-dyeing or be initiated into the art of the tarot. Numerous church offices were designated as "love-making salons" and were equipped with perfumes, incense, oils, lubricants, mattresses and colorful Indian bedspreads.

To capture the frenzied excitement in print, Richard Brautigan, Chester Anderson and Claude Hayward of the Communication Company busily printed flash news briefs the moment they occurred. "Reporters" careened through the maze of hallways like the steel ball of a pinball machine to gather the "news," and then skid back to the Gestetner duplicator to print it. Incredibly, innumerable news flashes were mimeographed and circulated instantaneously.

Michael McClure and Lenore Kandel read poems and at 9 p.m. a round table discussion was held in the Fellowship Room "On the Meaning of Obscenity" (Grogan 325). The panelists included a minister, a public relations policeman, a lawyer and Peter Berg.

According to Emmett Grogan's version of the event, Kent Minault chose this occasion to exhibit his penis on the shelf of a glass display case behind the panelists, wagging it around to the amusement of the audience, though the panelists couldn't figure out what everyone found so funny. After that, any attempt at a serious debate on profanity was doomed to failure.

The round table discussion came to a climax when a couple was carried into the room on a mattress by four bearers. When the mattress was lowered to the floor, the couple began copulating, then a group of belly dancers, some of which were topless, broke through a huge sheet of paper taped across the room and started shaking their hips and everything else. Coyote's blond girlfriend, Sam, led the way, naked except for a black scarf. Everyone danced in ecstatic delirium around the couple, to the frenzied rhythm of drums, evoking some fantastic pagan ritual.

No longer was anything sacred inside Glide Memorial Church as libidinous fantasies dwarfed the bravado of Federico Fellini at his best, or worst, depending on how you looked at it.

Winos, drag queens and a few Hell's Angels attended the bacchanalia, adding their splash of blasphemy. For hours on end it had been anything goes, with one person "performing cunnilingus" (Perry 147), others participating in group sex, fellatio or ritualistic flagellations. A procession was formed in the sanctuary, and as people passed each other they exchanged burning candles, spilling wax and dropping the candles on the crimson carpet.

The local media were tipped off and arrived with reporters, photographers and a news cameraman to cover the event. Yet strangely enough, The Invisible Circus was not mentioned in the local papers; probably because it was just too weird for the mainstream media, or perhaps because church officials discretely asked the papers to hush it up.

The San Francisco Police arrived, too, with fire marshals, and presented court orders to vacate the church immediately. By this time, the Glide Memorial officials had had enough of the Circus and announced that it was over and that everyone must leave at once. They must have figured that if things continued that way for two more days there would be no church left.

Emmet Grogan claimed that twenty thousand people went to The Invisible Circus, but that number has to be a huge exaggeration. Charles Perry's estimate of five thousand is probably closer to the mark. Even so, that number suggests how large the crowd was. Between four and five in the morning, things came to a halt.

People that were there wanted to continue and announcements were distributed to say where the Circus would be moved to. Most, however, simply went to Ocean Beach, sat around campfires, listened to conga drums and waited for the acid to wear off, while Michael McClure played his autoharp and read poems to greet the dawn.

Ronald Charles McKernan of the Grateful Dead, also known as Pigpen, sometimes played Sunday organ at Glide Memorial, but the Sunday after The Invisible Circus church officials made an exception. They had probably seen enough crazy hippies for awhile.

Claude Hayward and Chester Anderson printed a list of the church's principal grievances after the 24th of February: Firstly, there were too many people at the event; secondly, pornographic films were played; thirdly, the rug in the sanctuary was ruined by burns and candle wax; and finally, people were naked.

In the aftermath of the happening, one important question needs to be asked: was The Invisible Circus the liberating event it was supposed to be? The answer to that question probably depends a lot on what your idea of "liberating" is. For at least some of the Diggers, The Invisible Circus was a way of letting off steam and getting away from the routine of free food in the Panhandle, the Free Frame of Reference and all the hassles with the HIP merchants and public officials. The notion of *outré* had always been present in one sector of the psychedelic counterculture as a way of rejecting mainstream America and testing the limits of experience. Yet it is difficult to see how breaking the threshold of excessiveness merely for the sake of doing it could raise a person's level of consciousness, or how an orgiastic, anything goes attitude could create a feeling of harmony or inner peace.

The Diggers had a strong theatrical background and were very active in street and guerilla theatre. More than anything else, The Invisible Circus should be thought of as a theatrical presentation in which the participants were the players, and Glide Memorial Church was the stage.

Liberation is a tricky topic to discuss. One can become intrinsically bound to the thing one is trying to liberate oneself from, and it can also become a game, the goal of which may be ego satisfaction rather than "liberation."

6

The Monterey Pop Festival

According to Robert Santelli in his book *Aquarius Rising*, Alan Pariser was the person who first had the idea for the Monterey Pop Festival. Pariser, a concert promoter from Los Angeles, knew about the non-profit jazz music festival in San Remo, Italy, and wanted to organize something similar in California to promote rising talent, but unlike the Italian festival, he wanted it to be a rock and pop festival.

Pariser got in touch with Los Angeles booking agent Ben Shapiro, who showed interest in the idea, but wanted to organize a festival for profit. After discussing possible venues for the event, they decided that Monterey would be a good choice, because of the popular jazz festival held there annually and because Monterey was close to San Francisco. Eager to get the ball rolling, they reserved the Monterey County Fairgrounds for June 16 - 18, and signed a legal agreement in April, just two months before their reservation.

They knew they had their work cut out for them so they hired Derek Taylor, former press agent for the Beatles, to publicize the festival, which in itself was a shrewd move because of Taylor's know-how and relations in the music industry.

Pariser, it seems, had come to know quite a few musicians by selling them the best grass available (McNally 202), which at the time was Acapulco Gold and Panama Red. Heir to the Dixie Lily Sweetheart Paper Cup fortune, the mustachioed hipster had time and money to burn.

Shapiro and Pariser next went to see John Phillips—songwriter, musician and spokesman for the Mamas and the Papas—to ask his group to perform. Paul Simon, of Simon and Garfunkel, just happened to be at Phillips' house when they showed up, so they invited them to perform, too. But Phillips and Simon said they would only be interested if it were a nonprofit festival that could be used to promote current trends in the pop music scene.

Shapiro, who had already invested $50,000 in the venture, later told John Phillips he wanted to sell his interest (Santelli 23). At this point, Phillips called record producer Lou Adler who liked the idea of a nonprofit pop and rock festival on the California coast. It didn't take them long to elaborate plans to buy out Shapiro. Adler, Phillips, Simon and Garfunkel, Johnny Rivers and Terry Melcher each loaned the festival $10,000, which was then paid to Shapiro. The loans would be paid back from ticket sales. Lou Adler and John Phillips were now in complete control of the festival.

Just a month before Pariser spoke with Phillips and

Adler, there was a gathering of celebrities at Cass Elliot's house in Los Angeles. Cass Elliot, Lou Adler, Paul McCartney and John Phillips and his wife Michelle were talking about rock 'n' roll and how it wasn't considered a musical art form like jazz. But now that they were organizing a music festival, they felt it could be done in a way to change how people thought about rock music.

Pariser would stay on as a co-producer with Peter Pilafian, Chip Monck would take care of the lighting, Derek Taylor would be in charge of advertising, and a very prestigious and hip board of directors would be set up including Donovan, Mick Jagger, Paul McCartney, James Roger McGuinn, Terry Melcher, Andrew Oldham, Alan Pariser, Johnny Rivers, Smokey Robinson, Brian Wilson, John Phillips and Lou Adler. It was decided to schedule groups from various genres that would be representative of the past, present and future of contemporary music. Front money was lacking, so it was thought best to make it a charity; the performers would play for free, but first class travel expenses would be paid for all the acts.

It was fairly apparent that the organizers were riding on the coattails of the Summer of Love–Chet Helms had said as much–and they knew that for their festival to be a success, they would have to get the best San Francisco bands on board. Several well known groups from Southern California were already on the bandwagon and raring to go: the Byrds, Buffalo Springfield, the Mamas and the Papas, and hopefully the Beach Boys.

It is not exactly clear how the rumor was circulated, but in essence it said that the Haight-Ashbury Diggers would benefit from the charity, yet it is uncertain if they had been specifically contacted for such an event or not. A press release had been issued intimating that the Diggers would receive charity, but Taylor later recanted (Santelli 26). Derek Taylor says Emmett Grogan and Peter Coyote called the organizers "the scum of Hollywood" and didn't want to deal with them. The tough, streetwise Diggers were not in the habit of being used, especially by commercial "slickos" from Los Angeles.

Peter Berg, Emmet Grogan, Bill Fritsch (Sweet William) and Peter Coyote took a drive down to Bel Air, California, to meet Lou Adler at Phillips' mansion. Adler, Phillips, Derek Taylor and other bigwigs in the music industry were there, dressed in casual, but expensive clothes, many in white Nehru collar shirts. The Diggers, dressed in their dirty old leather jackets and worn out blue jeans contrasted sharply with the L.A. types who exuded wealth and self-assurance. Each Digger used a different tone of speech to let the money people know they could not use the word "Digger" to charge money: Coyote was polite, Berg was cool, Sweet William was threatening. While they were discussing things, Emmett Grogan reportedly disappeared in the mansion to see what could be ripped off. Then suddenly, perhaps realizing they could not dictate terms to the streetwise anarchists, Derek Taylor rose and left. After which the meeting simply disintegrated.

Paul Simon was pretty easy to talk to, so he acted as a buffer and go-between. Rock Scully and Danny Rifkin, managers for the Grateful Dead, gave Simon a guided tour of the Haight-Ashbury when he went there to persuade the San

Francisco bands to perform. Paul Simon was very eager to get the Dead to play at Monterey. Scully and Rifkin talked about the band's concerns, their worries about exploitation, and their fans. One could say they got along pretty well, because Simon gave Rifkin, the Dead's road manager, a set of keys to his New York apartment (McNally 203).

"Groovy" was a buzz word in 1967, and not only in the counterculture. The word was used long before the sixties and probably got its origin from the grooves on vinyl records. In any case, Rock Scully used it in almost every other sentence; so much, in fact, that Paul Simon immortalized it in his song "Feelin' Groovy." Mike Bloomfield, while addressing the audience before his group's set, and fairly stoned on Owsley's Monterey Purple, immortalized the word on Pennebaker's film documentary of the festival.

If Los Angeles bands were eager to sign with Adler and Phillips, that was not the case with the San Francisco bands that were a lot more apprehensive about committing themselves to people they called "wheeler-dealers." In an attempt to smooth any ruffled feathers, the organizers flew to San Francisco to meet the locals at the ultra posh Fairmont Hotel, at 950 Mason Street on Nob Hill. A lot of money questions were asked, but few answers were given (McNally 203). Who is going to own the film rights? Where are the profits going to go? Why can't it be a free festival? Will the fairgrounds be open to everyone for free? Why are the bands' expenses being paid first class?

Luckily, Ralph Gleason of the *San Francisco Chronicle* and Bill Graham, manager of the Fillmore Auditorium, were there, too, and they persuaded Adler to stick around and negotiate when he was on the verge of walking out after Danny Rifkin hinted that a free "antifestival" might be held a short distance from Monterey at Fort Ord. But Rifkin was mostly trying to scare the Los Angeles promoter. The decision to use the Monterey Peninsula College football field as a free stage and campground was a deciding factor. After that, the majority of the San Francisco bands agreed to play at Monterey.

The Pennebaker film documentary, on the other hand, posed a serious problem because of its potential for profit. Quicksilver Messenger Service, Big Brother and the Holding Company and the Grateful Dead refused to authorize Pennebaker to film their performances. Jefferson Airplane, however, managed at that time by Bill Graham, was not opposed to granting a performance release. Was this a shrewd move? Though it's true that the documentary probably helped the careers of some musicians, they did not receive a nickel from its sale.

Papa John Phillips understood that the best way to promote the festival was with a hit song and that's what he did when he wrote "San Francisco (Be Sure to Wear Some Flowers in Your Hair)." Phillips, who played guitar and coproduced the single, gave it to his childhood friend and folk singing partner Scott McKenzie, born Philip Wallach Blondheim, who, with that twinkle in his eye and his Sgt. Pepper mustache, could have passed for a hippie straight out of a Hollywood Boulevard casting agency. Paradoxically, the song could not have been written by a hippie from the Haight-Ashbury because it was too Sunset Boulevardish, though it echoed what many wanted to believe, that flower power was gaining ground, that this new generation had a new explanation for society's ills, that peace and love could change the world, and maybe even people over thirty. Scott McKenzie found the theme of the song that John Phillips knocked off in half an hour or so. It was cut at the Sound Factory in Los Angeles in one night and within days you could hear it everywhere on people's transistors (Phillips 230). The single was released on 13 May 1967, in time for Monterey Pop and the Summer of Love. The flip side was "What's the Difference," a folk song written by Scott McKenzie.

Media coverage of the festival was spectacular–about twelve hundred journalists from the underground and the establishment press covered the event. Anyone who was hip had to be there. Everyone who was anyone would be there. Monterey Pop said an awful lot about Northern California, as Bill Graham remarked. It could not have happened anywhere else (Graham 89). It couldn't have happened anywhere else because of the Haight-Ashbury, a unique, authentic, inventive and thriving neighborhood.

The damp, Pacific Ocean air notwithstanding, the festival goers said it was "far out." Apart from the orgy of music, there was plenty of pot, acid, food and camping space.

Friday evening, 16 June was opening day. 7,500 tickets were sold, priced from $3 to $6.50, which was reasonably expensive at that time. All the L.A. record moguls were up front: Jerry Ross from A & M, Jerry Wexler from Atlantic, Mo Ostin from Warner Bros., Clive Davis and Goddard

Lieberson from Columbia. Candice Bergen and Brian Jones were there, too, to check out the vibes.

A rumor spread that the Beatles would perform, maybe because Paul McCartney was on the board of directors for the festival. Those who spread the rumor apparently forgot that they had become a studio band and didn't play in public anymore. Their final performance would be on the roof of 3 Savile Row, home of Apple Records, on Thursday, 30 January 1969, when they sang "Get Back," "I've Got a Feeling," "Rainy Day Women # 12 and 35," "Don't Let Me Down," "One After 909," and "Dig My Pony." The London police put a stop to things, unfortunately, when they found out where the music was coming from. They didn't realize the Beatle's were making history and wouldn't have cared anyway.

For many, the festival got off to a rather inauspicious start with The Association, The Paupers, Lou Rawls, Beverly, Johnny Rivers, Eric Burden and the Animals and Simon and Garfunkel.

The Association, a six-member pop music band from Los Angeles, got the concert rolling with "Enter the Young," whose lyrics emphasize the importance of the youth culture. They were definitely not a band you would see at the Matrix or the Avalon Ballroom. They were followed by Albert Grossman's Toronto band, The Paupers, whose music was a kind of adulterated psychedelic rock.

The Paupers were followed by Lou Rawls, a Top 50 soul singer who released more than sixty albums in his long career as a recording artist, songwriter, record producer and voice actor. Beverly Kutner, an English singer and songwriter, took the stage after Rawls. Johnny Rivers, born John Henry Ramistella, continued the L.A. pop scene with a classic hit by The Beach Boys, "Help Me Rhonda." Having performed nine songs, many felt his set lasted way too long.

The Friday night concert was pretty much saved by Eric Burden and the (New) Animals, who led off their set with "San Francisco Nights," a song about the love generation in the Haight-Ashbury. The single was released in August 1967, two months after the Monterey International Pop Festival. The group said it was also meant to protest the Vietnam War, though many probably did not see that meaning in the lyrics. Eric Burdon finished with "Paint It Black," a Rolling Stones song written by Mick Jagger and Keith Richards, released on 6 May 1966. Brian Jones was in the audience during the performance and said he enjoyed their version of the song.

Paul Simon and Art Garfunkel, the iconic folk-rock duo that characterized a generation's protest, finished the first day with well known songs from their vast repertoire: "Homeward Bound," "At the Zoo," "The 59th Street Bridge Song," "For Emily," "Whenever I Find Her," "The Sound of Silence," "Benedictus," and "Punky's Dilemma."

It was about 1:30 in the morning when the performances ended. The air along the California coast was damp and chilly. The crowd milled about before heading to the campgrounds or wherever else they were going to crash.

The Grateful Dead were in L.A. on Friday for a gig. Shortly after arriving in Monterey, they spent some time strolling around the fairgrounds to check things out. Bob Weir went over to the Guild Guitars tent to see what was going on and found Paul Simon strumming on an acoustic guitar with a wiry, frizzy-haired black musician, so the three of them jammed together. Weir didn't know the guy he was jamming with, but he would blow everybody's mind on Sunday with a voodoo rendition of "Wild Thing."

Saturday afternoon, the people were so calm and orderly that Police Chief Frank Marinello sent most of his on-duty men home. The Hell's Angels were perhaps staying cool because Chet Helms promised them free tickets to Sunday afternoon's show, though they would have preferred to take in the blues sets on Saturday. John Phillips, however, tells a different story.

Following the afternoon show, it was reported that a group of the dreaded motorcycle gang was just a few miles outside of town. It wasn't clear what they were cooking up. Phillips decided that the best plan of action was to take the bull by the horns, so he and the police chief drove out to talk to them and see what they wanted (Phillips 238). As it turned out, the Angels wanted free tickets, as usual. Phillips politely informed them that the shows were all sold out, and that no tickets were available. When the Angels offered to work as security guards, they were told their services were not needed. The police chief interrupted to add that if they screwed up, they would all be busted and sent to jail. After that, the wild bunch pulled in their horns, got on their "hogs," and rode off into the California sunset.

Canned Heat, a blues-rock band from L.A. began the show. They were introduced by John Phillips. Bob "The Bear" Hite, more than three hundred pounds of Southern California blues, performed "Rollin' and Tumblin'," a traditional number first recorded by Hambone Willie Newbern in 1929, in Atlanta, Georgia, for Okeh Records. The band also performed "Dust My Broom," a traditional blues song first recorded by Robert Johnson during the Great Depression as "I Believe I'll Dust My Broom." It was based on the familiar themes of losing your woman and moving on. Johnson, like most bluesmen, used earlier recordings to write his song: "I Believe I'll Make a Change" by the Sparks Brothers (1932), Jack Kelley's "Believe I'll Go Back Home" (1933), Carl Rafferty's "Mr. Carl's Blues" (1933), and probably other songs, too, since blues singers often used "floating lyrics," or traditional blues verses. Johnson's song was recorded in a hotel room in San Antonio and was released in 1937 by Vocalion, ARC and Conqueror Records.

Hite was criticized for singing out of tune, but guitarists Al "Blind Owl" Wilson and Henry "Sunflower" Vestine kept it together musically for the band.

The big attraction of the afternoon was next–Big Brother and the Holding Company. They were introduced by Joplin's longtime friend Chet Helms, who brought her good luck. Janis' raw, passionate style hit the audience like a runaway freight train. The group played "Down on Me," an old freedom song that probably goes back to before the 1920s. The band performed three other songs, including "Road Block," before ending with the emotionally charged "Ball 'n' Chain," a traditional blues tune written and recorded by Big Mama Thornton (Willie Mae Thornton). The song was included on the album *Cheap Thrills*, released on August 12, 1968.

Janis' version of "Ball 'n' Chain" set the house on fire!

She was at her best—pure, authentic, supercharged emotion dished out in a bluesy, orgasmic rendition of Big Mama's gutsy song. Her performance clearly stood out at Monterey as one of the best. Cass Elliot and the critics Michael Lydon, Nat Hentoff and Greil Marcus were simply enthralled. The band realized they'd made the right choice when they changed the arrangement to suit their singer. Janis described it by saying there was this big hole in the song and she had to fill it with something; and fill it she did, with pure, fresh emotion, hot off the grill. The audience could see that singing for Janis was an expression of unbridled passion. She said she felt chills all over her body, like when you're in love for the first time.

The enormous impact she had on the audience was based more on her ability to express strong, tangible emotion than on her vocal technique, though that did not diminish her talent as a performer.

Big Brother's set was not filmed, however, on Saturday afternoon. Julius Karpen had refused to sign the authorization for film rights because no money, or promise thereof, was received in return. Karpen, an anomalous character to say the least, was nicknamed "Green Julius" because of the quantities of grass he smoked. He drove around San Francisco in a hearse because that was his means of transportation. If you wanted to sign a contract with the band, you had to smoke a joint with him. Karpen, like so many others, was extremely suspicious of the rock music industry, but maybe that was because ripping off musicians was like shooting fish in a barrel, and San Francisco musicians were typically naive and anticommercial.

Big Brother had turned to Ron Polte to take care of their business, but the manager of Quicksilver Messenger Service couldn't take them on because he was too busy. As a possible solution, he introduced the band to Albert Grossman who was in Monterey to see the Electric Flag and the Paul Butterfield Blues Band, and also to look after the Paupers. He urged Janis to authorize the festival organizers to film them. Confronted with Big Brother's desire to appear in the film, Julius Karpen relented. But the band figured they had had enough of "Green Julius" and after Monterey signed with Grossman, Bob Dylan's manager who seemed relentless in his efforts to sign the group. They would play again Sunday evening so they could be filmed for Pennebaker's documentary.

But John Phillips tells a different story. He says Janis went to him crying because Grossman would not let her go on again on Saturday night because he did not want her to get "overexposed." Phillips says he saw Grossman having a cup of coffee, so he sat down and started a conversation with him, insisting that she should be allowed to go on again that night. Then he says he tipped Grossman's cup so that the contents would spill on his hands. After threatening to sue him for misrepresentation, Grossman finally acquiesced (Phillips 238).

Ellis Amburn gives yet another version of the episode in *Pearl*, his biography of Janis Joplin. He says Grossman went to see Phillips in his office and bluntly informed him that Big Brother, the Grateful Dead, Quicksilver and the Airplane were boycotting Pennebaker's film, even though he was not officially managing the bands he mentioned (Amburn 126).

At that point, Phillips started getting really nasty and supposedly told Grossman where to go with his "two-bit" San Francisco bands.

Janis' Saturday set was not filmed because the organizers had no release to film her. Clive Davis was enthralled with her performance and promptly offered her a recording contract with Columbia Records. The hitch was that Mainstream Records had an option on Big Brother's next record. Davis knew that Janis had great potential so he invited Julius Karpen and the group's lawyer to the company's sales convention in Miami, in August 1967, and offered them a whopping $75,000, though he never went higher than $10,000 with new bands.

Backstage, after the show on Saturday, Kim Chappell brought Janis and Grossman together, and they started talking money right off the bat, though Karpen still represented Big Brother. The members of the band wanted to be filmed because it was a one-of-a-kind opportunity for them, but Karpen wouldn't let them since they had to relinquish all film rights to the festival organizers. Janis then spoke to Grossman, but he advised her not to sign anything and even told her to make a deal with him. Janis was feeling exasperated at that point, so she went to see Papa John, telling him Grossman wouldn't let her go on for the second performance (Amburn 127). Time was running out and Phillips still had no authorization to film Big Brother's performance. His blood was boiling at that point and he allegedly threw hot coffee on the promoter and threatened to take him to court for falsely representing Janis. Seeing that he was backed into a corner, he finally gave in.

Country Joe and the Fish was on stage after Big Brother. The musicians were a politically oriented group from Berkeley that played psychedelic rock. The word "fish" in the group's name referred to a quote by Chairman Mao Zedong: a revolutionary is like "the fish that swim in the sea of the people." The "Joe" alludes to Joseph Stalin, at least indirectly, since Joseph Allen McDonald was named in honor of the bloody Soviet dictator. The Fish wanted their music to be revolutionary and were outspoken in their criticism of the Vietnam War and American politics. Their style of music was revolutionary, too, and one of the best examples of psychedelic rock at the time in the San Francisco Bay Area.

They opened their set with "Not So Sweet Martha Lorraine," followed by "I-Feel-Like-I'm-Fixin'-to-Die Rag," a satirical protest song, and "Section 43." "Martha Lorraine" and "Section 43" were recorded on the band's debut album, released the month before Monterey Pop; before that the two tracks were first released on an extended play vinyl (EP) in 1966. "Section 43" was an innovative piece of psychedelic music with its uncanny electric sounds and eerie, numinous effect that simulated an acid trip. Monterey Pop was certainly not a political festival, but Country Joe and the Fish was one of the few bands, maybe the only one, that performed an explicit protest song.

Al Kooper, primarily an organist and keyboards player who had performed with Bob Dylan at the Newport Folk Festival in 1965, played two songs after the Fish: "I Can't Keep from Cryin' Sometimes," written by Kooper, and "Wake Me, Shake Me," a rhythm and blues song written by

Billy Guy and released by the Coasters as a single in 1960 on the Atco label. Kooper started the group Blood, Sweat and Tears after Monterey in 1967.

The Paul Butterfield Blues Band came on next and by most accounts played a tight set, beginning with "Look on Yonder Wall," first recorded on 24 October 1945, by James "Beale Street" Clark. Several songs in their set would be recorded on *The Resurrection of Pigboy Crabshaw*, released in December 1967. Those tracks included "Double Trouble," "Droppin' Out" and "One More Heartache." They closed with the standard blues piece "Driftin' Blues," first recorded by Johnny More's Three Blazers in 1945. "Driftin' and Driftin'," with an added horn section, was the band's extended version of the slow, mournful piece that was recorded on their third album.

Quicksilver Messenger Service, a San Francisco band created in 1965 by Dino Valenti, according to John Cipollina, played a five-song set: "Dino's Song," "If You Live," "Acapulco Gold and Silver," "Too Long" and their classic "Who Do You Love."

Although their performance at Monterey, like many others, was so-so, the band gave some outstanding shows at the Avalon Ballroom and the Fillmore Auditorium where they were pretty much a house band. Quicksilver was, in fact, one of the most popular bands in the Bay Area, though they resisted signing a recording contract until after Monterey. Their eponymous debut album was not released by Capitol Records until May of 1968. John Cipollina was on lead guitar, Gary Duncan (Gary Ray Grubb) on rhythm guitar, David Freiberg on bass and Greg Elmore on drums.

The Steve Miller Band, another San Francisco group, followed Quicksilver. They were a blues-rock and psychedelic-rock band, formed by Steve Miller in 1966. They played two songs: "Living in the USA" and "Mercury Blues," an old blues standby written by K. C. Douglas and Robert Geddins, recorded in 1948. The "Mercury" refers to the American automobile. Miller used a faster rhythm at Monterey, more of a rock rhythm than the slower blues tempo that he used on later versions of the song.

The Electric Flag ended the Saturday afternoon show. The blues and rock-soul band was put together by Mike Bloomfield, lead guitarist, who had just recently left the Paul Butterfield Blues Band. Monterey was apparently the first time they had played together. Bloomfield's whimsical panegyric on the "groovy" love generation was one of the lighter moments of the festival and seemed to epitomize the attitude of many festivalgoers. "Man, we're really nervous, but we love you all, man, 'cause this is very *groovy*, man. Monterey is very *groovy*, man. This is somethin', man, all you people, and we're all together, man, and it's really *groovy*, and dig yourselves, 'cause it's really *groovy*, man."

The Electric Flag played four blues songs: "Groovin' Is Easy," "Over-Lovin' You," "The Night Time is the Right Time," and "Wine."

The band played numerous concerts after Monterey in the San Francisco ballrooms. They played at Winterland on 9 December 1967, with the Byrds and B. B. King; on 26 April 1968, with Albert King and the Collectors; on 26-27 January 1968, with Big Brother and the Youngbloods; and on 14 July 1968, and 29 August 1968, at the Fillmore.

Saturday evening was a long concert with Moby Grape, Hugh Masekela, The Byrds, Laura Nyro, Jefferson Airplane, Booker T. and the M.G.s and Otis Redding. Moby Grape began the evening show amidst rumors the Beatles were going to appear, creating some agitation and expectancy at the fairgrounds. The light show that evening, provided by Head Lights from San Francisco, helped to create a psychedelic ballroom atmosphere.

What's big and purple and lives in the ocean? You guessed it, Moby Grape. The joke was how the group's name came about, and like so many rock bands of the late sixties, the image was meant to be psychedelic. Their music was a refreshing mix of psychedelic rock, blues and jazz with some folk. It was one of the most original and innovative bands of the San Francisco scene.

Unfortunately for the members–Skip Pence, Jerry Miller, Bob Mosley, Peter Lewis and Don Stevenson–Matthew Katz, the goateed, quixotic manager, hindered their success considerably. Before Moby Grape, Jefferson Airplane revolted against Katz's questionable ethics.

The group played a number of concerts in 1967-1968 at Winterland and the Carousel Ballroom. Its first studio album was released just before Monterey Pop on 6 June 1967. This explains why the five songs they performed at the festival were on their debut album: "Indifference," "Mr. Blues," "Sitting by the Window," "Omaha" and "Fall on You." Their album was deftly-produced and is still highly-listenable today.

Hugh Masekela, a black jazz trumpeter from South Africa, was next on stage that evening. The group opened their set with a Paul McCartney tune "Here, There and Everywhere," first released on their *Revolver* album on 5 August 1966, followed by "Society Child." "Bajabula Bonke" (The Healing Song)–a meld of jazz-blues and wild African rhythms–was highlighted by Masekela's staccato double tonguing. The audience, expecting shorter pieces during the set, failed to appreciate his long trumpet solos and some people walked out; others actually booed his performance at the end. Masekela was probably best known for his pop jazz hits "Up, Up and Away" and "Grazing in the Grass," released respectively in May of 1967 and 1968.

The Byrds were next and performed a longer set of seven songs including "Renaissance Fair," "Have You Seen Her Face," and "So You Want to Be a Rock 'n' Roll Star." Many compared the Byrds–composed of David Crosby, Michael Clarke, Chris Hillman and Jim (Roger) McGuinn–to the Fab Four of Liverpool, but at Monterey they lacked energy and stage presence to be really convincing. The Los Angeles group was probably more of a studio band than anything else. The Byrds had just come from the Fantasy Fair and Magic Mountain Music Festival on Mount Tamalpais, billed as the first outdoor music festival.

Before the band performed "He Was a Friend of Mine," David Crosby made a remark about the assassination of President John F. Kennedy, though it is difficult to estimate how many people in the audience were truly interested. Crosby said that Kennedy had been shot from different angles by different assassins, thus refuting the official version of the Warren Commission, and advancing the idea of a conspiracy. Mark Lane's *Rush to Judgment*, published in 1966, criticized the Warren Commission's belief in a lone gunman, and gave proof there were shots fired from different directions. But this is not what the lyrics in "He Was a Friend of Mine" say. Crosby perhaps felt it was time to correct the error. Jim McGuinn rewrote the lyrics to this old folk song which was first recorded in 1939 by John and Ruby Lomax with the title "Shorty George." It is interesting to note, too, that the other three members of the Byrds reproached Crosby for what he said.

David Crosby also agreed with Paul McCartney of the Beatles that LSD could end war, and that it would make the lion lie down with the lamb. That seemed to be an appropriate thing to say at Monterey with so many people–on stage and in the audience–popping Owsley's Monterey Purple.

Crosby and McGuinn were often quarreling and their bickering intensified after Monterey, often over which direction the group should take, and which themes they should choose for their songs. David Crosby soon left the band to form Crosby, Stills and Nash. He bought a fifty-nine foot schooner, named *Mayan*, with the cash settlement he received from the group.

Laura Nyro was a talented, though at the time relatively unknown singer, songwriter and pianist from The Bronx. She was just nineteen when she took the stage at Monterey. Unfortunately, her backup musicians made a mess of her rather complex arrangements, making it difficult for the audience to follow her set, and some people started hissing and heckling. Distraught, she left the stage in tears. Her immense talent, however, would not be denied and shortly after the festival recording artists such as Barbara Streisand, Peter, Paul and Mary, Blood, Sweat and Tears, The Fifth Dimension, Three Dog Night and Maynard Ferguson would record hits with songs she had written. Laura Nyro was inducted into the Rock 'n' Roll Hall of Fame in 2012.

Saturday evening, the much awaited Jefferson Airplane took the stage, and lived up to its legendary reputation. The lightshow by Headlights attempted to create a ballroom atmosphere in Monterey, but the Fillmore and the Avalon were inimitable.

The band performed several of its hits including "Somebody to Love," "White Rabbit," "Today," "She Has Funny Cars" and ended their set with "The Ballad of You and Me and Pooneil."

"Pooneil" is a portmanteau word for Winnie the Pooh and Fred Neil, the singer and songwriter who was born in Cleveland and raised in Saint Petersburg, Florida. Neil was particularly well known for the song that was used thematically in *Midnight Cowboy*, "Everybody's Talkin'."

"The Ballad of You and Me and Pooneil" was totally different from the previous songs of the group, beginning as it did with screechy feedback from Kaukonen's Gibson, before accelerating into a wild rhythm that conveyed corybantic paroxysms of joy. Equally impressive were the group's improvisational dexterity and vocals by Grace Slick and Paul Kantner. Jefferson Airplane gave proof that they were a top performance band.

Booker T. and the M.G.'s, a rhythm and blues band composed of two Afro-Americans–Booker T. Jones and Al Jackson–and two whites–Donald "Duck" Dunn and Steve

Cropper–performed four songs, including their instrumental hit "Green Onions." They were the house band for Stax Records and thus performed on innumerable recordings by Otis Redding, Wilson Pickett, Sam and Dave, Albert King, and a score of other performers.

Otis Redding, the act that everyone was waiting to see, closed the Saturday evening concert. Otis performed five songs: "Shake," "Respect," "I've Been Loving You too Long," "Satisfaction" and "Try a Little Tenderness."

The critics were unanimous in their acclaim for the black performer: "Otis was 'King' at Monterey." As an experienced showman, he knew how to move a crowd the moment he walked on stage. More than his voice, it was his boundless energy, charisma and soulful generosity that excited the audience.

Redding, a rhythm and blues man, was not well known outside of the black music circuit, so it was a challenge for him to give a show at Monterey where the audience was predominantly white. But when he got into his act and began stamping and shaking, his exuberance awed the sea of faces before him.

Contrary to what has been claimed, Otis Redding was not the only black performer at Monterey. There were also Hugh Masekela, Booker T. Jones, Al Jackson, Lou Rawls, Buddy Miles and Jimi Hendrix. It is true, however, that the Motown Sound had been forgotten. Diane Warwick was invited, but could not come because of a conflict in her performance schedule. Chuck Berry was cordially invited, but when he was told it was for charity, his response was that the only charity Chuck Berry recognized was Chuck Berry.

Lou Rawls got a lot of static for performing at Monterey because many black artists felt it was a honky festival. On Saturday afternoon it would have been nice to see bluesmen like Muddy Waters (McKinley Morganfield), B. B. King, Albert King, Howlin' Wolf (Chester Arthur Burnett) or Lightnin' Hopkins (Sam John Hopkins).

Sunday afternoon was devoted exclusively to the Indian musician and virtuoso Ravi Shankar.

Indian music played a significant role in sixties popular culture, and in the second half of the decade the sitar became a permanent feature of psychedelic rock. The first songs to use a sitar were perhaps "See My Friends" by the Kinks and the Yardbirds' "Heart Full of Soul."

George Harrison of the Beatles became a competent sitar player and took lessons with Ravi Shankar and Shambhu Das. He played sitar on "Norwegian Wood," a track on the *Rubber Soul* album released in 1965. He also played tambura in several songs including "Within You, Without You" and "Love You to."

Brian Jones, a versatile musician, played sitar on "Paint It Black." Other recordings in which sitars were used include The Chocolate Watch Band's "In the Past" (1968), Donovan's "Hurdy Gurdy Man" (1968), Traffic's "Paper Sun" (1967) and Scott McKenzie's "San Francisco" (1967). In light of the influence of Indian music on psychedelia, it was not surprising for Ravi Shankar to be invited to perform at the Monterey International Pop Festival. He was the only performer to be paid.

Beyond any doubt, his performance received the loudest and the longest ovation at the festival, and he didn't need to smash his sitar or invoke Shiva and torch it to do so. For spiritual reasons, he asked the audience not to take photographs or smoke during the performance.

Sunday evening, June 18, was the final concert of the festival. On the program were The Blues Project, Big Brother and the Holding Company, The Group with No Name, Buffalo Springfield, The Who, The Grateful Dead, The Jimi Hendrix Experience, The Mamas and the Papas, Scott McKenzie and, finally, The Mamas and the Papas with Scott McKenzie.

A Greenwich Village group, The Blues Project, specializing in psychedelic rock and blues with jazz riffs interposed, began the evening calmly, opening their set with "Flute Thing," featuring Andy Kolburg on electric flute.

Next, Big Brother and the Holding Company was back to be filmed for Pennebaker's documentary. Many felt, however, that their second set was not quite up to their first performance on Saturday. Wearing a gold pantsuit, Janis screamed and wailed "Ball and Chain" to the delight of the audience. Many men seemed to be aroused by her raw sexuality. The *Los Angeles Free Press* ran an article entitled "Big Brother's Boobs," referring to the way Janis turned men on. Richard Goldstein of the *Village Voice* spoke about her grinding sexuality. This is not to say that the women in the audience did not appreciate her performance. Cass Elliot was deeply impressed by the way she "stripped her emotions" in front of the crowd. Music was an aphrodisiac for Janus and the shows brought her into contact with other musicians and singers, with several of whom she would have brief flings. Country Joe McDonald, Jimi Hendrix and Jim

Morrison are three names that come to mind.

The Group with No Name made about as much of an impression as their name. Cyrus Faryar, songwriter and folk musician, led the band that wished to remain anonymous. The *Berkeley Barb* in its June 23-29, 1967, issue did suggest a few names however: "The Bummer, The Mistake, The Shits."

Buffalo Springfield, the folk-rock group from Los Angeles, followed them, with David Crosby replacing Neil young. Their set included "For What It's Worth," "Nowadays Clancy Can't Even Sing," "Rock and Roll Woman," "Bluebird," "A Child Came to Fame" and "Pretty Girl Why." All in all, their performance was rather lukewarm, a far cry from their stunning studio performances and their rich vocal harmonies.

Many spectators were anxious to see The Who, the British group they'd heard so much about, mostly because of their outrageous acts at the Marquee Club in London where they developed a bad boy reputation by trashing their instruments. The band had previously played at Murray the K's show at the Academy of Music, in New York City (Graham 188), but they were not very well known in the United States.

They started their set with "Substitute," written by Peter Townshend, followed by "Summertime Blues," the traditional fifties rocker written by Eddie Cochran and his manager Jerry Capehart. The 45 rpm vinyl was released on 21 July 1958, and recorded on 28 March 1958, at Gold Star Recording Studios in Hollywood. Eddie Cochran took care of everything–vocals, guitar parts and hand clapping. Connie

"Guybo" Smith was on electric bass, with Earl Palmer on drums. "Summertime Blues" was in fact on the flip side (B side). Cochran joined other immortal rockers in 1999 when he was inducted into the Grammy Hall of Fame.

The Who followed Cochran's song with "Pictures of Lily," "A Quick One, While He's Away," "Happy Jack" and ended their set with "My Generation," also written by Townshend. Released on 29 October 1965, it was one of the songs most closely identified with the group and associated with adolescent angst and rebellion. One verse rants about hoping to die before you get old, though Townshend affirmed it was not meant to be taken literally.

At the end of their set, The Who lived up to their bad boy reputation by going on a rampage. The lightshow bubbled up to a boil in the background as smoke bombs went off and Townshend began hammering his guitar against the stage. Keith Moon kept rhythm to the frenzy on his drums as though it were some satanic ritual, amidst the freakish approval of the spectators. Stage hands, not anticipating the modish madness, rushed to recuperate the expensive microphones just in time. After Moon Kicked over his drums, the band exited as though nothing out of the ordinary had happened. Just another day on the job.

Watching the mind-boggling finale from the wings, Phil Lesh of the Grateful Dead asked in disbelief, "You mean we have to follow that?" Jerry Garcia knew it would be hell to perform after the overt display of rock 'n' rage. John Phillips, who had to deal directly with the group, said they were supercilious and fastidious (Phillips 241), and Townshend was described as "surly." According to Phillips, his ego and superiority complex were overwhelming. He was playing the "Man"; all the other jerks were just "pussy." Townshend, like many other recording artists of his time, ran into serious problems with booze and drugs, though he did manage to solve those problems.

The Grateful Dead came on after the Who. They were not violent, but they were admittedly weird. One of the weirdest, if not *the* weirdest San Francisco band. They lived together in a Victorian Lady at 710 Ashbury Street, along with their girlfriends and managers Rock Scully and Danny Rifkin. Everybody knew seven-ten, a veritable hippie monument.

Naturally, the Dead did not want to do a set sandwiched in between The Who and The Jimi Hendrix Experience. Just as they were heading for the stage, Papa John arrived out of nowhere to pressure them into allowing their set to be filmed (Scully 106). But the timing was bad and the Dead didn't sign the paper. As a result, they were not in the documentary film. As a matter of fact, Phillips and Adler waited till the bands had arrived in Monterey to ask them to sign the contract that gave all the film rights to the festival organizers.

The Dead performed "Viola Lee Blues," "Cold Rain and Snow" and "Alligator/Caution." The set was performed like an Indian raga, some songs lasting twenty minutes. With Jerry Garcia on lead guitar, Phil Lesh on bass, Bob Weir on rhythm guitar, Bill Kreutzmann on drums and Ron "Pigpen" McKernan on organ, they built a rocking, steam roller rhythm meant for dancing, and Phil Lesh encouraged the audience to do just that: "You're sitting on folding chairs and folding chairs are for folding up and dancing on." Grateful Dead fans knew that their music was meant to be danced to, but this was Monterey Pop, not the Avalon Ballroom, and dancing was strictly forbidden. It seems Papa John was afraid things might get out of control if hundreds of hippies stoned on acid got carried away and started expressing love. Lou Adler pushed people who were dancing off the stage, and the ushers out in the house made the audience sit down. Outside, people were climbing over walls to get in for free. Peter Tork of The Monkees, the television band that wasn't one, came out to say that the Beatles were not there, so there was no point in trying to get in for free. On hearing that, Phil Lesh suggested that they be let in anyway, since it was the last concert. The audience was on Lesh's side and the doors were opened wide, letting in people who watched from the back of the audience. The prohibition on dancing notwithstanding, the audience enjoyed the performance and Jerry Garcia was particularly effective on guitar.

The next group on the bill, The Jimi Hendrix Experience–Jimi on guitar, Noel Redding on bass, Mitch Mitchell on drums–seemed to come from another dimension, for their music, emblematic of psychedelia, came on like a rush of Owsley Purple. The set was an epiphany–a continuous surge of vibrations and sounds that transcended reality. Several of the songs performed were recorded on the *Are You Experienced* album, released a month before the festival on 12 May 1967.

Hendrix and Townshend argued over who would play first. A toss of a coin decided it would be The Who, but Jimi had an ace up his sleeve. The performance by the Experience was a mind blower: Hendrix playing his Stratocaster with his teeth, humping it against an amp in ritualistic coitus, and doing a backward roll without losing a note, but the best was yet to come. Kneeling before it at the close of "Wild Thing," "the English and American anthems combined," like some voodoo shaman in a trance, he squirted it with lighter fluid, and then set it ablaze. The audience, mesmerized, roared for more, though they weren't sure how that fit in with the "peace and love" ethic.

The Mamas and the Papas ended the Sunday show. The set list included songs from the *If You Can Believe Your Eyes and Ears* album: "Straight Shooter," "Spanish Harlem," "Somebody Groovy," "Got a Feeling," "California Dreaming," "I Call your Name" and "Monday, Monday."

Mama Cass assumed her *de facto* role as waggish performance leader, establishing a humorous contact with the audience. Before the group sang "Monday, Monday," her witticisms flowed freely as she said a few words about John Phillips. Few in the audience would have understood the derogatory slant to her verbal sallies. Cass Elliot had a sharp wit and knew how to use antiphrasis to her advantage. She praised John as the guy who wrote their original stuff as well as the stuff they stole. John Phillips was truly "a fine man, a *great* musician," and to top it all she ironized by saying he was an outstanding American. Cass was laying it on pretty thick to make John look foolish.

It was no secret among those who knew the band that Cass's popularity irritated Phillips, the group's ostensible leader and songwriter, though Cass was the fans' favorite.

Phillips was forever taunting her about her size and bullying her, forcing her to do innumerable takes in the studio for no good reason (Fiegel 195).

As far as the pop festival was concerned, Cass Elliot and Denny Doherty were not that interested in doing it, not in the beginning at least (Fiegel 229). The band members were each going their separate ways. Moreover, they hadn't sung together as a group for three months–a long time considering the rehearsals needed to maintain their subtle and intricate harmonies. The animosities and lack of working together showed at Monterey. They sang out of tune from start to finish and Papa John was wired on speed (Phillips 244). But the audience, stoned on grass and LSD, was apparently too high to notice, or to care.

The Mamas and the Papas embodied the image of peace and love, the *fons et origo* of the psychedelic counterculture. But sometimes the idealized image becomes more important than the reality behind it. Appearances are sometimes deceiving. Within a year after Monterey, Cass Elliot went solo. On 21 October 1967, *Melody Maker* announced their performing quietus: "Mama's and Papa's Concert cancelled–Group Split up."

The summer of love festival could not end without Scott McKenzie singing the Star Spangled Banner of Hippiedom: "San Francisco." Backed by the Mamas and the Papas, he gave the audience its balloons and cotton candy, though his singing was an anticlimax.

The festival came to a close with the Mamas and the Papas singing "Dancing in the Street"–though there was not much dancing at Monterey Pop–a song written by Marvin

Gaye, William "Mickey" Stevenson and Ivy Jo hunter, and popularized by Martha and the Vandellas in 1964.

The media lavishly showered encomium on the Monterey International Pop Festival. The *Berkeley Barb* called it "a tremendous success" (June 23-29, 1967). Thousands of people attended the festival; some journalists claimed there were more than ninety thousand, though an official count was not taken.

It's certain that people enjoyed themselves. Smashed or torched guitars on stage were the most violent things that happened. Even Monterey police Chief Frank Marinello had a change of heart and was "beginning to like these hippies." Fortunately, the police did not harass people for marijuana, which was everywhere, and LSD was free and in abundance. It was a hippie's dream come true.

Lou Adler simplistically compared Monterey to Woodstock. "Monterey was about music," while "Woodstock was about weather." Let's assume he missed the exceptional performances at Bethel and the bland, uninspired and just plain lousy ones at Monterey.

In truth, Monterey Pop is often remembered because of a few sets that were also the artists' first major American performances. Such was the case with The Who, The Jimi Hendrix Experience, Ravi Shankar and Janis Joplin with Big Brother and the Holding Company, though Chet Helms affirmed Janis had already gained a reputation outside of San Francisco.

Grace Slick reminisced about Monterey in her autobiography cowritten with Andrea Cagan. She said it was the only festival she could think of that was excellent in every way (Slick 132).

The Carmel coast is a paradise in itself. There was grass (the kind you sit on) and cypress trees for shade, and there were decorated booths where you could get hand-crafted sandals or earrings, or get soul food, corn on the cob or hot pastrami sandwiches. There were functioning toilets and meditation rooms in the Seminar Building. Add to that a veritable cornucopia of music: pop, rock, blues, soul, folk, jazz, psychedelic rock and rhythm and blues, music from the East and music from the West, from Northern California and Southern California. It was convenient for those who lived in San Francisco or the suburbs because they could drive home when it was over.

Charles Perry compared the festival to the Human Be-In in San Francisco because it was "huge," "exhilarated" and "peaceful" (Perry 209). The ambiance was what people would have liked for the summer in the Haight: no deaths, no injuries, no arrests, but Monterey was a paradoxical harbinger for the Summer of Love.

Monterey Pop is supposed to have symbolized the idea of change in America that had begun a couple of years earlier involving a shift in attitudes. It couldn't be called a revolution because it was not about radically changing or subverting the system. Monterey Pop was very much part of the old system, but with marijuana, acid, and a few hippie clichés thrown in for good measure. The reality behind or in between the clichés was different. Whether the idea went further than the symbol is a different question. That question would be answered in the seventies when disco became popular. Monterey did help to make live rock a mainstream phenomenon, but that was already happening and would have continued with or without the pop festival. The downside is that Monterey and the other festivals eventually killed the small ballroom dance concerts that were so popular in San Francisco.

Monterey Pop has been eulogized by some as the model rock music festival, and in many ways that is probably true. But the city of Monterey refused permission for a repeat festival in 1968, and that seems to say it all. There were the usual complaints about noise, drugs and lack of respect for private property. Some young people were "doing it" in the most unusual places, but the folks in Monterey were not used to that kind of behavior and found it shocking. "Why Don't We Do It in the Road?" by Paul McCartney, released on 22 November 1968, described the primal act, though he claimed he was inspired by the behavior of two monkeys.

Monterey was organized as a charity, but some made money off it. On Sunday, the final day of the festival, the gate receipts suddenly disappeared. The amount was estimated at $50,000 (Scully 107). Of that amount, $35,000 was recovered. $25,000 went to the Sam Cooke Scholarship fund. The Los Angeles free medical clinics got $5,000 each. But there was also money from the television and film rights, plus the future double album.

For their part, The Grateful Dead were pissed off and looking for a way to get even. They felt their music and the San Francisco vibes had been ripped off in broad daylight. In fact, they saw an opportunity to do just that with the outrageously expensive musical equipment donated by Fender. After the festival and after having dosed the two rent-a-cops with Owsley's best, Danny Rifkin and Rock Scully calmly drove a delivery van up to the stage and started loading. They managed to get away with more than a million dollars in twin reverbs, speaker boxes and power amplifiers.

They were careful to leave a note to let the owners know they would get their property back. They sent telegrams to Fender and Ralph Gleason of the *Chronicle*, stating that the equipment would be used for a few free events, and then returned at the end of the week (Scully 109). Do unto others before they do it to you!

7

The Diggers

A lot has been said about the Diggers in the decades that followed the Summer of Love. Since then, they have been wreathed in an aura of myth, sometimes making it difficult to separate fact from fiction. Emmet Grogan published *Ringolevio: A Life Played for Keeps* in 1972, Peter Coyote published *Sleeping Where I Fall* in 1998, and there have been numerous interviews with the original members.

The Diggers operated in San Francisco's Haight-Ashbury, but there were people calling themselves Diggers in other American cities as well. They were an idealistic group of young people that believed in anonymity, community and communal living. Many in the establishment found them subversive because of their antipathy for capitalism and consumer culture. They were sometimes referred to as "radical anarchists," and when considered in the perspective of their guerilla theatre and marginal living, this epithet seems valid. As part of the counterculture of the sixties, they embraced the ideas and feelings of many. They were, for example, opposed to the Vietnam War, American imperialism in Southeast Asia, and an economic system that exploited the lower classes by keeping them in a state of perpetual poverty. Promoting civil rights was an obligation for many and some Diggers worked with the radical Black Panthers, which was unusual even for white radicals because the Panthers didn't like to see too many whites around and because a lot of whites felt intimidated by their gun-toting machismo and violent, revolutionary rhetoric.

One of their seminal ideas involved the notions of money and buying. For them, it was simple: everything should be free, so they initiated a free food program in the Panhandle of Golden Gate Park and created free stores and crash pads. Since they were also into drugs, they gave that away, too.

The Haight-Ashbury Diggers borrowed their appellation from the seventeenth century English Diggers, whose rich and remarkable story evokes the quest for human freedom and equality.

England was in social turmoil in 1649, after the trial and execution of Charles I, which resulted in a scramble for political control and power. The Diggers, as they were metaphorically called, came about as a result of civil wars: 1642-1646 and 1647-1648. Royalists sought to put Charles II on the throne; others, like Oliver Cromwell, called for the organization of a parliamentary government in which the head of each household could vote; others believed a theocracy should rule. For his part, Digger Gerrard

Winstanley was adamantly opposed to the idea of a plutocracy governing the country.

The Diggers, also known as the "True Levellers," were led by William Everard, a soldier in the New Model Army. Their goal was to use the land–dig up the soil–to reclaim the freedom they felt they had lost as a result of the Norman Conquest. They exhorted Englishmen everywhere to seize the land and own and work it collectively in egalitarian communities, to challenge the slavery of property, with the ultimate goal of creating a classless society founded on economic equality.

At Saint George's Hill, then in Cobham, Surrey, a group of people took over the land and cultivated it, in direct defiance of the law, the army and the wealthy landlords. Men such as Gerrard Winstanley travelled around England to rally support, advocating a secular, classless, democratic society as described in the pamphlet "The Law of Freedom in a Platform," written in 1652.

All men were equal, so government must be elected by the "people," which at the time meant the men. Women did not vote. The Diggers were opposed to the House of Lords because it represented the ruling, moneyed class.

Apart from the right to vote, they believed in free speech, freedom of religion and equality before the law, something that certainly did not exist in seventeenth century England. For these radical idealists, the land belonged to all people as a right, because God created all men equal. In light of these beliefs, the English Monarch and the House of Lords were seen as oppressors that must be ousted from their position of power.

In 1647, they drafted "The Agreement of the People." This document affirmed that power was invested in the people. It called for one year Parliaments, the right to vote for all men who worked independently for their living, the right to recall any or all members of Parliament at any time, abolition of the House of Lords, the democratic election of Army officers, religious toleration and, most importantly, the immediate redistribution of land to the common people.

It is not difficult to imagine the extent to which the ruling class felt threatened by this text. However, the Diggers were unable to mobilize sufficient numbers of Englishmen to seriously menace and eventually extirpate the ruling class.

A Declaration from the Poor Oppressed People of England drafted in 1649 by Gerrard Winstanley was a radical pamphlet that addressed the issue of poverty and the idea of buying without money, as is stated in Isaiah 55:1: "Come, all you who are thirsty, come to the waters; and you who have no money, come, buy and eat! Come, buy wine and milk without money and without cost."

The San Francisco Diggers would incorporate these ideas into their activities and philosophy.

It is impossible to know the names of all the San Francisco Diggers because they tried, for the most part, to remain anonymous, but the better known were Lynn House (Freeman), Peter Cohon (Coyote), Peter Berg (the Hun), Emmett Grogan, Kent Minault, David Simpson, Richard Brautigan, Lenore Kandel, Bill Fritsch (Sweet William Tumbleweed), Siena Riffia (Natural Suzanne), Phyllis

Wilner, Judy Goldhaft, Nina Blasenheim, Cindy Small, Jane Lapiner, Bill Lyndon, Eva Bess (Myeba), Roselee and Vicky Pollack.

Having studied with the San Francisco Mime Troupe, at least a few of the Diggers had solid acting backgrounds. Ronnie Davis founded the controversial group in 1959, after which it distinguished itself for its political and social satire. The Mime Troupe gave free shows in San Francisco and the Bay Area using the time-honored techniques of the Commedia dell'Arte and farce. Literally, the expression means "comedy of professional actors," as the *arti*, in Medieval Italy, were groups of artisans, though the origins of the genre certainly go back to Roman civilization.

Performances were adapted, or crafted, so to speak, to specific needs, and as a result were largely improvised using stock characters such as Pantaloon, Harlequin, Inamorata and Scapino.

Davis' group gained notoriety with its free performances in Golden Gate Park, during which the sacred cows of America were slaughtered. Needless to say, local authorities indulged in knee-jerk conservatism and sought to put an end to the satire that ridiculed the notion of American exceptionalism by attacking imperialism, political lies and hypocrisy.

During a performance of *Il Candelaio* in Lafayette Park on 7 August 1965, Davis was arrested and officially charged with performing without a permit, although those in the troupe, or associated with it, knew they were harassed for political reasons.

The script by Peter Berg addressed the issue of the

gender of two characters, one gay and one bisexual. The trial, widely covered by the media, drew attention to the Mime Troupe, but it wasn't until July 1966 that it was authorized to perform again. In an important free speech ruling, Superior Court Judge Koresh declared that the San Francisco Park Commission could not censor the content of performances, since that constituted a violation of free speech. This was a big victory for The Mime Troupe.

The Diggers had several influential members working in the Mime Troupe: Emmett Grogan, Peter Berg, Peter Coyote and Kent Minault. It is obvious that their theatrical experience with the Troupe revolutionized their world view with regards to money, property, power and social class. Peter Coyote has stated that because of it, he analyzed the world according to "Marxist principles." It helped him to see things in a different light and closed the gap between a person's intellectual and artistic life.

Ronnie Davis organized a meeting of writers, artists, actors and musicians to defend a popular, democratic vision of art. The Artists Liberation Front (ALF) was established as a result of this reunion. Several members of ALF would later become Diggers.

One of the things ALF did was to organize street fairs with art and rock bands that drew large numbers of people. It considered having booths at its fairs to sell food, crafts and psychedelia. The Diggers, however, were opposed to this. To their way of thinking, the counterculture should set an example for the rest of the community by opposing all forms of commercialism.

The goal of those in the Haight-Ashbury, as far as they were concerned, was to "do your own thing," which in part meant not living to make a profit or acquire too much private property. The two groups were unable to reconcile their differences on this matter and in October 1966, the Diggers left ALF. This clash of wills and creeds would foreshadow their *hejira* from the Haight in the fall of 1967.

The Diggers were spurred into action by a tragic police shooting in the Hunter's Point ghetto, sparking a week of riots in the city's black neighborhoods. Matthew Johnson, an Afro-American aged sixteen, was shot and killed by the San Francisco police on 27 September 1966.

Mayor John Shelley ordered a curfew in the city and Governor Edmund "Pat" Brown mobilized the National Guard to quell the rioting and looting. Students for a Democratic Society (SDS) told residents to disregard the curfew as a sign of solidarity with the black community. Haight merchants, on the other hand, urged people to stay indoors and to avoid confrontations with the police or National Guardsmen. The Haight-Ashbury borders on the Fillmore district, a predominately black neighborhood, so it was in the line of fire of racial violence.

The Diggers disseminated one of their earlier broadsides advising people to do what they wanted to, either stay indoors or go outdoors, thus seeming to run with the hare and hunt with the hounds. The police were actively looking for curfew violators and arrested 124 people for such violations, while the Diggers accused the "hippie merchants" of hobnobbing with the local police to promote their commercial interests.

The Digger broadsides, whose success was variable, were a grassroots attempt to change people's attitudes, or at least get them to question their viewpoints in the interest of the community.

Since they were not part of the flower power movement, nothing prevented the Diggers from criticizing hippies for their political apathy. This is what the broadside "Time to Forget" essentially does when it says "Forget the war in Vietnam. Flowers are lovely." The idea was that wearing flowers in your hair wouldn't stop the war. The hippies in the Haight or elsewhere, though opposed to the war, were not politically active like the politicos across the Bay in Berkeley, so they were not inclined to demonstrate.

The broadsides, printed by the Communication Company–abbreviated Com/co–were a kind of condensed pamphlet, haiku for pamphleteers, if you will, that gave the Diggers a voice in the neighborhood, while at the same time allowing them to remain anonymous, or "enfranchised." These broadsides also played an important role in establishing certain standards of ethics and integrity in the Haight.

"Money Is an Unnecessary Evil" summarized their intentions and underscored their predilection for satire and humor. Asking upright citizens to turn in their money was a sneer at capitalist America. "Responsible citizens" were reassured that "no questions [would] be asked." Your friendly neighborhood Digger was anxiously waiting to "liberate its energy."

"In Search of a Frame" was a broadside reprinted on page six in the *Berkeley Barb* on November 25, 1966. Unlike

Abbie Hoffman and Jerry Rubin of the Yippies, the Diggers felt publicity was iniquitous. Big Brother and the Holding Company was photographed in *ID* magazine, and the photograph was placed next to commercial advertisements that, according to Grogan and others, co-opted the band's countercultural image. They similarly chastised the Charlatans for promoting hair tonic. If you were selling your image, an aspect of your identity, you were at the same time compromising your freedom by fettering it to material gain. But this was something that all rock bands did, in one way or another. The same could be said about signing a record contract, and all bands dreamed of signing a big contract so their music could be heard by as many people as possible.

The Diggers were quick to point out the paradoxes of the rock stars, who though appearing to be part of the counterculture, shared the establishment's motivations. The hippie accouterments were merely a façade, a means of achieving their capitalist ends. In reality, their hit tunes about love, revolution, and getting together were just so much hype. "Let me live in a world pure," said the Diggers, which in part meant that people should stand up for what they believed and not cop out.

From the very beginning, the Diggers expressed a great deal of antipathy towards the Haight-Ashbury merchants and were merciless or even vindictive towards them.

The mid-sixties saw a proliferation of shops with catchy names catering to psychedelia: The Psychedelic Shop, In Gear, Far Fetched Food, House of Richard, Annex B, Rhinoceros Leather Goods, Malcolm's Granary, The I-Thou Coffee House, Blushing Peony, Wild Colors, The Print Mint,

Quasars, Silver Things, Mnasidika.

The Haight Independent Proprietors (HIP) created their own organization because the Haight Street Association refused to admit them in their older group. City Hall put pressure on the psychedelic merchants as a way of getting at the hippies that they hated in the Haight-Ashbury. In October 1966, the Psychedelic Shop was threatened with eviction because of loiterers and poorly dressed clients. As far as the Diggers were concerned, the HIP merchants were only interested in making money; beggars were the flotsam and jetsam of Haight Street that scared customers away. But things were not as one-sided as some Diggers liked to believe. The HIP merchants did help to organize a job co-op, though this also came under attack as a form of exploitation because the pay was so bad.

"Take a Cop to Dinner" was conceived of as a means of improving relations between the HIP merchants and the police. Things had deteriorated as a result of increased drug arrests in the Haight. Ron Thelin posted a sign in the window of the Psychedelic Shop with those words on it, and other merchants did likewise.

The Diggers attacked "Take a Cop to Dinner" as bribery and compared the merchants who posted the signs to pimps, racketeers and drug dealers. The broadside pursued its metaphor by describing how different groups and institutions bribed the police, from businesses and clubs to neighborhood committees and social organizations and, finally, the police themselves. The impression one got from reading the text was that society was rotten to the core.

Racketeers take cops to dinner with payoffs.

Pimps take cops to dinner with free tricks.

Dealers take cops to dinner with free highs.

Business takes cops to dinner with graft.

Unions and Corporations take cops to dinner with post-retirement jobs.

Schools and Professional Clubs take cops to dinner with free tickets to athletic events and social affairs.

The Catholic Church takes cops to dinner by exempting them from religious duties.

The Justice Department takes cops to dinner with laws giving them the right to do almost anything.

The Defense Department takes cops to dinner by releasing them from all military obligations.

Establishment newspapers take cops to dinner by propagating the image of the friendly, uncorrupt, neighborhood policeman.

Places of entertainment take cops to dinner with free drinks, and admission to shows.

Merchants take cops to dinner with discounts and gifts.

Neighborhood Committees and Social Organizations take cops to dinner with free discussions offering discriminating insights into hipsterism, black militancy, and drug culture.

Cops take cops to dinner by granting them immunity to prosecution for misdemeanors and anything else they can get away with.

Cops take themselves to dinner by inciting riots.

The leaflets and broadsides, printed for almost nothing, captured the imagination of the Haight. Who were these Diggers, anyway? Being anonymous gave them a kind of mystical power, at a time when mysticism was an ace up one's sleeve. The anonymity was a significant aspect of Digger philosophy; if you received recognition for what you did, then it wasn't free, because your ego was being paid.

In "The Ideology of Failure," "failure" was equated with the refusal of participating in mass consumer culture. To circumvent consumer capitalism, which was developing at a rampant pace in the prosperous sixties because of television, McLuhan's "timid giant," the Diggers advised people to do their own thing for nothing.

"Do your own thing" was one of several catchwords the Diggers contributed to the counterculture. Often repeated on the street and by the media, it represented a desire for freedom, individuality and, by implication, acting outside of capitalist culture, which was usually a lot easier said than done, and often involved a considerable amount of fantasizing.

"We live our protest," they asserted, which meant implementing their participatory ideology in the here and now. Some were idealists, some were perhaps visionaries. They sometimes squabbled over their goals, but shared enough in principle to seek a common means of pooling their energy.

Among the social actions undertaken in the Haight, the free food ritual was undoubtedly the most publicized. It did feed hungry people, though not everyone lining up to eat was a starving, barefoot hippie. But that was also an objective of the program, because apart from feeding people, they wanted to change their attitudes towards money. Notices like this were posted and distributed in the Haight-Ashbury: "FREE FOOD EVERYDAY FREE FOOD. IT'S FREE BECAUSE IT'S YOURS."

The Panhandle in Golden Gate Park was chosen because it was on a busy street. People driving by would see the show. "The Frame of Reference" was a double-entendre that expressed both literal and figurative meanings–the tangible wooden frame and one's personal perception of reality.

Billy Murcott built the frame with wooden two-by-fours bolted together and painted a bright orange so you couldn't miss it. Before being served, you stepped through the frame; in other words, you changed your attitude because you were symbolically in a different space where money didn't count.

The frame was twelve feet by twelve feet, so it was easy to see at a distance, and when people drove by they saw a "picture" of people being served free food in a new kind of non capitalistic society. According to Digger ethos, if you did something for free, you did it in a "free frame of reference."

Free food also implied that you were taking responsibility for what you did. The Diggers believed they were taking responsibility by taking care of people in the community, and by stepping through the frame you were taking the responsibility of changing your attitude and behavior, becoming aware of the real meanings of the words "money" and "free." Free food could also be associated with the concept of a "free life," which meant not having to work to feed yourself.

Most of the food served had been thrown away, donated or pilfered. Emmett Grogan was arrested on at least one occasion for stealing food: prime round steaks from Armour Meat Company, figuring that a slice of a cut cake is never missed. According to Lenore Kandel, "It was good hearted." It also involved a lot of work, especially for a group of people that rejected institutions and well organized projects.

The idea was noble, but given their concept of doing what you felt like doing, it could not have lasted forever, since doing something on a regular basis required planning, organization and commitment. But Free Food in the Panhandle ended shortly after the Free Frame of Reference Store on Frederick Street closed on February 5, 1967, so several months before the Summer of Love. To make matters worse, Grogan had a monkey on his back, so he had other things to worry about.

Part of the Diggers' ethos involved creating a condition to solve the social problem at hand–putting your money where your mouth is, so to speak, acting rather than just talking about it. "Create the condition you describe" was the way they put it. The condition described by the Diggers was "eternity is now," so if a person had a dream or a fantasy that they wanted to see come true, then they had to "take responsibility for it," make their act real to the point of creating a "society," and then take a step back to see if the "condition" had taken root and grown.

It should be remembered, too, that they were not trying to eliminate poverty in the short run, but rather to create a situation that if pursued on a larger scale could help to eliminate it.

The Diggers did, on occasion, burn money, an act which symbolized the end of capitalism, though they did not burn every greenback that came their way, since they also had a practical sense of necessity.

For all intents and purposes, the notions of mutualism and sharing were corrupted when based on money. Money corrupted because it inherently changed the relationship between people. It changed their motivations and opened the door to power games and the desire to control and manipulate rather than do things for the general good.

The obvious problem was getting from a money-based society to one that was not. Part of that problem involved the myriad traditions and habits ingrained in people's minds. For Peter Berg, there must be an intermediary position, a step in between. The so-called "Digger Do" was intended to create the interjacent perspective involving a different social contract. "Do your own thing," which meant "being free," came within the framework of mutualism and sharing. Culture was the foundation for society, everything was built on it. The theory behind the Digger concept of social change was that if you could change the culture, the politics and the economics would naturally follow.

Housing, too, should be free. That belief explained why the group created crash pads like the Digger garage on Page Street. But these were easy prey for city building inspectors who cited them for various sanitary violations. The same thing occurred with the Free Frame of Reference Storefront at 520 Frederick Street that was used as a crash pad.

The first Free Frame of Reference Store was opened at 1762 Page Street in November 1966, but it was closed the following month on December 30.

The Radha-Krishna Temple was established next door to the Diggers at 518 Frederick Street, but the Krishna devotees and the Diggers did not see eye to eye. Both gave away free food and were recruiting members, though their philosophies, goals and plans of action diverged. Adepts of Krishna wished to transcend the senses to achieve spiritual perfection, whereas the Diggers believed in gratifying the senses to the fullest.

The San Francisco police were quick to go "shopping" at 520 Frederick Street–shopping for runaways, so they said, but also for drugs and stolen property. Though they were denied entry three times, they returned in the evening to disrupt the screening of *Poon Tang Trilogy*, which was being shown for free on an old bed sheet. Emmett Grogan and three others were arrested, and the apartment was thoroughly trashed by the police for good measure (Hjortsberg 283).

The "Full Moon Public Celebration of Halloween" was an exercise in guerilla theatre as provocation and exemplified their penchant for sailing close to the wind. One thousand five hundred leaflets were passed out to advertise it. At half past five on Halloween in 1966, twenty Diggers carried the cumbersome Frame of Reference up the hill to the intersection where the public celebration was to be held. As expected, the Mime Troupe's eight foot puppets soon drew a large crowd. Dozens of six inch Frames of Reference were passed out that people hung around their necks as a sort of amulet.

The fun really began with an impromptu version of "Any Fool on the Street," a kind of guerilla sit-in used to tie up traffic and take over an intersection to show that pedestrians had precedence over automobiles. The crowd was a colorful, multifarious organism, and included children dressed up for Halloween, with their trick-or-treat bags full of goodies. But then five police cars and a paddy wagon arrived with sirens blaring.

The humorous part of the incident is that without realizing what was happening, the police became part of the farce when they started addressing a puppet as though it were a real person, warning it and the other puppets that they would all be arrested for blocking traffic. The puppet (with a Digger inside) immediately responded to the cue by asking who the public was, and then answered his own question. Of course, *he* was the public, and in a democracy the streets, like everything else, belonged to the people, so the streets were "free."

When the puppets tried to leave, they were grabbed by the police. Five Diggers were arrested and thrown into a paddy wagon: Robert La Morticella, Emmett Grogan, Kent Minault, Peter Berg and Brooks Butcher. Unknowingly, the police had sown the dragon's teeth. Now it was time for the crowd as chorus to get into the act by booing and chanting: "Frame up! Frame up! Frame up!"

Those arrested were booked at Park Station for creating a public nuisance and spent the night in jail singing, among other songs "Avanti Populi" (C. Perry 105). They were released in the morning on their own recognizance.

It was free publicity for the arrestees who were praised as heroes in the Haight-Ashbury and across the Bay in Berkeley where political activism was the *sine qua non* of social and economic change. The *Berkeley Barb* ran an article in its November 4, 1966, issue and advertised the free food in the Panhandle, as well as other Digger projects such as the "24-hour Frame of Reference Exchange."

The *San Francisco Chronicle* put the story on the front page on November 30, 1966, and the photograph of the five Diggers on the steps of the Hall of Justice transformed them into living legends, though their names were withheld.

"The Death of Money" was another major street theatre event which took place on Saturday afternoon, 17 December 1966. It was organized to condemn capitalism and money. Those who took part in the "circus parade" created a happening with whistles, bells, flowers, incense, lollipops and signs that said "NOW!" Rearview mirrors were distributed to show people they were watching themselves (C. Perry 114), or maybe to create the blinding light of social truth.

A coffin with coins in it was carried through the street by six pallbearers wearing very large animal masks. The unwonted procession was preceded by a Diogenes-like character with a kerosene lamp. It was pure phantasmagoria from Petrarch's world, complete with dwarves and cripples leaping and lurching and "oooooing!" and "aaaahhhing!" down Haight Street. Amidst the sweet scent of incense and maryjane, penny whistles screeched, and toga-clad maidens threw daisies to the crowd. It was just all make believe.

The cortege brought traffic to a standstill as Hell's Angels roared down the road, "NOW!" signs flapping wildly in the wind. Phyllis Wilner let it all hang out when she stood up screaming "Free!" on Hairy Henry Kot's Harley. Several thousand people had assembled in the rollicking romp through the Haight. It was a lot of innocent fun until the police arrived.

Like most Digger events, it was an unlawful assembly. But it's difficult to arrest several thousand boisterous paraders, so Hairy Henry was singled out. Allowing Phyllis to stand up on his bike was a traffic violation. The police could have ignored it, but they didn't.

A radio check on Kot's driver's license soon revealed that he had recently been paroled from San Quentin prison. Bingo! Henry was summoned to accompany the police to Park Station where he could supposedly recover his license. But he told them to keep it and walked off. Upon which a horde of uniforms submerged Kot, who was collared for resisting arrest, though not properly informed of his rights, and dragged by force to the paddy wagon. Seeing what was happening to his brother in arms, George Hendricks, better known in the Haight as "Chocolate George," plunged head first into the foray to pull him out. Both were then piled on by a swarm of angry uniforms that were more ferocious than the Green Bay Packers defending their goal line. Chocolate George, one of the best known Angels in the Haight, was so named because of his unusual appetence for chocolate milk. The crowd, that had witnessed the entire episode, got into the act as best it could by yelling in chorus: "The streets belong to the people!"

Both Angels were dispatched *illico presto* to Park Station and booked: Hairy Henry for resisting arrest and Chocolate George for interfering. The Death of Money Parade, or what was left of it, was redirected towards Park

Station, but upon arriving there they were informed that the two bikers had already been sent downtown to city jail, so the parade continued downtown, with poet Michael McClure leading the way. Donations to pay for bail were put in the Death of Money coffin. Chocolate George was released on bail, but Hairy Henry remained in jail as a parole violator. Some of the police guarding Park Station were reportedly the first to make a contribution to the bail money. The Hell's Angels, who were grateful for the generosity of the hippies, paid them back by organizing a New Year's Day party.

The Summer of Love had come and gone and the hippies of the Haight turned a whiter shade of pale. The "Death of Hippie" parade took place on 6 October 1967. One of its intents was to comment on the sinister change in the neighborhood that everyone was aware of and attempting to understand. The date was meant to be symbolic since it was one year, day for day, after the California State ban on LSD.

The parade was in fact a ritualized funeral procession, with pall bearers carrying a wooden coffin filled with beads, flowers and other hippie fetishes, and bearing the sardonic inscription: "Hippie, Son of Media." In effect, Death of Hippie rebuked the mass media for creating and disseminating a false image of the counterculture and the Haight-Ashbury. Epitomized by the Summer of Love, hippies were distorted out of proportion into easily recognizable stereotypes. In short, "hippie" was in reality a huge media fabrication. From then on, the Diggers proposed to use the expression "Free Man."

Several organizations participated in the Death of Hippie Parade including The Free Clinic, Happening House, Free

City, The Switchboard and the Flame.

At the end of the mock funeral cortege, the coffin, draped in black crepe, was put on a funeral pyre and set ablaze. Someone played taps on a shrill trumpet while remembrance cards were handed out with the following text: "Once upon a time, a man put on beads and became a hippie. Today the hippie takes off the beads and becomes a man, a Freeman."

Both the mainstream and underground press published articles on the event and many could not resist replacing "Freeman" with "Freebie."

Not everyone, of course, embraced the Digger gospel. Some underground papers such as the *Berkeley Barb* and the *Haight Ashbury Maverick* felt a need to vindicate the underground press, protesting that the Diggers used media events to impact society, too, and that they even had their own personal pamphlet called Com/co.

People looked around and could see that the neighborhood was going to the dogs, and more and more the general attitude was the devil take the hindmost. Not surprisingly, many community services such as the Free Clinic were closed, while others were steeped in debt. The Switchboard, victimized by embezzlement, owed $1,000, The Psychedelic Shop owed an incredible $6,000, prompting the Thelin brothers to give everything away, and the Diggers' Trip Without a Ticket was $750 in debt and confronted with numerous building code violations which could not be remedied. Nothing short of a miracle could save the Haight. To make matters worse, black youths were preying on and bullying the hippies, particularly hippie girls and women, sometimes committing violent acts of rape, robbery and assault (Grogan 516-17). The police were not letting up on the hippies either with a significant increase in "haul-ins" and "sweep-ups."

Those that had places to go left the Haight or were making preparations to do so. There was a massive urban exodus. Even the Diggers were leaving after all the sound and the fury. Some went to Marin Country, across the Golden Gate to Lagunitas - Forest Knolls, moving into the Red House. Grogan went back east to New York. Others set up numerous communes around the country: Olema, Salmon River House, Black Bear, Trinidad. There was no one left to turn to.

A lot of people asked where the Diggers were, now that things had gotten so violent and degrading, and the question of responsibility and accountability was raised. Leaving the Haight-Ashbury in the lurch seemed to be proof of their indifference to the results they had previously advocated.

The notion of responsibility is a complicated issue. Of course there was no written agreement between the Diggers and the community, just a lot of leaflets, broadsides, parades, guerilla theatre and free food. Yet one wonders. Didn't their involvement in the different programs and street happenings imply a tacit agreement of accountability?

If you ask them, most people will say they want to be free and that they value freedom more than anything else. But freedom involves responsibility, and most people shun it. But there can be no real freedom without moral responsibility, just as there can be no real love without a belief in the moral principles of allegiance, conscience, compassion and respect.

It could be argued that the Diggers never claimed to be doing anything for the rest of their lives as a committed political or cultural group. They said that what they were doing was "life acting the theatre of free." Coming from a Digger that might sound acceptable, but coming from anyone else it would sound like a cop-out. Some have said the group did little things that changed the world. They did do things to make the Haight-Ashbury a better place to live for people lacking financial means and that because of the things they did, it was, in many ways, a better place for a while. But is our world a better place because of what the Diggers did? It behooves us to be prudent when comparing the Haight-Ashbury of the mid-sixties with the complex world of the twenty-first century. There were enormous social and economic problems in the sixties, and many of them are still with us.

Responsibility is an important theme in literature and the Russian writer Fyodor Dostoyevsky thought seriously about it in *The Brothers Karamazov:* "Everyone is really responsible to all men for all men and for everything. I don't know how to explain it to you, but I feel it is so, painfully even."

A sense of universal responsibility is undoubtedly a key to happiness and that feeling did exist in the Haight-Ashbury in the beginning and up to the Be-In, but it was lost afterwards for different reasons.

8

The Communication Company

The Communication Company, also known as Com/co, was a well known component of the Haight-Ashbury in 1966 and 1967. It collaborated with the Diggers by printing and distributing their messages, broadsides, leaflets and handbills spontaneously, quickly and on a regular basis.

The Digger broadsides, which first appeared in the Haight-Ashbury in October 1966, were often used to criticize specific groups, named or unnamed, to exhort people to do certain things in the community, or simply assess particular problems and situations. The tone used by the authors was particularly aggressive, sarcastic and militant. People reacted to them with surprize and curiosity, wondering who was behind the anonymous announcements.

The range of subject matter for the different communications was virtually limitless, but was generally based on events related to or occurring within the Haight such as police brutality, homelessness, health problems, unsanitary living conditions, overcrowding, the basic needs of indigent youth and the deterioration of the basic standard of living in the Haight-Ashbury. Other topics might include the HIP merchants and the shops on Haight Street, notably Ron and Jay Thelin and their Psychedelic Shop, or capitalism and exploitation.

The subjects were often decided upon after heated discussions between the key figures of the group: Emmett Grogan, Coyote, Peter Berg, Sweet William and Kent Minault.

The first printings were signed George Metevsky, alluding to George Peter Metesky, the notorious Mad Bomber who terrorized New York in the forties and fifties by planting bombs in public places. Metesky's life is a tragic story of exploitation and rage. The bombings were a form of revenge for Metesky who was permanently disabled after a boiler accident on a worksite. He lost his job and developed tuberculosis, but never received any disability compensation despite his numerous protests and trials.

By signing their broadsides with the Mad Bomber's name, the Diggers were making an appeal for "justice" in the Haight and intimating that a failure to comply could have serious consequences. The authors of the messages signed Metevsky were Emmett Grogan and his friend Billy Murcott.

The Digger texts can be seen as a reaction against the content, style and tone of *The San Francisco Oracle*, which the radical anarchists believed failed to address the important issues of the community. The Digger texts can also be seen as a reaction against Timothy Leary and all the hippie gurus who profited from the media hype about peace and love.

The Communication Company

After the Love Pageant Rally, the "Free Food Leaflet" was handed out to passersby on Haight Street.

> FREE FOOD GOT HOT STEW
> RIPE TOMATOES FRESH FRUIT
> BRING A BOWL AND SPOON TO THE
> PANHANDLE AT ASHBURY STREET
> 4 PM   4 PM   4 PM   4 PM   4 PM
> FREE FOOD EVERYDAY FREE FOOD
> IT'S FREE BECAUSE IT'S YOURS!
> the diggers

Warren Hinckle, the executive editor of *Ramparts* magazine, well known for the black patch over his left eye and his acerbic prose, wanted to know who was behind the leaflets and who the Diggers were.

Claude Hayward was working for the muckraking magazine at the time, and because he looked like a hippie and seemed to know something about their subculture was sent by Hinckle to investigate bohemia. Unbeknownst to the twenty-one-year-old Hayward, the assignment would change his life.

As a child, Hayward had lived in Greenwich Village and was well up on the beat poets and writers. He later moved to Venice in Southern California, where some of the beats had relocated.

Born in 1945, Hayward liked to think of himself as an average American youth. He didn't get along with his stepfather and like so many baby boomers was plagued by an angsty feeling of alienation.

While in Southern California, he worked for Pacifica Radio Station KPFK as a volunteer and also for the *Los Angeles Free Press*, also called "Freep," that was edited by Art Kunkin. Hayward eventually became the advertising manager there.

Hayward moved to San Francisco with H'lane Resnikoff, his pregnant companion, in the autumn of 1966. The couple lived in a slummy apartment near Third Street and Mission Street. Hayward luckily found a job as advertising manager for *Sunday Ramparts*, a weekly that Hinckle had recently created, with the first issue in print on 2 October 1966. The paper ceased publication in 1967 because of severe financial difficulties.

Ramparts sought to be a committed, veracious political voice of the New Left. It was the first radical glossy, but the extravagant publishing costs proved to be the demise of the magazine that ceased publication for good in 1975.

Hinckle's weekly staunchly opposed the Vietnam War, published the diaries of Ernesto Che Guevara, the prison diaries of Eldrige Cleaver and in August 1966, "Napalm: Small Town Diary" by James Colaianni, the first article published in the United States to condemn the use of napalm in Vietnam. William Raborn, director of the CIA, asked for a complete report on the paper's personnel in 1966 because the government suspected a direct communist connection with Cuba or elsewhere.

In many ways, the radical magazine was representative of the counterculture with Eldrige Cleaver and Jann Wenner, the rock critic, on the staff. Jann shared an office with Claude Hayward. It was while investigating the Diggers that

Hayward met Chester Anderson.

Chester Anderson moved to San Francisco on January 7, 1967, a week before the Human Be-In. Novelist, poet and editor, Chester Valentine John Anderson was born on August 11, 1932. Though he grew up in Florida, he became a coffee house poet in Greenwich Village and North Beach. He published several novels including *The Butterfly Kid*, a work of science fiction and the first part of the *Greenwich Village Trilogy*, which was nominated for the 1968 Hugo Award. Anderson was fascinated by the emergence of the psychedelic counterculture in the Haight-Ashbury, particularly since the Beats had emigrated *en masse* due to violent police harassment.

In December 1966, Hayward and his companion moved to a second floor apartment at 406 Duboce Avenue, southeast of the Haight. It is uncertain exactly how they met, but about that time, Chester Anderson moved in with Claude Hayward and H'lane Resnikoff.

Anderson, eager to get involved in the excitement of the Haight-Ashbury, suggested they procure a mimeograph machine and the necessary printing equipment to start publishing. Since he was deeply influenced by the Canadian media scholar, Marshall McLuhan, Anderson wanted their publications to respond to the immediate needs of the community, to report the news of the neighborhood as it was happening, something that no one else was doing or apparently wanted to do. The *Oracle*, though integrated in the Haight community, was publishing its issues on an irregular basis. Anderson felt there was a need to publish on a daily basis, even several times a day if need be.

For those who knew mimeograph machines, the Gestetner Company showroom was the logical place to start looking because of its state of the art technology, so Anderson and Hayward went there to see what they could buy. Gestetner was a German manufacturer that built reliable and efficient mimeograph equipment, the most advanced machines at the time.

The Gestefax was a stencil cutting machine that reproduced a stencil for the mimeograph machine. It could print both texts and halftones quickly and cheaply. Anderson and Hayward were immediately sold on it and the Communication Company was born.

The Gestetner 366 silk-screen stencil duplicator and the Gestefax mimeograph machine were set up in the Duboce Avenue apartment. Now they could make their stencils and duplicate as many copies as they wanted to–texts, photographs, graphic designs, whatever they wanted to print. They also used an IBM electric typewriter that may have come from Hayward's office at *Ramparts*.

Com/co distributed the following printed announcement of the company's birth:

> The Communication Company
> Haight/Ashbury
> OUR POLICY
> Love is communication.
> OUR PLANS & HOPES
> + to provide quick & inexpensive printing service for the hip community.
> + to print anything the Diggers want printed.
> + to do lots of community service printing.

\+ to supplement The Oracle with a more or less daily paper whenever Haight news justifies one, thereby maybe adding perspective to The Chronicle's fantasies.

\+ to be outrageous pamphleteers.

\+ to compete with the Establishment press for public opinion.

\+ to revive The Underground, old North Beach magazine of satire & commentary that was instrumental in ending a police harassment routine very like the present one.

\+ to function as a Haight/Ashbury propaganda ministry, free lance if needs be.

\+ to publish literature originating within this new minority.

\+ to produce occasional incredibilities [*sic*] out of an unnatural fondness for either outrage or profit, as the case may be.

\+ to do what we damn well please.

\+ to keep up the payments on

OUR MAGNIFICENT MACHINES

* one brand-new Gestetner 366 silk-screen stencil duplicator.

* one absolutely amazing Gestefax electronic stencil cutter.

WITH WHICH WE CAN

\+ print up to 10,000 nearly lithographic quality copies of almost anything we can wrap around our scanning drum.

\+ on any kind of paper up to 8-1/2 by 14 inches (this being basically an office machine).

* with any kind of art, including half-tones.

* on both sides of the page.

+ in up to four colors with adequate registration (office machine).
* with all manner of outrageous innovations.
* all in a very few hours.
>   WE NEED ALL THE HELP WE CAN GET!
>   WE NEED

+ printing orders.
+ Haight Street reporters.
* a whole lot of scripts for maybe publication.
+ writers for The Underground.
>   claude & chester

626-2926
we deliver

The fliers, broadsides and other printings by Com/co were always free, thus adopting the Digger dictum against commercial profit. But since it didn't get its paper, ink, stencils and other materials for nothing, they solicited funds to cover their printing costs. No addresses were indicated, only their first names and a telephone number where they could be reached.

For the most part, the layout of the broadsides was austere, since the primary goal was to disseminate information, not to seduce its readers with sophistication. The *Oracle* and Com/co were antipodal neighbors, yet Hayward and Anderson's publications came to be emblematic of the Haight-Ashbury. Emmett Grogan thought it was a great paper, the best a community could have.

Hayward and Anderson, like their printed texts, dressed in a plain if not austere fashion. Both had a predilection for black clothes. Hayward usually wore a black, high-crowned hat reminiscent of the Far West, and Anderson was known for a pair of thick-lensed sunglasses.

Peter Coyote gave a rather negative description of Claude Hayward and H'lane Resnikoff in *Sleeping Where I Fall*. Claude was described as a "ferret-faced" individual, while H'lane was "condensed hostility" with unkempt hair. She could swindle a street hustler and steal a cripple's "wooden leg," or anything that wasn't firmly tied down. Claude was said to be anarchistic and a "thief" (Coyote 86). Coyote claimed the mimeograph machines were stolen, which is somewhat intriguing because the Diggers had a reputation for sticky fingers and helping themselves to whatever they needed. Maybe this was a case of the pot calling the kettle black.

Hayward operated and maintained the press and stencil machines since he was mechanically more inclined than Anderson who liked to ramble through the Haight in search of newsworthy items to print, meticulously writing down information in the notebooks he kept in his beat up canvas bag.

Hayward kept his job with *Sunday Ramparts* to have a steady source of income to support his family. Anderson and Resnikoff often ran the machines during the day; sometimes volunteers right off the street would lend a hand in the printing and distribution of hundreds of broadsides that were posted everywhere you could imagine.

The collage of subjects printed says a lot about the Diggers' goals. Since they believed that everything should be free, there were naturally leaflets against money and commercialism. "Money Is an Unnecessary Evil" was one such leaflet, which visibly echoes the first book of Timothy 6:10: "For the love of money is a root of all kinds of evil." Desire for wealth has long been recognized as a source of temptation that results in the loss of compassion. Innumerable verses in the Bible refer to the "love of money," "bribes," "vanity," "greedy dogs," and princes whose companions are thieves. The Diggers, for their part, were aware that materialism tended to make people selfish and coldhearted.

Other printings made announcements for free acid, fish, comestibles, or just plain everyday necessities. Some evoked the FBI's list of radical subversives, of whom the Diggers were included, or how we spend our time and what we do with our meaningless lives: "What Part of the Day Do You Spend Running," or who decides what in a neighborhood: "Who Wants Haight Street." Poems and poetic texts were also printed, such as "War Is Décor in My Cavern Cave" by Michael McClure, and *All Watched Over by Machines of Loving Grace* by Richard Brautigan.

Com/co did quite a bit to make the Haight-Ashbury poet and novelist a household word by printing collections of the writer's works. It was responsible for the first printing of *All Watched Over by Machines of Loving Grace*, an important transitional work that signals Brautigan's development as a hippie writer. Brautigan's typescript was printed and distributed for free in a matter of days; about five hundred copies in all were printed. Naturally, there were a number of printing errors in the text due to lack of proofreading, but today the original Com/co publication is a rare collector's item.

Commended by the hippies for its generosity and sincerity, in spite of or perhaps because of its flaws and simplicity, Com/co redefined publishing in the Haight-Ashbury.

The Underground Press Syndicate (UPS) helped to mobilize underground papers in the United States. It was created in mid-1966 by the *Berkeley Barb*, the *Los Angeles Free Press*, *Fifth Estate*, the *East Village Other* and *The Paper*. There was hope UPS could unify the underground press, but most members were disappointed with the syndicate and realized that it had not created a feeling of unity. UPS existed for a year before it finally organized a powwow at Stinson Beach, California. Thorne Dreyer, editor of *The Rag*, said there was too much bombastic twaddle and self-admiration at the powwow, so not much was done.

Only six out of nineteen papers in UPS sent representatives. A mission statement was drafted, but it was "vague and hubristic" (McMillian 91-92).

Com/co became a member of UPS simply by submitting a request. Members exchanged articles as they did subscriptions and listed the addresses of member papers. The accomplishments were modest, but before that there was little contact between different underground papers.

In truth, Com/co functioned more like a group of pamphleteers than as an underground paper, but its role in the community of the Haight was reel, though short-lived like the Haight itself. Anderson and Hayward freely admitted this role when they said they wanted to function as "outrageous pamphleteers" and as a ministry of propaganda in the neighborhood.

Relations with the Diggers were often problematic and dissension arose between Emmett Grogan and Chester Anderson. Moreover, Com/co's role in the neighborhood was complicated by the fact that Hayward and Anderson had moved from 406 Duboce Avenue to 742 Arguello Street in the Richmond district in May 1967, a time when thousands of young people were arriving in San Francisco with no money and no place to go.

A conflict arose over the machines. The Diggers wanted complete control of the mimeograph equipment and demanded that they be used exclusively for their specific purposes. Chester Anderson could not believe his ears, and felt it was time for a serious reality check. So he said "no." Hayward, the younger of the two, apparently sided with the Diggers. Anderson, who had paid the down payment for the machines tried to get them back, but without success (Barber 116). The Diggers pulled the rug out from under him, and by the time the Summer of Love arrived, Anderson was no longer a part of Com/co. The machines were ensconced in the basement of the Diggers' store (Carlson 55), the Trip without a Ticket, and Chester Anderson, disgruntled with the turn of events and perhaps the general decline of the Haight, left the city. Hayward, for his part, continued to print for the Diggers as he had in the past.

The dramatic rupture was officially announced by Anderson on 15 August 1967, in a text entitled "Hippie Siamese Twins Split" (Perry 230). Anderson had hoped to start another Com/co in San Francisco, but was unable to do so. He kept himself busy by editing Paul Williams' *Crawdaddy*, the first rock magazine in the United States, even though that job was short-lived. Williams was the literary executor of science fiction writer Philip K. Dick, and as such he published some of Dick's works posthumously.

It was as though everything were disintegrating right before your eyes. Soon the Diggers broke up, too, changing their name to the Free City Collective. It was over.

Agenda setting is about controlling the topics discussed by the media. If a given topic is covered often enough, it will be considered more important by those who are exposed to it than topics that are covered less. Agenda setting is used by the mass media and all media to sway public opinion. The media create images in the minds of the public, and these images determine how people think and feel. It is a way of creating "reality," and an individual's "reality" will be greatly determined by what they read and what they watch and listen to. By repeating certain images, they become engraved in people's minds and can thus be used to trigger predetermined thoughts and behavioral patterns. Vance Packard, the American journalist, was probably one of the first to discuss this mode of manipulation in his meticulously researched books on behavior molding and motivation research.

Some groups and individuals have greater access to the media than others, and that makes it easier for them to set the agenda and thus influence public opinion. Certain persons act as opinion leaders, which also helps them to impact particular events or issues.

When people feel that a specific issue is relevant, they tend to feel a need to be oriented, informed, or guided.

Agenda setting plays a significant role in telling people

what to think about, but on another level it also tells people what to think and, ultimately, how to feel about a given issue and what to do about it.

The most active members of the Diggers, those that decided what topics and issues should be discussed in the Com/co broadsides, were setting the agenda. They were controlling, to some extent, what people thought about certain issues, particularly since the tone of their texts was slanted and somewhat sectarian in that it was confined to the dogmatic limits of their group. With their fliers and broadsides, the Diggers were telling their audience what to think about the HIP merchants, the Psychedelic Shop, the Human Be-In, Timothy Leary, the dance concerts, money, and the other issues they addressed.

Com/Co stood out in the Haight because of its position in the community and because of its position with regards to the establishment. It often opposed what the *status quo* stood for and stood for what the *status quo* was against.

Like the counterculture in general, Com/co was opposed to the Vietnam War and favored the use of recreational or spiritual drugs such as LSD and marijuana. But it also castigated elements of the hip culture that exploited the psychedelic community. A noteworthy example is "When You Come to San Francisco Wear a Flower in Your Hair," which chided John Phillips as songwriter for capitalizing on the Summer of Love. Papa John was also mistrusted because he lived in La La Land. "Uncle Tim'$ Children" affords another example. It reproved those who sold the Haight-Ashbury to the mass media. Ostensibly it attacked the former Harvard professor turned High Priest, but it also flayed the merchants on Haight Street and the Diggers' old nemesis *The San Francisco Oracle*.

The text succinctly related the story of a pretty teenage girl who went to the Haight–allured by the media hype–expecting to meet gentle people with flowers in their hair. The reality, however, was completely different. When she got there, she was preyed upon by the kinds of people that have always taken advantage of the more naïve, trusting individuals. She was shot with speed again and again before being raped by a gang of hoodlum "hippies." "Rape is as common as bullshit on Haight Street" said the broadside.

Chester Anderson's text, which would never have been published by the mainstream press, was admittedly crude and shocking, but purposely so. He knew it was the most effective way of moving his readers on a deeper level. In the final analysis, the Haight-Ashbury, thought Anderson, was really no better than anywhere else, and you could find dishonest, immoral people there like you could anywhere.

Com/co was for and about the Haight-Ashbury. It attempted to cut through the mainstream hype that did not understand the community. Being free from commercial ties, it was able to tell the plain unvarnished truth, and to some extent mobilize opinion. Com/co, unlike many sources of information, was produced in the neighborhood, by the neighborhood, and for the neighborhood. And that explained why it was a respected institution of the underground.

9

The San Francisco Oracle

The San Francisco Oracle was a psychedelic underground paper in the Haight-Ashbury that was published from 1966 to 1968. It was edited at different times by John Brownson, George Tsongas, Gabe Katz, Ron Thelin and Allen Cohen.

For many, including Abbie Hoffman, the paper was a "mind blower." It fed the dreams of the psychedelic counterculture, the "Flower Children," as they were called, in quest of a deeper meaning to life. For some, it was a cosmic voyage through the doors of perception into a garden of earthly delights.

The colored pages of the *Oracle* showed how far a generation had gone from the fifties and how much further it needed to go to make the dream come true. For Allen Cohen, staff member and editor of the paper, "it began as a dream and ended as a legend."

In the spring of 1966, he dreamt he was flying around the world, and as he looked down, he saw people reading a multicolored newspaper with rainbows printed on it. How remarkable, he thought, a rainbow newspaper.

He went to the Psychedelic Shop owned by Ron and Jay Thelin at 1535 Haight Street, a place where you could find the accouterments of psychedelia: hash pipes, rolling paper, incense, beads, posters, books on astrology and mysticism, and sometimes more, if you knew how to ask for it.

When Ron Thelin heard about Allen's project to create the rainbow paper, he eagerly supplied the start-up money. This was in the spring of 1966, before the mainstream media had really heard about the Haight-Ashbury and began concocting and mass-producing their phony, counterfeit image. At that time it was a haven for poets and artists, a seemingly Edenic bohemia, with a good number of students and alumni from San Francisco State College who were drawn there by a surplus of cheap housing.

Many have wondered why a social revolution occurred at that time in the Haight-Ashbury. One significant reason was the rapid dissemination of psychedelics, including LSD, across the entire country. The Harvard drug scandal involving Timothy Leary and Richard Alpert was brought to national attention when Boston newspapers seized the affair in March of 1962. Yet well before that, Henry *Luce's* magazines had published articles on LSD and other hallucinogens, with the first appearing in 1954 in *Time* entitled "Dream Stuff," and three years later *Life* published "Seeking the Magic Mushroom."

LSD was often considered a shortcut to transcendence by many because it helped to see through the social roles and psychological games inherent in human relationships, and thus realize that the ego was a barrier to higher consciousness.

In late 1965 and early 1966, on any given day, you could be sure that all and sundry were "tripping out" in the Haight. Michael Rossman of the Berkeley Free Speech Movement (FSM) stated that many students at "Cal" were smoking grass and dropping acid when the FSM began (Torgoff 227). But LSD was not at all like smoking pot. George Harrison of the Beatles compared grass to having a couple of beers, whereas acid was like a rocket trip to the moon.

When young people started smoking marijuana in the sixties, they realized that almost everything the establishment had said about it was wrong. It was not the "Devil's weed," as described by government agencies and the mass media that indulged in scare tactics to create taboos and condition public opinion. Users saw through the hype right off the bat. Either the government was talking through its hat, or it had decided to lie. The Office of Strategic Services (OSS) had chosen marijuana as a truth drug because it made some people talkative, but average individuals smoked it when listening to music, watching movies or just going out to have a good time because of its capacity to enhance awareness and help you relax, or as some would say, "get in the groove."

Tripping on lysergic acid diethylamide is a completely different ballgame because of the rush and the intensity of the drug. It can induce moments of profound awareness, cosmic epiphany or personal quietude. Many users have felt it helped them to understand the deepest mysteries of human existence. But LSD is not to be taken lightly because a trip may take you into the depths of the human psyche, for better or for worse. As the eponymous protagonist remarks in Oscar Wilde's *The Picture of Dorian Gray*, "Each of us has heaven and hell in him." Moreover, a trip can last up to ten or twelve hours, depending on the dosage and the purity of the dose. Sometimes it might be cut with other chemicals like speed that could induce a "bummer" or bad trip. Clearly, taking this hallucinogen does not involve the same commitment as smoking a joint.

Although millions of young people were having fun with grass and acid, the establishment perceived the change in attitudes and behavior as a threat to society and the nation's ambitions in the world. Some leaders in government actually saw it as a communist plot to corrupt American morals and destroy the nation. For J. Edgar Hoover, even Martin Luther King was a communist, because he couldn't conceive of anyone challenging the establishment unless they were.

A lot has been said about the "revolution" that had begun in the Haight-Ashbury—the world's first psychedelic supermarket—but this was a different kind of revolution, for it was an inchoate movement based on mind expanding drugs. Nothing like that had ever happened before in the country, or anywhere else for that matter.

Some imagined a peace and love revolution that could expand exponentially and transform not only a district or a city into a peaceful, loving community, but perhaps the entire human race as well. These visionaries sought to change the parochial, humdrum format of newspapers and explore new themes and layouts.

After some wrangling and arguments, the politicos and

McLuhanites got hold of Jay Thelin's $500 contribution to get the presses rolling, though they slurred over their specific goals, and began work on *P.O. Frisco* in a Frederick Street storefront. The filmmaker Bruce Conner had suggested they call the paper the *Psychedelic Oracle*, a name that foreshadowed the radical changes that would shortly occur in the underground paper.

A lot of people were disappointed with *P.O. Frisco*, particularly the front page that oriented the paper in a confrontational direction that many wanted to avoid. It showed a naked girl kneeling on a couch with a swastika armband. There was a story on concentration camps for subversives and another on a GI back from Vietnam. Other articles included "The Craft of Masturbation," Richard Alpert talking about Meher Baba and LSD, and a couple of articles thrown in on the neighborhood.

The Thelin brothers felt their money had been wasted and withdrew their support for Dan Elliot and Dick Sassoon, the editors. From then on, Ron and Jay wanted decision making to be more democratic and specific ideas to be adopted by consensus. After some discussion, *The San Francisco Oracle* was chosen as the name for the paper.

Oracle number one was published on 20 September 1966. John Brownson and George Tsongas edited the first two issues, using traditional tabloid layout with vertical columns and black and white print, though more graphic art was included, with Bruce Conner and Michael Bowen having entire pages devoted to their work. The paper ran ads for In Gear, B'tzalel, the Mojo Navigator, City Lights Books, plus subscription information for the *Oracle*. The editors were incredibly optimistic because it was possible to subscribe for seventy-eight issues at the bargain rate of seven dollars.

The front page was an "us vs. them" piece entitled "Haight-Ashbury Meets Police" by Allen Cohen. "Affirming Humanness" was a Timothy Leary apology for "turn on, tune in, drop out." It asked its readers to reflect on the sapience of acid's High Priest by dropping out of the social game, flowing with evolution and joining the revolution. Traditional protest, the article said, had not changed anything in the world: the Vietnamese continued to be killed and ethnic minorities were still oppressed, proof that the United States was a destructive juggernaut. People were urged to survive "independent of the system" to implement lasting change.

The *Oracle* attempted to create an "open voice" for those pursuing a "life of art." The staff wished to motivate people to take part in the on-going revolution and quoted Marshall McLuhan to justify its departure from the traditional mass media format.

There were also letters in support of Michael McClure's controversial play *The Beard* and an article on a play entitled "Search and Seizure," described as "an investigation into the police machine."

On the back page was a declaration of independence, formulating certain inalienable rights: freedom to use one's own body the way one wanted to and freedom to pursue joy and to expand one's consciousness. This was in fact an announcement for the Love Pageant Rally, reportedly "the first public outdoor rock concert." The *Oracle* even went so far as to perceive the event as a second Boston Tea Party, though it was obvious the hippies did not have the overwhelming support of Americans on that issue. People were not going to overthrow the government to defend LSD. The Prophesy of a Declaration of Independence was to be held on October 6, 1966, the day LSD became illegal in California. Hundreds of people attended the event to protest the penalization of acid. The three sixes in the date supposedly symbolized evil, but it was meant to be a fun event and not one of violent confrontation.

Oracle number two, which was undated, pursued the political tone with the front page headline "Youth Quake," referring to the Bayview-Hunters Point riot that began when Matthew John, a sixteen-year-old black, was shot in the back for allegedly stealing a car.

The riot and the curfew provoked the Diggers' first public act. Emmett Grogan tore down Michael Bowen's signs urging hippies to stay home during the riots, and put up his own signs calling for hippies to "Disobey the Fascist Curfew."

In a different vein, a health food store operator wrote "Back to Food," an article on the importance of eating natural foods and avoiding processed, commercialized food.

There were more ads in this issue than in the preceding one, with larger announcements as well. These included ads for The General Store, The Blushing Peony, Sunset Health Foods, 40 Cedar Alley, Inner Space, Mnasidika, Quasars, In Gear, The Phoenix, Wild Colors, Vanguard, B'tzalel and House of Richard. There was also an advert for the Avalon Ballroom concerts on November 4th and 5th featuring the

Grateful Dead, Country Joe and the Fish and Oxford Circle, and shows at the Juke Box and the Armenian Hall. The advertisement section also ran the Diggers' announcement for free food at Oak and Ashbury in the Panhandle.

The centerfold, a pen and ink drawing by Bruce Conner, established the tradition of using the centerfold for artwork. It was fairly obvious, at this point, that the paper was still in search of itself.

Oracle number three was apparently published on November 7, 1966, or thereabouts. The basic format was traditional, though some changes were made. A bare-chested acid Christ (Ken Kesey), with microphone in hand, was featured on the front page, thereby stressing the importance of LSD in the Haight as well as for the *Oracle* that sought to represent the community.

Gabe Katz edited the issue with George Tsongas. Katz, an adman from New York, had dropped acid like Allen Cohen. Both agreed the layout of the underground paper needed to be changed, and both lauded Leary, maybe Katz even more than Cohen, who saw him as the guru of the psychedelic counterculture, whose "religion" would help mankind to transcend its primitive, ego state of mind.

During an argument over an article on Kesey's Acid Test and the tabloid's layout in general, John A. Brownson and George Tsongas walked out in a huff, giving Katz and Cohen free reign over the paper. As a result of their greater freedom of action, they were able to orient the paper towards the oneiric, rainbow design that would become its hallmark in the months ahead.

Cohen had lofty ambitions for his paper, wanting it to

provide the symbols and guidance for the psychedelic trips its readers were routinely taking, and on a much broader plane, he sought the paradigms needed to change the world to their cosmic vision of peace and love.

One extensive article, "Ken Kesey and the Great Pumpkin," reported on his mediatized return from Mexico. "Acid is a door. We must graduate from acid," declared Kesey. The counterculture was rife with rumors after hearing that. Was the acid Christ copping out? Had he made a deal with the FBI to save his skin?

Apart from the main story about Kesey, there was an article by Gary Snyder entitled "Buddhism and the Coming Revolution," which was framed by a Michael Bowen collage. In "Yogi and the Commissar," staff artist Alan W. Williams spoke about his being arrested and beaten by the San Francisco police. Though the police did not like to hear about its brutality, or worse yet, read about it, even in a "rag," these were not isolated incidents.

Oracle number four, "Dr. Leary and the Love Book," was published on December 16, 1966. About 15,000 copies were printed.

Leary had gone to San Francisco to make a pitch for "The Death of the Mind" show. Gabe Katz's admiration was apparent in his graphic eulogy of the former Harvard professor, though the rest of the staff would have preferred a soberer depiction of acid's High Priest. According to Allen Cohen, Katz's first drawing depicted Leary with halos and rays of divine glory, but that version was scratched.

In the interview, Leary not surprisingly advocated the use of psychedelics and predicted that more and more young people would be using them in the future as America turned on, tuned in and dropped out. "Psychedelic drugs are sacraments," said Leary, insisting that they should be used as such. Before taking LSD, users should be "in a state of grace," which involves something akin to a confession. Those who are not, he said, risk experiencing the "LSD temporary psychosis" and "an ontological panic." When asked if Leary's new religion, The League of Spiritual Discovery, offered the promise of heaven and the threat of hell, he said it did, but you had to take LSD. Announcing heaven and hell's irruption into our daily lives was a way of translating eschatology into psychedelics for the turned on masses. The fiery evangelicalism of a Southern Baptist minister could not have been more effective.

The Death of the Mind celebration was held at the Berkeley Community Theatre on Friday, January 27, 1967, and on Saturday, January 28 at Winterland. Tickets ranged from $2.25 to $4.75. To put theses prices in perspective, the average price of a movie ticket was $1.25 in 1967.

There was also a feature story about Lenore Kandel's *Love Book*, which had caused such a stir. Local and state authorities decided to attack the counterculture in the Haight-Ashbury because it had openly declared itself opposed to mainstream America. Kandel's book on the spirituality of sex was a pretext to harass the Psychedelic Shop at 1535 Haight Street, and *The San Francisco Oracle* that they had never liked anyway.

Ronald Wilson Reagan had just been elected governor of California by promising "to clean up the mess at Berkeley" and by putting "the welfare bums back to work." His victory gave the local police the go-ahead to start "cleaning up" the Haight-Ashbury. Two officers from the San Francisco Vice Squad bought the book in The Psychedelic Shop and then promptly arrested Allen Cohen.

On November 23, 1966, six English professors at San Francisco State College–James Schevill, Patrick Gleason, Jack Gilbert, Leonard Wolf, Mark Linenthal and Maurice Bassant–read Lenore Kandel's *Love Book*, along with passages from *The Beard* by Michael McClure, in protest of police actions against so-called obscenity laws. The San Francisco police had seized both works it seems in "a wave of homebred puritanical neo-fascism" (*Oracle* 66).

In "Notes of a Dirty Bookseller," Allen Cohen described his arrest and trial in prose somewhat reminiscent of Henry Miller. A kind of trial was held and The Psychedelic Shop and City Lights Books were found guilty of violating state obscenity laws. The book was judged obscene in 1967, but this ruling was later overturned by a higher court as a violation of First Amendment rights to freedom of expression. At the time, numerous porn shops in San Francisco were making sizeable profits with impunity, not to mention the pornographic newspapers sold in vending machines on the streets of the city for everyone to see, including children. They put everything you could imagine on the front page. Clearly, there was a double standard on pornography in San Francisco and other major cities in the United States.

"At the Handle of the Kettle," by Steve Leiper, discussed the Diggers of the Haight-Ashbury, whose philosophy was so radically different from that of the *Oracle*. The author, who attended a Thanksgiving feast offered by the local anarchists, was surprised by the positive vibrations during the meal, until he wandered into the backroom kitchen and witnessed "the brink of cosmic horror." There was so much garbage that it seemed to be crawling up the walls like some primordial mire. This was the flip side of the good vibrations in the outer room.

The Diggers provided food, shelter and clothing for free and they did it anonymously, in most cases. They did not believe in "peace and love," nor did they believe people should grovel before authority or lick the boots of government. The Diggers were neither hippies, nor political radicals, but somewhere in between.

Carl Helbing, artist and astrologer, was "The Gossiping Guru." His column sought to be an open forum of ideas about anything remotely related to the Haight and the psychedelic counterculture. His style was like a multitudinous stream of thoughts and feelings running down the page, evoking such ideas as collective consciousness, the interest in new ways of turning on, survival in the depths of the counterculture, or "commune-ication" [*sic*]. There was also a letter to the editor by Robert Duncan to praise Lenore Kandel and *The Love Book* as an expression of the "divine nature of sexual love."

The centerfold was a contribution by North Beach poet Lawrence Ferlinghetti, "After the Cries of the Birds Has Stopped" [*sic*], enframed within a religious collage by Michael Bowen.

Oracle number five featured the Human Be-In. The issue came out in early January 1967 to advertise and promote the large happening in Golden Gate Park. About 50,000 copies were printed in the format that came to be associated with the paper. This issue marked its first use of color–eight pages using purple ink. The technique of color printing would be augmented and perfected in the issues that followed, becoming the tabloid's trademark. Text and graphic art coalesced in a symbiotic nexus to depict the visionary state of expanded consciousness.

The staff was committed in their effort to be the harbinger of the psychedelic revolution, of which the Haight-Ashbury was thought to be the nucleus of the avant-garde movement. It was with this in mind that they heralded a return to the halcyon days of tribalism, modeled after the culture of Native Americans, and based on an ethos of peace and love which they believed would assure harmony within and without, and stave off the impending apocalypse that many feared would arrive some terrible day in the history of the Cold War.

The front page in purple of the Hindu holy man, or sadhu, was a familiar motif of the hippie counterculture and became a poster for the Be-In at the Polo Field. *Oracle* number 5 was given away for free at the "gathering of the tribes," as it was quixotically called.

Michael Bowen spent a lot of time and energy organizing the Human Be-In and took advantage of his personal contacts to persuade Timothy Leary and a couple of underground poets to participate. Ostensibly, one of the goals of the gathering was to bridge the growing gap between the hippies in San Francisco and the radicals in Berkeley, a somewhat ambitious task that could not be achieved overnight.

This issue also featured an interview with Dick Alpert, former Harvard psychologist and Leary collaborator, entitled "Ees Setisoppo," which spells "See Opposites" backwards. For Alpert, the Haight was unique in its expansion of consciousness, way ahead of other American cities because of its "softness" and "gentleness." In a rambling talk, with neither head nor tail, he echoed such topics as revolution, dropping out, the establishment, using LSD and marijuana, his friends Ginsberg and Leary, and so on.

"The New Science" spoke about astrology and ancient medicine, spiritualism, and also announced the arrival in the city of "His Holiness, A. C. Bhaktivedanta Swami, a 71-year-old Sannyasi," which is to say an authentic spiritual guide (*Oracle* 96). The centerfold was devoted to Allen Ginsberg's speech "Renaissance or Die," in which he suggested that everyone in good health over the age of fourteen should take LSD at least once, in order to see what lies beyond their individual selves, their institutions and their deadly social conditioning. Only then could they unite in peace.

Several poems were printed in an attempt to maintain literary interest in the paper: "The God I Worship Is a Lyon," by Michael McClure, and works by Geoff Brown, Ted Berk, Don Lewis and Leland Meyerzove.

The lion is an important motif in McClure's poetic works. He supposedly read poems from *Ghost Tantra* to the lions at the city zoo, and they responded favorably. Animals and nature play a significant role in McClure's poems and demonstrate his strong attachment to them. These motifs are also present in such works as "Hummingbird Ode," "For the Death of 100 Whales," "Rare angel," "Love Lion," "On Organism," "99 Theses," "Maybe Mama Lion," and others. His verses also exalt our sensory awareness and the fusion of body and spirit.

The back page was a mandala drawn by Dangerfield Ashton, a young man who was AWOL (absent without leave) from the armed service. Some 50,000 American servicemen are believed to have deserted during the War in Vietnam.

The front page of *Oracle* number six, "The Aquarian Age," is emblematic of what the paper stood for: a Christ-like figure with angel wings, symbol of the Aquarian age, pours the waters of life. This cosmic messenger, framed by rays of divine light, is draped in a white robe, with a purple and red blanket wrapped over his shoulder and around his waist. Rick Griffin, the psychedelic poster artist, drew this memorable cover.

Three staff astrologers–Rosalind Wall (Gayla), Ambrose Hollingsworth and Gavin Arthur–explained what the Aquarian Age meant. All three were rather eccentric personalities of the counterculture. Gayla claimed to be clairvoyant and said she could perceive people's auras, something that hippies in the Haight liked to say they could do, maybe because it was difficult to prove them wrong. Ambrose Hollingsworth, who was confined to a wheelchair, belonged to an esoteric association called The Brotherhood of Light, and had created a school for the occult sciences called the Six Day School.

Eclecticism was the paper's trademark and this issue was

no exception. Chester Anderson, co-founder of the Communication Company and mouthpiece for the Diggers, contributed a diatribe on rock music. According to Anderson, it possessed many forms of baroque music. In 1967, rock music's aspirations were "total freedom, total experience, total love, peace and mutual affection." Rock was not just a form of music, but "a way of life" and "a tribal phenomenon."

Rock, especially psychedelic rock, or acid rock, depending on what you wished to call it, was an integral part of the Haight-Ashbury. It engaged "the entire sensorium" and was part and parcel of the communal experience. The Haight could not have been the Haight without rock, and rock would never be the same after the Haight. Rock music, as it was played in the ballrooms, was a physical experience. It permeated one's body and one's mind. It piloted one's trip to a different level of consciousness and physical awareness. Drugs and music went hand in hand. People took drugs when they went to a dance concert, as did the musicians on stage.

It was no secret that the *Oracle* promoted the use of psychedelics, but the paper also criticized bad drugs such as methamphetamine, or speed, that keeps you from sleeping while it destroys your nervous system: "Ecstatic Isolation and Incarnation," by Kent Chapman, warned of its dangers.

There was also an interview with Paul Krassner, editor of *The Realist*, in which he discussed the *Oracle's* favorite topic: lysergic acid diethylamide. John Sinclair, who hailed from the Motor City, spoke about rock music in "Five Music," referring to bands such as the MC-5 and the DC 4, and musicians like Sun Ra, Pharoah Sanders [*sic*], John

Coltrane and Marion Brown.

Alan Watts, noted Zen scholar, contributed his first article to the paper entitled "The Basic Myth," in which he discussed the "Self," something we are all familiar with, yet find it difficult to describe.

The Self is what exists and all that exists. It has no opposite, like white and black, form and emptiness, but it has two sides: an inside and an outside. In Sanskrit, *nirguna* is the inside and *saguna* is the outside. It is a sort of eternal reality, consciousness and "joy."

The Self is always at play and this is called *lila*. The play of the Self involves losing and finding itself, as though it were a game of hide and seek, without beginning and without end. When the Self forgets that it is the one and only reality and pretends it comprises the multitude of beings that people our world, it is disjoined. When it finds itself, it is remembered. It sees that it is "the one behind the many," knowing that its seeming to be many is *maya*, illusion or magic.

The play of the Self is a rather unusual drama, with the Self as both performer and audience in a theatre of life. The performer creates an illusion of reality so the audience can experience joy, fear and pity, which is similar to Aristotle's definition of tragedy involving pity, fear and catharsis. The Self is seemingly enthralled by the joy and suffering of all beings, if that is possible, and that is the Self. I am that and that is me. My breath is the creation, the preservation and the end of all illusion. This story is without beginning or end and continues forever and ever.

All sentient beings pass through the six paths of the

Wheel of Becoming: *naraka-gati* is the path of aggression, *preta-gati* is the path of hungry ghosts, *tiragyoni-gati* is the realm of animals, *ashura-gati* is the path of constant anger and conflict, *manusya-gati* is the realm of mankind (both good and evil), and *deva-gati* is the realm of gods and heavenly beings.

We are all bound to the Wheel of Becoming by karma, the principle of cause and effect where our intentions, actions words and thoughts have an effect on our future.

But there is no "I" and no "Self" except that which is beyond time and space. *Jivan-mukta* is the name of one who has been liberated from the illusion of "Self" and "Other."

Returning to *The San Francisco Oracle*, we find Steve Levine's column "Notes from the San Andreas Fault." He described the Human Be-In as a "baptism" and "a reaffirmation of the life spirit."

The centerfold reiterated the theme of the Be-In with a collage of the so-called gurus: Leary, Snyder and Ginsberg, with the Grateful Dead squeezed in between.

Lenore Kandel contributed her poem "In Transit," framed by naked women lounging sensuously around the text. The motifs of infinity and the perpetual movement of existence are accentuated in Kandel's poem. Since we live in a world of perpetual change, she says, there is no point in trying to hang on, you just have to "Let it Go!"

The graphic art in this issue was sometimes noteworthy, expressing a special feeling for the Haight-Ashbury counterculture, notably in the cover by Jim Phillips' "Dr. Mota's Medicine Show," which waggishly depicted hippie attitudes about cannabis and LSD. The picture deftly depicted a rickety old truck metamorphosed into a travelling medicine show to suggest how grass and acid could "cure" western civilization of its malaise. It also emphasized the importance of psychotropes for the counterculture by depicting a veritable cornucopia of dope. The truck is appropriately parked at the loading zone.

Oracle number seven was devoted to the Houseboat Summit and published in February 1967. At fifty-two pages, it was the longest issue.

The front page shows the four countercultural sages–Timothy Leary, Alan Watts, Gary Snyder and Allen Ginsberg–smiling broadly for the camera and appearing rather chummy, though Leary was put on the spot to explain what he meant by "dropping out." According to Allen Cohen, Gabe Katz, art editor of the paper, was the person who came up with the idea for the Houseboat Summit, and when Alan Watts was approached about it, he agreed to host it on the S.S. *Vallejo*.

The centerfolds were a good indication of what the staff felt was important, and for this issue they chose the *Prajna Paramita Hridaya* sutra, boldly colored in red, white and blue, with a hybrid female angel/butterfly occupying the center, a hippie invention that has nothing to do with the sutra.

This Buddhist doctrine is used as a chanted prayer to perfect wisdom. It is the best known and most popular Buddhist sutra. The text, which dates back to the seventh century CE, refers to the liberation of the bodhisattva, one who out of divine compassion forgoes nirvana to enlighten others in our world. The term is derived from Sanskrit and has two roots: *bodhih*, "perfect knowledge" and *sattvam*, "reality." Repetitive chanting of the mantra is said to reveal its deeper message and promote enlightenment.

Lucifer Rising, a Love Vision announced Kenneth Anger's underground film at the Straight Theatre, 1748 Haight Street–an ironic name for a theatre in the Haight-Ashbury if there ever was one.

Rick Griffin did the artwork, borrowing from Gustave Doré (Paul Gustave Louis Christophe Doré), the nineteenth century French artist, famous for his romantic engravings and illustrations. Griffin's poster depicted an eagle ascending heavenwards with a body enshrouded in a cloth. The macabre tone suggested the darker ideas associated with Anger's group.

Kenneth Anger accused Bobby Beausoleil, who played Lucifer in the film, of stealing the footage after the showing, though the actor/musician strongly denied the accusation. Anger was reported by some to be a Satanist, which is debatable, but he was motivated by Aleister Crowley's description of Lucifer as the angel who brought light to mankind. Taken from Latin, *Lucifer* means "light-bearing."

Robert Kenneth "Bobby" Beausoleil was associated with the Charles Manson "Family," though he categorically denied being a member of the cult group. He is currently serving a life sentence in prison for the murder of Gary Hinman on July 27, 1969. As described in *Helter Skelter* by Vincent Bugliosi, Hinman was reportedly murdered because of property and money he owed the Manson Family.

Oracle number eight was devoted to the American Indians, and was perhaps the densest issue as regards its content. There were two printings in the summer of 1967 and it sold for twenty-five cents in the State of California, and thirty-five cents outside the State.

There was a common belief shared by many hippies that they had been reincarnated from Native Americans. According to another belief, hippies were supposed to live in tribal communities as part of their atavistic heritage, to get back to the land, to live in harmony with nature, as the Native Americans had done, before they came into contact with European culture.

Hetty McGee designed the front and back covers depicting Chief Joseph at Mount Shasta, though she did not sign her work. Flying saucers can be seen hovering over the summit.

Bob Schnepf designed the Summer of Love poster with the warm, vibrant colors representing Saint Francis and the Christian prayer expressing (hippie) piety:

> Lord, make me an instrument of thy peace.
> Where there is hatred, let me sow love;
> Where there is injury, pardon;
> Where there is doubt, faith;
> Where there is darkness, light;
> Where there is sadness, joy.

The prayer is often attributed to Saint Francis of Asisi, but, in fact, it apparently dates to about 1912.

Throughout the issue, in articles such as "Tuwaqachi: The Fourth World," "Kiva," or "Living with the Land," the Native Americans and their tribal culture were glorified, while mechanized, technological America was censured. "Living with the Land" reiterated the desire to "get back to nature"; the preposition "with" conveying an idea of harmony, "regard for the environment" and "respect for nature," rather than a Baconian concept of domination.

The centerfold was a poem by John Collier Jr.: "Who is an Indian?" It was dated April 1967. The artwork in blue and green was by Ami Magill. According to Allen Cohen, Collier, half Zuni Indian, was one of the founders of visual anthropology. When he was a young boy, he was involved in a tragic automobile accident; his brain was seriously injured and his speech and hearing were impaired, resulting in learning disabilities. Yet despite these handicaps, Collier became a renowned anthropologist and photographer.

A poem by Bob Kaufman, "Plea," taken from *Golden Sardine*, published by City Lights Books in July 1967, was included in this issue. Kaufman was one of the more colorful poets of San Francisco, but his story is tragic. He was often arrested in North Beach and brutalized by the police who misunderstood his Homeric iconoclasm. In New York he was arrested and given shock treatment in an effort to cure him. It is more than likely that it contributed to his alcoholism. He died on January 12, 1986. His funeral procession was a memorable event in San Francisco and a worthy homage to his poetry: dozens of poets and a jazz band led the colorful procession through the streets of North Beach, stopping at the poet's well known haunts to read his poems.

The artwork for "The American Indian" was inspired and imaginative. In "1984," Armando Busick imagined a return to a rural, more primitive mode of existence. The art of collage–a word that Georges Braque helped to coin with Pablo Picasso–was often explored in the *Oracle* and a work by Bruce Conner vaguely suggested the justapositional imagery used by Max Ernst.

Buried in the fine print near the end of the issue was a plea for young pilgrims coming to the city to bring money for rent and food, sleeping bags and rucksacks, brown rice, camping equipment, warm clothing for the foggy weather, and a personal identification card with a photograph (*Oracle* 234).

Oracle number nine, published in August 1967, entitled "Psychedelics, Flowers and War," continued the exploration of color and aesthetically designed texts and graphics, while augmenting diversity in content. The early goal of creating a visual and cerebral stimulus for its readers seemed to have been achieved.

"On programming the Psychedelic Experience" by Timothy Leary and Ralph Metzner was a reprint from the *Psychedelic Review* number 9, 1967. The white letters on a colored background did not make for easy reading, but were part of the rainbow effect that the editors desired.

The featured article was about LSD and was largely promotional. Unlike Ken Kesey, who believed acid tripping should be random, Leary and Metzner advocated a controlled trip in order to induce a positive experience. In other words, a tripper needed an experienced guide, someone who had been there before to show the way and prevent the person from having a bummer. It was a role that called to mind the sage archetype of Carl Jung; someone whose main quest in life would be the Truth.

To achieve this end the "set" and the "setting" needed to be controlled. Basically, the "set" referred to the person's state of mind, whereas the "setting," an expression taken from literature, referred to the specific physical surroundings. The role of the guide was decisive since he was supposed to create and maintain a state of serenity. For Leary, Metzner and Alpert, the *Bardo Thodol*, translated as the *Tibetan Book of the Dead*, and the *Tao Te Ching*, or *Dao De Jing*, symbolized the psychedelic trip.

Composed in the eighth century by Padmasambhava, the *Bardo Thodol* is a description of the different experiences one's consciousness has in the *bardo*, or the period between death and rebirth. The text is also meant to be a guide as one travels through the *bardo*. There are, in fact, three *bardos*: the *chikhai bardo*, the moment of death, the *chonyid bardo*, involving visions and forms, and the *sidpa bardo*, the bardo of rebirth.

The Psychedelic Experience, written by Leary, Metzner and Alpert, and published in 1964, was based on the *Tibetan Book of the Dead*. It was meant to reveal the deepest parts of the human mind and guide those seeking spiritual liberation. John Lennon of the Beatles was profoundly influenced by this book and wrote "Tomorrow Never Knows" in response to it. Lennon took hundreds of acid trips, though they did not seem to help him come to terms with his personal problems.

The *Tao Te Ching* is the primary document for Taoism. It may be translated as "the way of integrity." It is meant to help a person live and act with integrity and virtue in the physical world, which essentially means being self-aware. "Know thyself" (gnothi seauton) said numerous Greek sages, and before them the ancient Egyptians.

For those living in the Haight-Ashbury, it had become

painfully obvious that the Summer of Love was an egregious misnomer. "In Memorium for Superspade and John Carter" was written by Allen Cohen.

On Thursday, August 3, 1967, John Kent Carter, whose nickname was "Shob," was found dead in his apartment in Parnassus Heights. Carter, a flutist who sold acid to make ends meet, was brutally stabbed to death and his arm above the elbow was hacked off. Two days later, Eric Dahlstrom, an acid dealer, was arrested as he drove the stolen van through Sebastopol. All the stolen items, including the severed arm, were found in the van. Dahlstrom blamed his ultra-bad trip on LSD.

William E. "Superspade" Thomas, a twenty-six-year-old African-American, was very well known on Haight Street because of the acid he sold. He wore a badge that read "superspade, faster than a speeding mind." But Carter apparently wasn't fast enough to elude his assassins. He was reported to have gone to Sausalito with as much as $55,000 in cash to score acid. Later, his body was found in a sleeping bag, hanging from a cliff in Point Reyes. Somebody shot Superspade through the back of the head, and to make sure the job was done stabbed him in the heart. The money was of course long gone. This case remains unsolved to this day.

The unsigned Alice in Wonderland drawing was donated by a curious character named "Owen." Alice was depicted as a young woman rather than a child, and she was surrounded by two motifs held dear by the hippies: the hookah smoking caterpillar and the mushrooms.

The centerfold was an antiwar poem by Michael McClure, "Poisoned Wheat," which begins with the line:

"There is death in Viet Nam." Although not political activists, the staff of the *Oracle* was resolutely opposed to the War in Vietnam, as it was opposed to all wars. Other poems included in the issue were "The Rainbow Warrior's Quest" by Page Brownton and "The ; ; ; ; ;" by George Tsongas.

Oracle readers were curious about eastern religions such as Buddhism and the teachings of Gautama Buddha who believed the middle path was the way to enlightenment. This means one should avoid the extremes of self-indulgence and self-mortification. Dane Rudhyar analyzed some key aspects of Buddhism in "The Buddha Mind." He pointed out that Buddha only achieved illumination after leaving his family and rejecting the ritualistic traditions of his culture.

Nirvana is seen as the ultimate goal in Buddhism because it releases a person from *samsara*, the endless cycle of rebirth. To achieve Nirvana, one must extinguish all passion, aversion and ignorance. Understanding the meaning of opposites, too, is an essential step along the path of enlightenment, because of their relationship to existence and form. The Buddha mind is the mind of clarity, illumination and beauty, "it is the mind of perfect relatedness," said Rudhyar. The Buddha mind neither rejects, nor embraces tradition or conformity. The Buddha mind accepts the perfect form of the whole. Gautama Buddha attained Nirvana, and yet he returned to teach others what he had found. Perhaps he did this out of compassion for humanity. If such were the case, then compassion must be greater than even Nirvana.

The back cover in blue and red was a drawing by Bob Branaman that was supposed to depict Kali. To fully appreciate the picture's intricacies, you needed to view it under a black light. Etymologically, "Kali" is derived from the Sanskrit word *kala*, which means time. Kali, a powerful goddess, represents many things: Time, Change, Power, Creation and Destruction. Representations of the divinity are in blue or black, since her name also signifies "the black one." She has four arms, although the Mahakali form has ten. The upper left arm brandishes a sword or knife that is used to decapitate her victims, whose heads she wears in a garland. She also wears a skirt of severed arms. Kali is sometimes depicted with fangs, with her bright red tongue hanging loosely out of her mouth. Branaman's divinity is obviously not based on a strict interpretation of Hindu religion.

Oracle number ten was entitled "The Politics of Ecstasy." There were several printings of this issue that were done at the time of the Pentagon demonstrations and "exorcism" on 21 October 1967. Bob Branaman created the blue and red mandala for the cover that is evocative of the paper's cabalistic style.

The artwork, color and layout reached their apogee in this memorable issue. Like so many other underground papers in the sixties–*The Great Speckled Bird*, *Berkeley Barb*, *Rat* or *Kaleidoscope*–the *Oracle* was a nexus for innovation. Most of the writers gave their work for free or refused to sign their contributions, happy just to be part of the cultural underground, since their goal was to support the general growth of artistic consciousness.

A "Call to Celebration," an unsigned article written in the idiom and slang of the Diggers, proposed to supply the human race with the basic necessities: food, clothing and housing. Revolutionary in tone, it declared the time had come to dismantle our outmoded social and economic systems, referring to capitalism and America's social institutions of health, education and welfare, which failed to provide the basic needs of a growing number of Americans. It went on to say that the country was hindered by the obsolete structures of the industrial age.

William S. Burroughs–icon of the beat, or perhaps upbeat and beatific counterculture, alongside Allen Ginsberg, Jack Kerouac, Lucien Carr and Herbert Huncke–contributed "Academy 23: A Deconditioning." The author of *Junkie* and *Naked Lunch* spoke about drugs, always a favorite topic in the tabloid, and more specifically about the criminalization of drug use. He warned against the undesirable effects of LSD that could create a feeling of obsessive warm-heartedness (*Oracle* 299). Ever the controversialist, he affirmed that the drug could be dangerous, and advocated the establishment of official academies to teach students how to get really high.

Burroughs castigated the mainstream press for its lurid descriptions of drugs that aroused curiosity as much as they misinformed, and was opposed to the manufacturing of Benzedrine. Surprisingly, he did not have an opinion about the legalization of cannabis, but said that if English doctors could prescribe heroin and cocaine, it seemed reasonable that they be able to do the same with marijuana. Burroughs preferred smoking hashish and marijuana to taking LSD or psilocybin because he found hallucinations unsettling.

Timothy Leary was back with an article entitled

"Another Session with Tim Leary." Interviewed in the *Oracle* offices about LSD and claims of chromosomal damage, he responded by saying they were merely hoaxes and government scare tactics. In regard to a completely different topic, he praised the Sufis for having "the highest form of psychological wisdom" (*Oracle* 283).

Science magazine published an article in 1967, entitled "Chromosomal damage in human leukocytes induced by lysergic acid diethylamide," authored by Cohen, Marinello and Back. The *New England Journal of Medicine* published a similar article that same year entitled "In Vivo and in Vitro Chromosomal Damage Induced by LSD-25," by Cohen, Hirshhorn and Frosch.

For several years, the media were crying wolf about the dangers of chromosomal damage in peer-reviewed scientific journals. The broadcasting media followed suit with hair-raising stories about future mutations of the human race. It wasn't until the mid-seventies that science put its house in order and revised its earlier claims, admitting that LSD did not cause chromosomal damage or birth defects. It nonetheless leaves a bad taste in one's mouth to think that supposedly reputable research teams could knowingly publish lies at the behest of sectarian groups.

Staff reporters interviewed Chinmayananda, a Vedantist teacher giving lectures in the United States. He spoke about a variety of issues, including repression in the Haight-Ashbury, creating Ashrams, sensuality, birth control, the deterioration of India and western society, the law of karma, nuclear weapons and a host of other topics. Spirituality, he said, is the only way to overcome the social problems of domination and exploitation.

The centerfold was a poem by Lawrence Ferlinghetti, "Temporary Flight," and a text describing a performance of "Fuclock," which was supposed to be performed at a "Mantra Rock dance on an elevated platform." At a quarter to midnight, a naked man is bound to the hour hand and a naked woman is bound to the minute hand. But they can both move their arms and legs, and at midnight they become one in "ecstatic bardo embrace" (*Oracle* 289).

"Pentagon Rising," by Richard Honigman, announced the exorcism of the Pentagon. According to Allen Cohen, he and Michael Bowen had originally suggested the idea that would later be used by the Yippies Jerry Rubin and Abbie Hoffman, the Abbot and Costello of the New Left.

1967 was a high-water mark for mobilizing against the war. Organizers from the National Mobilization Committee to End the War in Vietnam (MOBE) announced a huge march on Washington D.C., which was part of a larger movement called Stop the Draft Week. On 21 October 1967, 100,000 protesters assembled at the Lincoln Memorial. David Dellinger and Benjamin Spock gave rousing speeches, Peter, Paul and Mary played folk music, after which some 50,000 protestors crossed the Memorial Bridge to take on the Pentagon. Ed Sanders of the Fugs had written an exorcism text and people chanted. But federal soldiers and U.S. Marshals were in place and well prepared for the marchers; 647 demonstrators were arrested and 47 were hospitalized for injuries. Yet the war not only continued, it escalated. In December 1967, there were at least 510,000 American soldiers in Vietnam and no light at the end of the tunnel.

Oracle number eleven, "The City of God," published in November 1967, attempted to suggest ways of changing society, its values and institutions. The staff wondered if it was possible to live in harmony with the environment and with other people and societies.

The cover, drawn by Steve Schafer, represented a divine trinity with a child, a young man and God in the center of the drawing. Between their legs stands a stone tower with the words "City of God" on the facade. An all-seeing eye, emblem of rebirth and the transformation of man into a superior being, is situated at the top of the tower. It was a symbol redolent of the idealism that permeated Cohen's underground paper, though this ingenuous optimism was running out fast in the Haight-Ashbury, a neighborhood that once represented a genuine feeling of hope for the psychedelic counterculture.

An interview with Buckminster Fuller, the well known architect, designer, author and inventor who made geodesic domes popular in the sixties, was a welcome addition to the tabloid. Fuller was an environmentalist and an activist who advocated ephemeralization, which means doing more with less. He also advocated sustainability.

Always a thought provoking speaker, he spoke about a new kind of telepathy by wave propagation at ultrahigh frequencies, and actually claimed he knew what audiences were thinking when he lectured. According to Fuller, Man is almost completely automated and his consciousness is minute. When answering a question about overpopulation, he replied that the world, at that time, was not overpopulated, but rather "overconcentrated."

Bryden did the artwork for the centerfold, the City of God, with the Revelation of Saint John, chapter 21, verses 9-27. This chapter referred to scenes beyond the judgment and described the joyous state of the redeemed church once the conflicts had all been resolved and the enemies had been vanquished. For the ancient Hebrews, Jerusalem symbolized the heavenly world, the dwelling place of God. Yet it was a city that had no temple, because the whole city was a temple; a city that needed no light, because God was its light. Nothing impure could pass through its gates. Jerusalem thus represented Paradise regained, an image that many hippies in the Haight dreamed of reproducing.

Alan Watts, a brilliant speaker, writer and philosopher, contributed a waggish text entitled "Food is God." It was a pleasant article that said profound things in a seemingly lighthearted manner. Life was a paradox and people were capable of doing the most appalling things "in the names of the highest ideals." History's greatest dictators and greatest mass murderers had the highest ideals when they were sending millions away to be exterminated in gulags or death camps.

Watts was English, but he adopted the United States and Sausalito as his place of residence. Owing perhaps to his detached objectivity and the fact that he had emigrated to the United States, he probably understood the country better than many Americans. He was well aware of its high ideals and beliefs in exceptionalism and was thoroughly convinced that because of its ideals the United States represented a real threat to the rest of the world. How could a nation that baked such insipid, tasteless bread, pretend to be capable of ruling the world and deciding the fates of millions of others? Moreover, how could it possibly enact intelligent legislation, since the congressmen were "blithering idiots?" And if the country cared so little about the global food problem, it was because Americans were not really interested in food.

For the author of *The Joyous Cosmology*, Chinese cooking was the best, and French cuisine was a close second. But if Watts had known the epicurean delights of dining at L'Épicure au Bristol, Le Pré Catelan et Guy Savoy or L'Ambroisie, he might have had a different opinion.

Good cooking is directly related to the Tao, the way of nature, and the art of life is to cooperate with nature, not violate it or attempt to subjugate it. For those who were interested in putting their recipes into practice, Watts suggested a good book on Chinese cooking: *Secrets of Chinese Cooking* by Tsuifeng and Hsiangju Lin.

Oracle number twelve, "Symposium 2000 A.D. and the Fall," printed in February 1968, was the paper's last issue. Its demise coincided with the social and cultural collapse of the Haight-Ashbury.

The winter of 1968 was a hard time in the Haight and it marked the end of a unique period in American history. It was the year the dream died. The fact that peace and love could provoke so much hate on the part of the establishment says a lot about that establishment.

Things changed when Joseph Alioto was elected mayor of the city. Allen Cohen said Joseph Alioto hated the hippies (*Oracle* li). The same was true of mainstream America, which felt that the ungrateful hippies were destroying the nation's values and the American way of life. Cohen also believed FBI and CIA programs were committed to destroying the counterculture in the Haight-Ashbury, where peace and love had vanished to be replaced by hard drugs and violent crime. But that was no skin off the mayor's nose.

The last issue of the *Oracle* reflected the feelings that had swept through the Haight. After the intense feelings of joy, freedom and community people had known, the prospect of returning to the alienated world of straight America was dust and ashes in the mouths of the hippies, many of whom were leaving the city to live in communes.

Drop City, outside Trinidad, Colorado, became well known for its geodesic domes, which were simple and cheap to construct. The story of the commune began on May 3, 1965, when Gene Bernofsky bought six acres of goat pasture for $450 from a farmer about to retire in the hamlet of El Moro near Trinidad, Colorado, not far from the New Mexico border.

Gene and Jo Ann Bernofsky moved there right away. Clark Richard joined them when he finished his master's degree in fine arts. They wanted to do something outrageous. After devotedly proclaiming the land Drop City, they began developing their commune according to the sixties model that was based on anarchy, drugs, promiscuity, peace and love, and art.

Drop city communards devoted themselves fully to making life an art. They refused paid employment, declared their commune a seminal civilization, gave themselves new names and identities and rejected traditional establishment mores; as a result, the commune became a haven and a pilgrimage for way-worn hippies in quest of a new American narrative. The geodesic domes were made from car roofs, bottle caps and scraps of wood. Buckminster Fuller, who popularized these constructions, sent the struggling commune a check for $500 after receiving pictures of the domes and a cordial invitation to pay a visit.

Bob Schnepf did the cover design for the last issue. It shows a woman lying flat on her back on Mount Tamalpais. The design is redolent of a poster by Stanley Mouse or Rick Griffin with the flowing letters and the photograph framed in a circle. The perspective elongates the woman's limbs, thereby creating an eerie, unnatural effect. The human body has become one with the earth, and is an extension of it. The observer might be tempted to say that it suggests part of the universal peace symbol designed by Gerald Holtom in 1958, calling for nuclear disarmament. Holtom's symbol is in fact a combination of semaphore signals for the letters "N" (nuclear) and "D" (disarmament). The "N" is formed by holding two flags in an inverted "V"; the "D" by holding one flag straight down and the other straight up. The "N" was clearly present in the poster by Bob Schnepf, but the "D" was missing, perhaps implying that the counterculture had not achieved peace.

The Esalen Institute in States Hot Springs, Big Sur, California, was founded in 1962 by Michael Murphy and Dick Price. The goal was to develop "human potentialities" by helping individuals to realize their full human capabilities, learn about themselves, others and their environment. A wide variety of courses were taught including personal growth, meditation, massage, yoga, organic food, ecology, spirituality and encounter groups. It was no secret that many of the courses challenged the *status quo*. Some of the celebrities involved with the institute were Buckminster Fuller, Carl Rogers, Arnold Toynbee, B.F. Skinner, Robert Nadeau, Timothy Leary, Richard Alpert and Virginia Satir.

The *Oracle* staff formed an Esalen-led group, experimenting with psychodrama, dream theatre, encounter groups and sensory awakening experiments. They were hoping to publish their results, but unfortunately this was their last issue so nothing ever came of their experiments.

"2000 A.D." was a symposium at which Alan Watts, Carl Rogers and Herman Kahn were invited to give talks. The purpose of the symposium was to attempt to foresee the future of the world in the year 2000, which, at the time, seemed very far away. The entire transcript of the symposium was printed in the *Oracle*. Alton Kelley and Hetty McGee did the artwork and design.

Carl Rogers was well known for having helped to create and utilize encounter group techniques. For Rogers, accepting rapid change was one of the greatest challenges facing the human race, and he believed that religion, as practiced at the time, would be replaced by a more creative group experience. Rogers also spoke about overpopulation, a favorite topic for discussion in the sixties. He was forced to admit that population growth would result in overcrowding and that this would have negative consequences on social behavior, provoking apathy and lack of compassion. He also felt that people would be more aware of what was going on inside themselves (*Oracle* 354).

Alan Watts began his talk with a provocative statement

that would have been brought to the attention of J. Edgar Hoover and Richard McGarrah Helms, whose agents were closely monitoring the activities of the counterculture. He predicted that in the year 2000, the United States would no longer exist (*Oracle* 355). It was a perfect opportunity to lambaste the government, so Watts went one further when he said that if the United States still existed in the next ten years, there would be a "holocaust." Watts also said that money did not represent wealth, nor was it real (355), and he criticized the country for investing in war, rather than in basic human needs.

In a somewhat digressive talk, Herman Kahn discussed economics and the possibility of world starvation. Kahn, futurist and military strategist, founded the Hudson Institute, a conservative think tank. He was the author of *On Thermonuclear War*, in which he argued that civilization could survive a nuclear holocaust. One of his favorite topics was nuclear war scenarios, or prognosticating the consequences of certain hypothetical situations during a nuclear war.

An unsigned collage and drawing depicting the mushroom cloud from a nuclear explosion in the United States evoked the anguish and fear felt by many Americans in 1968, the year of the Tet offensive in Vietnam on January 30, when more than one hundred cities and towns were simultaneously attacked. Below the cloud are photographs of President Johnson, who eyes the viewer with an intimidating stare, and on the other side is his secretary of state, Dean Rusk. Within the mushroom cloud, naked human bodies writhe in the deadly horror of the explosion above a map of the continental United States (*Oracle* 364).

A newspaper's advertising reveals information about its readers, and that was the case with the *Oracle*. In the classified ads section of the paper there were advertisements for studying classical yoga, an H. P. Lovecraft poster for one dollar, wife swapping, waterpipes, a paperback entitled *Lysistrata in the White House*, a mansion for sale, job ads, poetry books, cheap food at Bishops Café on Divisadero Street, a list of underground buttons, several messages asking children to call home, aphrodisiacs, lists of psychedelic shops, a Hell's Angel looking for a RICH old lady, a mutual self-help association for women with an undesired pregnancy, commune ads, an artist experienced in black velvet, growing cannabis, psychedelic glasses, personalized posters, a wannabee bullfighter looking for a sponsor, and more. There were also a few miscellaneous adverts. One was for the "Dimensions of Consciousness" symposium, and another was a warning to speed freaks–Park Emergency Hospital reported that some unscrupulous dealers were cutting their drugs with talcum powder, which could be fatal.

A host of new album releases were also advertised for Ultimate Spinach, Jefferson Airplane, Richie Havens, Rotary Connection, Leonard Cohen, Scott McKenzie, Ravi Shankar, The Chambers Brothers, The Peanut Butter Conspiracy and The Don Ellis Orchestra.

The last page was the "Cosmic Village"–a "cosmically attuned village designed for rehabilitation." Below the drawing was part of a text from the *I Ching*, which was frequently used by the *Oracle* staff: 43 Kuai: Breakthrough,

Danger. "The best way to fight evil is to make energetic progress in the good" (*Oracle* 378).

The sixties represented many things to many people, and at the risk of stating the obvious, it must be said that they were a time of profound social mutation. Berkeley students were smoking pot, dropping acid and demanding freedom of speech; Martin Luther King was leading protest marches and denouncing the War in Vietnam; the MOBE marched on the Pentagon; the Weathermen declared war on the United States. Revolution and revolutionary ideas were doing more than just blowing in the wind across a nation in turmoil-establishment values and beliefs in the American Dream were swept aside by a generation.

The San Francisco Oracle represented a rare symbiosis of community and communication, and a creative process motivated by philosophical needs and psychotropic stimulants.

"What is art in the age of mechanical reproduction?" The modest tabloid at 1371 Haight Street sought to answer this seemingly simple question, just as it sought to let the voices of the counterculture be heard, read and viewed. The *Oracle* represented an interesting experiment with the tabloid medium in mass communications, at a time when they were undergoing a revolution. *Understanding Media* by Marshall McLuhan had been published just a few years earlier, in 1964. The electronic age translated people into information that was an extension of their consciousness, and by expanding their consciousness, it was easier for them to extend information. "People don't actually read newspapers, they get into them," said McLuhan. This seemed to be what the staff of the *Oracle* was interested in helping its readers to do.

Yet hidden in the shadows of psychedelia were powerful forces ready to wreak havoc with the generation of peace and love. Local and federal authorities at the highest levels became extremely interested in the underground press, a huge phenomenon in the second half of the sixties. On the day that Richard Milhous Nixon was elected president of the United States, FBI director J. Edgar Hoover sent a memorandum to FBI bureau offices nationwide instructing agents to gather detailed information on publications of the New Left with respect to staff, printers and sources of advertising (McMillian 115). Before that, agents were instructed to do everything that was necessary to force papers to cease publication. War had been officially declared on the underground press. The FBI, CIA and Johnson administration had a whole new idea of what American democracy should not be. It is no secret that the U. S. government, within the framework of COINTELPRO, used illegal practices such as wiretaps, forged documents and smear campaigns to discredit and destroy New Left leaders and radical papers (McMillian 115-16). These programs were enlarged to include, as targets for sabotage, an incalculable number of countercultural papers.

The Haight-Ashbury was decimated by hard drugs, essentially speed and heroin. The question is who introduced these drugs into the neighborhood and who had the means of producing them?

Everyone knew weird drugs were circulating in the Haight. Owsley used to be the main source of LSD there and his colored batches were usually pure. But things started getting wild and crazy. The mafia set up a network of production and distribution, and the quality of LSD suddenly got very bad (Lee 188).

The CIA, too, never abandoned its interest in LSD. On the contrary, Agency personnel reportedly assisted chemists to set up labs in the San Francisco Bay Area during the Summer of Love, supposedly to establish a surveillance operation (Lee 188-89). At the time, there were a lot of bad trips, and claims that the Agency was "poisoning the acid."

Look magazine ran an article on September 23, 1969, claiming that Mayor Joseph Alioto had ties to Jimmy Fratianno, but Alioto sued the magazine and was awarded several hundred thousand dollars.

In *The Last Mafioso*, Ovid Demaris had quite a bit to say about the former mayor in chapter fourteen. In it he explained how Alioto represented Tony Lima as his tax lawyer (Ovid 168), and later he worked for Emilio "Gam" Georgetti. Georgetti was widely known as the "Gambling Czar" of San Mateo County. In 1953, Alioto helped to keep Georgetti out of prison (168). Alioto even became a partner in the Holly Meat Packing Company, owned by Georgetti (168). Moreover, the San Francisco mayor knew Angelo Marino and Jimmy Lanza (169). FBI agents reported that Jimmy Fratianno and Angelo Marino had an appointment with Alioto on November 3, 1964 (172). Jimmy liked to "bullshit" with Joe when he was in the city, so he would go to see him. Alioto's bank gave him five sizeable loans for the Fratianno Trucking Company, at a lower rate of interest. But one hand washes the other, so Alioto asked Jimmy if Babe

Goldberger, a Teamsters official, would deposit pension money in his bank (174).

George Orwell, for his part, noted that politicians have always been good at making "lies sound truthful and murder respectable."

10

The San Francisco Music Scene

San Francisco's underground rock community wanted to listen to live music, but it was a matter of fact that there weren't too many good places to go. The city needed permanent venues, places that were large enough so people could dance, that sold refreshments, whose acoustics were at least adequate, and were places where people could feel at home and let their hair down.

Mother's, created by Tom "Big Daddy" Donahue, born Thomas Coman, has been described as the first psychedelic nightclub anywhere (Seay 43). Located at 430 Broadway, it was the trip, the place to be cool, where people got together to hang out and do their thing. But what kind of trip was it?

Tom Donahue bought a place called DJ's, squeezed in between Carol Doda's, of topless fame, and the Swiss Hotel on Broadway–decidedly not a good place for hippies–and had the place renovated. Everything inside was done in purple, including the walls that were covered with three-dimensional murals. Sheb Wooley, who wrote and performed "The Purple People Eater" in 1958, would have liked it, but not many others did. People didn't care much for the lighting either, because of the claustrophobic atmosphere it created. The Lovin' Spoonful played there when "Do You Believe in Magic" was a hit, and the Grateful Dead and the Great Society played there, too. But Mother's didn't draw large crowds and it closed within a year. It clearly wasn't the type of place the psychedelic crowd was looking for.

The Matrix, located at 3138 Fillmore Street, opened on Friday, 13 August 1965. The date was chosen for good luck. The club was initially intended to showcase Jefferson Airplane. Marty Balin persuaded three associates to contribute $3,000 each to transform a pizza parlor into a dance hall. Hunter S. Thompson, the gonzo journalist, said it was his favorite haunt in San Francisco. The music played there was essentially rock, blues and jazz. There was a mural painting on the left wall near the rear, depicting the Four Horsemen of the Apocalypse. Members of Jefferson Airplane supposedly painted it. There was a bar near the entrance that served beer and wine, a dance floor and a stage one step above the floor.

A number of live albums were recorded there, worthy of the most demanding vintage rock enthusiasts. The Great Society recorded *Conspicuous Only in Its Absence* (1966), *How It Was* (1966) and *Collector's Item* (1966). *Early Steppenwolf* was recorded in 1967, *Live at the Matrix* by the Doors in 1967, and *Cheaper Thrills* by Big Brother and the Holding Company in 1966-1967.

Eliot Sazer is said to have coined the name of the new

ballroom. Sazer, who helped finance it, explained that "matrix" was a word used in mathematics and that a wall at the club was covered with pages from matrix algebra books (Tamarkin 24).

Apart from Jefferson Airplane, a lot of popular groups and well known performers played there including the Grateful Dead, Big Brother and the Holding Company, Quicksilver Messenger Service, Country Joe and the Fish, Sopwith Camel, the Steve Miller Blues Band, the Doors, the Youngbloods, the Chambers Brothers, Electric Flag, the Charlatans, Lightnin' Hopkins, the Great Society, Wildflower, the PH Phactor Jug Band, Little Walter and His Band, the Blues Project, James Cotton and His Chicago Blues Band, Moby Grape, Junior Wells, Howlin' Wolf, and others.

The Matrix caught on fast, but the local establishment was not happy with a dance hall opening in a conservative, bourgeois neighborhood, and so the harassment began. Building inspectors made their rounds hoping to find flagrant violations, but to their amazement they couldn't find any. The first Matrix poster reads: "Coming to the Bay Area! The Matrix. San Francisco's First Folk Night Club. Opening August 13. Performances Start at 9:00." Jefferson Airplane was not mentioned.

The Matrix was meant to be something new for the nascent psychedelic movement in the Haight-Ashbury and the Bay Area.

The atmosphere was an important ingredient in the ballroom's success, and the music was supposed to be secondary to it, at least that was the idea in the beginning.

The musicians often mingled with the audience because things were pretty casual and they were not yet thought of as rock stars that you couldn't get close to. The Matrix was a good place to socialize and meet people, hip or otherwise, but dancing was not allowed because of a strange city ordinance requiring food to be served, so the club was refused a dance permit. The large pizza ovens were removed to make room for the dressing room, and tables and chairs were set up because it was a requirement in places where music was the main attraction.

Opening night was sold out without a hitch. John Wasserman wrote a long article to promote the new club entitled "The Matrix: Social blues via the Jefferson Airplane." It was published in the *Chronicle* on 29 August 1965, with a picture of Marty Balin on acoustic guitar. Ralph Gleason also covered the music scene with his "On the Town" column. In "Jefferson Airplane–Sound and Style," he predicted the group would sign a recording contract.

The Fillmore Auditorium at 1805 Geary Street, on the corner of Fillmore and Geary, was one of the most popular places for dances and concerts. From January 1966 to July 1968, Bill Graham, "Fillmore Bill" as he was sometimes called, operated the ballroom upstairs, making it synonymous with rock music and the San Francisco sound.

The building was first opened as the Majestic Hall and Majestic Academy of Dancing in 1912. Charles Sullivan, a six foot five inch black promoter who Graham said looked a lot like bluesman Albert King, took over in 1952 and renamed it the Fillmore Auditorium. Top black performers of the day played there including Duke Ellington, Ray Charles,

Little Richard and the Temptations. Sullivan knew quite a few people and had some influence with black performers since he also booked the Pacific Coast tours of James Brown, the "Godfather of Soul," Ike and Tina Turner and Bobby Bland (Selvin 103).

Bill Graham was looking for a large dance hall for the second Mime Troupe benefit on December 10, 1965, to be organized for the legal defense of the theatrical group he managed.

It is uncertain who first suggested the Fillmore to Bill Graham for the second Mime Troupe benefit. Perhaps it was Ralph Gleason (Graham 128), or more probably he heard about it from Chet Helms and the Family Dog, though Ronnie Davis says he found the Fillmore and was planning to put on the Minstrel Show there. In any event, Graham knew what he was looking for and fell in love with the large ballroom that had a real stage.

During the first Mime Troupe benefit, that took place in their Howard Street loft on 6 November (Perry 31), Graham noticed that people were dancing who had probably never danced before. That gave him the idea of organizing rock concerts, though he did not know very much about the genre at the time and was not a rock music fan. Bill loved Latin music and musicians like Esy Morales, Pupi Campo, Xavier Cugat, Machito, Tito Puente, Tito Rodriguez and the like, and loved to go dancing at the famous Palladium at 53rd Street and Broadway in New York City (Graham 44-49).

For the second benefit Graham got Sam and the Gentleman's Band, the Great Society with Grace Slick, and Mystery Trend. Frank Zappa reportedly dropped by. Bill got a lucky advertising break when Bob Dylan held up a placard announcing the show while being interviewed on KQED television, so thousands of people knew about it. The second benefit was an even bigger success than the first, bringing in perhaps as much as $6,000.

The third benefit took place on January 14, 1966, and featured the Great Society, Mystery Trend, the Grateful Dead (formerly the Warlocks) and the Gentleman's Band. Graham realized that he was into something big because he was making money hand over fist; just thinking about the shows made dollar signs flash in his eyes like strobe-lights.

The story about the first benefit is fairly incredible. Graham was running around with a clipboard in a frenzy, checking on everything: the front and back doors, the ashtrays, the ice. . . . The place was so packed they couldn't have squeezed Twiggy in there, but people were still lined up all the way down the block, waiting to get in. At eleven o'clock, four policemen arrived and a Sergeant told Graham they had to shut it all down right away. Bill went into his routine, trying to get the Sergeant to yield, but he replied that there was too much smoking and too many people. It was a fire hazard and as such was dangerous. Then Bill had a brainstorm. He told the officer a cock and bull story about Rudy Vallee and Frank Sinatra arriving to put on a show; then he used the magic word, calling the Sergeant "Captain," and that changed everything. The "Captain" grew about three feet taller, the tone of his voice changed, and he acquiesced (Graham 125-26). You had to admire Bill for his chutzpah in situations like that, but for him it was natural, he had never been the kind of person that gives in.

Bill Graham and Ronnie Davis, the director of the Mime Troupe, both had strong personalities and didn't see eye to eye on a lot of basic issues since their ideas and egos were diametrically opposed. They exchanged a few words over the organization of benefits and the conflicts of interest involved. On the one hand, there was the tenacious defense of art as an ideal of freedom of expression; the oppositional voice was the staunch capitalist more than eager to take advantage of a golden opportunity to make money. Davis said the Mime Troupe was in the business of doing plays, not in the business of doing benefits. That answered Graham's question about whether he should stay or not.

Bill Graham left the Mime Troupe, of course, "for political reasons," affirmed Peter Berg. Graham's talk about not using the theatre to make a "political statement" was either a pretext so he could get out, or a deep-rooted belief that he voiced in one of his famous tantrums.

Political theatre, in various forms, has existed since the Greek *polis*, and political themes permeate the plays of Euripides and other Greek playwrights. Theatre represented an important means of self-criticism and a means of improving democracy. William Shakespeare's plays were political plays that describe the guile and stratagems of Machiavellian characters plotting in the shadows for power, and Bertolt Brecht has had an enormous influence on political playwrights. In fact, theatre by its very nature is political. Bill Graham was a stage, film and television actor, so he knew what the theatre was about and that to make it big it helped to be apolitical and not make enemies. Ronnie Davis could have cared less about making enemies; he was involved in theatre as an art, and also because he wanted to bring about social change.

In looking back over Graham's career, it is clear that he preferred making money to engaging in protest. He was not interested in changing society as a whole, nor was he a political activist. Bill Graham saw where there was money to be made, and he went running after it. But if Graham is remembered for anything, it is because of his contribution to music in San Francisco and later in New York. To expose his audience to different kinds of music, Graham started mixing genres, putting blues, rock or soul on the same bills. He brought in a number of black performers, too, such as Otis Redding, Count Basie, Muddy Waters, the Staples, Jimmy Reed, Howlin' Wolf, Roland Kirk, Chuck Berry and Albert King.

Lenny Bruce's last performance was organized there and a number of live performances were recorded at the Fillmore, including Cream's *Wheels of Fire* and Chuck Berry's *Live at the Fillmore.*

There were some highly original names from the sixties and "The Family Dog" is one that calls to mind a multitude of images and anecdotes. Contrary to what Bill Graham first believed, it was not a dog act.

At the very beginning it involved four people–Jack Towle, Alton Kelley, Ellen Harmon and Luria Castell–who knew nothing about promoting or organizing dance concerts.

2125 Pine Street was known as the "Dog House," a highly unusual urban commune and psychedelic-rock promotion and production group. Why was it called The Family Dog? There are several hypotheses. Some say it came from the idea of creating a pet cemetery to make money. Others say it was because of all the poor dogs getting run over on Pine Street because people were driving so fast. Or maybe it was because of the commune's mascot–a street dog, part shepherd and part Mexican named "Sancho."

Jack Towle was an honest dope dealer who would not rip you off. He sold his lids for ten dollars on Haight Street in 1966. Some say he established this price as the rule of thumb in the neighborhood. It is true that an ounce of grass usually sold for ten dollars on Haight Street from 1965 to early 1968, and that most dealers adhered to this unwritten rule.

Alton Kelley was a former commercial designer who would become well known for his remarkable concert posters and his artistic collaborations with some of the hottest bands at the time.

Ellen Harmon was Kelley's girlfriend from the Motor City. She liked to read stories from Marvel Comics about Spider-Man, the X-Men, Doctor Strange, Doctor Doom, Daredevil and Captain Marvel.

Luria Castell liked to hang out with the Beats. She had been to Havana, Cuba, where she discussed politics with Che Guevara and Fidel Castro, and she spent a lot of time with her hip friends on the Sunset Strip in Hollywood.

All four had taken in the casual performances at the Red Dog Saloon in Virginia City, Nevada, where the Charlatans played their hybrid form of music, which was something like country-folk music from the twenties with something else added to spice it up (Seay 29).

The hippie counterculture had something in common with the bebop culture–the uncontrollable urge to dance when people heard music they liked, that *moved* them, but certainly not in a bar with all its establishment sex-games. Besides, the hippies smoked grass and hashish, rather than drink alcohol.

The Family Dog wanted to do something. They thought about it for a while, and it seemed the obvious thing to do was to put on a rock show. Ironically enough, their parents ended up financing it, while their hippie sons and daughters called people up, opened a checking account, made psychedelic posters and passed out handbills.

The dance/concert on 16 October 1965, produced by The Family Dog at Longshoremen's Hall, was billed a "Tribute to Dr. Strange." It sounded like a lot of fun, but there was a fly in the ointment: the acoustics were terrible there. Despite that drawback, it was a place for freaks to get together and get it on.

Luria Castell was quick to get in touch with Jefferson Airplane and the Great Society. The master of ceremonies was none other than Russ "the Moose" Syracuse, one of the zaniest, wackiest DJs on the radio. The Moose worked graveyard, regarded by many as a dead end for DJs, but he used the night shift to explore different possibilities of broadcasting and invented "The Love Line" on radio station KYA. His alter ego was simply called "Your Captain," and the program was "The All-Night Flight."

Quite a few people in the San Francisco Bay Area stayed up late to take the All-Night Flight and listen to the bombs falling on the records the Moose didn't like, or the moronic voices of Barnyard Benny and Cy Lo.

The Primary means of publicity for the concert was a

thousand eight by ten inch handbills that were given out at strategic locations such as Sather Gate and Telegraph Avenue in Berkeley, San Francisco State campus and Haight Street. Ralph Gleason gave a lending hand by mentioning Dr. Strange in his "On the Town" column.

The attire for the event amply conveyed the zeitgeist of the sixties, when costumes served to recreate one's self and alter reality. There were all kinds of freaks: Beatniks, exotic Orientals, Easy Riders, Robin Hoods and Flower Children attired in the latest Goodwill chic. Some of the crowd had been at the Vietnam Day Peace March. The sweet smell of Acapulco Gold wafted around the Hall, but there wasn't very much alcohol. Chet Helms, ever the Haight hippie, characterized the general feeling as one of "sanctuary" and newfound freedom of doing what you like with the people you like. The acid heads were out in numbers that night.

A Tribute to Dr. Strange was a watershed in the psychedelic movement and an occasion for acting out fantasies. Even if the sound system was Paleolithic and playing the Hall itself was like playing in an airplane hangar, the vibrations were good and would create the impetus for the psychedelic movement in the Haight-Ashbury, which never could have been what it was without the concerts, the dances and the psychedelics.

The Trips Festival took place from January 21 to 23, 1966, at Longshoremen's Hall. According to Chet Helms, the original idea for it came from Zack Stewart, though others say it was Stewart Brand. It was put together by Ramon Sender from the Tape Music Center, Stewart Brand, an American Indian scholar, and Zack Stewart, a Stanford biology graduate. They decided to bring Ken Kesey into it, and where he went, Neal Cassidy and the Merry Pranksters followed.

The Grateful Dead and Big Brother and the Holding Company played and Loading Zone was scheduled to play; poet Allen Ginsberg was also there, as was photographer Gene Anthony. Ken Kesey, who had been arrested the night before on Stewart Brand's roof, was out on bail after being charged with the possession of marijuana, trespassing and assaulting a police officer.

Kesey was involved in a bold publicity stunt in Union Square on January 20, 1966. He stepped off the bus named "Further" with "Hot" and "Cold" written on his pants, "Tibet" stenciled across his rear, and played the clown in Union Square as he gave details for the Trips Festival. Stewart Brand was there, too, with a Prankster lady dressed up as a *danseuse* from the Moulin Rouge. The ambiance was sublimely carnivalesque. Kesey released several weather balloons into the sky as a large banner with "Now" written across it was held up. The story made for good reading in the morning *Chronicle*.

Thousands of people showed up for the three-day saturnalia that was in essence an Acid Test with music, dancing, electronic multimedia and a feast of madness.

An article in *The Oakland Tribune*, dated Friday, January 21, 1966, announced "A mammoth three day trips festival." But some of the announcements could be misleading, to say the least. America Needs Indians was little more than a tepee and a few slides on a projector. The parachutes and banners that were hung could not eliminate all the echoes that added to the weirdness, in a hall that was supposed to hold 1,700 people, but must have been holding twice that many.

There were at least two handbills for the festival. One was designed by Wes Wilson. Another reads: "This is the first gathering of its kind anywhere. The trip–or electronic performance–is a new medium of communication and entertainment. In this festival, audience and participants will see how the trip has been developed for theater, music and dance, education, light and sound, rock 'n' roll, sculpture, novelists and poets." People were asked to come the way they were usually dressed.

This was the first time Bill Graham saw the acid thing at close quarters, forced to dance cheek and jowl with psychedelics, so to speak. A shopping bag full of Owsley's tabs was being passed around and people were greedily helping themselves. Large tubs of fruit-flavored drink spiked with LSD were set up for people to use, including children, but there was no way of knowing how much you had taken afterwards. Driving home was a test in itself for those who came from the suburbs.

Aside from that, the thing that really got Graham's goat was that people were getting in for free; he went into huge conniptions. Owsley Stanley III couldn't help but notice how shocked he was because of the crazy, totally uninhibited way people were behaving. A few, including the "Henry Ford of LSD," would have loved to get Graham stoned, but couldn't figure out how to do it.

The "unparalleled chaos," as Charles Perry described it, was in fact an initiation, a psychedelic ritual in which rational thought surrendered to the unimagined forces of the id. Without a doubt, the multimedia extravaganza was a feast for your eyes and ears and everything else. It was madness with a thousand faces amidst movie projectors flashing visions around the hall, strobe lights dazzling the mind, Anna Halprin's dancers leaping and spinning, closed circuit TV groping for monads, ultraviolet lights creating new spatial dimensions of Day-Glo, Ron Boise's thunder machine booming from within, a Moog synthesizer machine-gunning sound from sixteen speakers, the Merry Pranksters vandalizing reality, Paul Foster wrapped up in tape like Griffin in *The Invisible Man*, irrelevant announcements, running commentaries of unremitting, polymorphic dementia, girls dancing braless in the vertiginous spinning, throbbing whir of the kaleidoscopic vortex that surged and spumed like the riptide of your bloodstream. "Anybody who knows he is God go up on the stage," read a message from Kesey in the control tower. Voyeurism was reserved for the balcony. The psychedelic madness, vintage 1966, was thought to be a way of transcending self via electronics.

Kesey, who believed the Acid Tests would become an everyday form of entertainment, was soaring in the exosphere with his gold lamé space suit and helmet, trying to hide from reporters and police, though everyone knew it was him. Early in the evening, Bill Graham, clipboard in hand, accosted the spaceman for letting in Hell's Angels for free. That was his first encounter with the quixotic author of *One Flew over the Cuckoo's Nest*. When Graham raised his voice and demanded to know what the hell was going on, Kesey simply closed his visor and went about other "pranks." Stewart Brand was supposed to keep Kesey and Graham separated.

Ken Babbs, Prankster de luxe, was typically obnoxious, clashing with conga drummers because of their "jungle bunny music" and trying to cut short Big Brother's set, until Chet Helms intervened and addressed the audience to be sure the band would play a four-song set.

Jerry Garcia couldn't play because somebody broke the headstock to his guitar. It was funny seeing Bill Graham trying to fix the unfixable. That was the first time they met. Many thought that the best part of the largest Acid Test ever was the music. In any event, psychedelia was born from this primordial soup.

Chet Helms, who hitch-hiked to San Francisco with Janis Joplin in January 1963, and Bill Graham, born Wulf Wolodia Grajonca, were about as different as two people could possibly be. Helms was the naïve, trusting, long-haired hippie; Graham was the cabby from the Bronx who had fought in the Korean War and escaped the Holocaust by the skin of his teeth. Both were promoters, but their styles and motivations were light-years apart.

Helms and The Family Dog did collaborate with Graham, however. On 19 February 1966, The Family Dog did a show with Bill featuring Jefferson Airplane and Big Brother and the Holding Company. On February 26, they organized another show together with The Great Society, Grass Roots, Big Brother and Quicksilver on the bill. On April 8th and 9th of the same year, they were associated for a concert with Love, the Sons of Adam and the Charlatans. Chet emceed Graham's concerts as well as his own, while

John Carpenter sold tickets. Helms and Carpenter, who had a long list of people, actually phoned them to fill the ballroom.

But their association was not meant to last and Helms got the short end of the stick. With the pretext that Helms and Carpenter had not provided their own tape and thumbtacks to pin up dance posters in the Fillmore, Graham got rid of them lickety-split (Seay 69). However ridiculous the incident may seem, it gives some insight into Graham's character.

The Avalon Ballroom, located at 1268 Sutter Street, was another important venue. It had a capacity of sixteen hundred. On June 3-4, 1966, Big Brother and the Holding Company played at the Avalon with Janis. Also on the bill were The Grass Roots, The Buddha from Muir Beach and A Stone Facade. Victor Moscoso did the poster work with a gargoyle from Notre Dame of Paris. This may have been Janis Joplin's first public performance with Big Brother.

For the psychedelic counterculture and the real hippies, Chet Helms' concerts at the Avalon Ballroom were the real thing, superior to Graham's Fillmore, in part because Helms was a folksy sort of promoter and his shows were examples of grassroots psychedelia. April 22 and 23, 1966, the first concerts were organized at the Avalon featuring the Great Society and the Blues Project from New York. Chet Helms and the Family Dog organized concerts from April 1966 to November 1968. Their contribution to the creation and development of the San Francisco music sound was enormous.

The building that housed the ballroom was built in 1911 and originally called the Puckett Academy of Dance. The

Family Dog had a lot of fun finding facile rimes for "Puckett." The wooden dance floor was upstairs. It had an L-shaped balcony, mirror, gilded booths, columns and red-flocked wallpaper. It was beautiful.

But times changed and Helms lost his dance permits because people started complaining about the noise. A big part of sixties culture was swept away when the Avalon ballroom became a Cineplex in the seventies.

The advent of the Fillmore Auditorium and Avalon Ballroom ushered in a new era for San Francisco music. Helms didn't give apples away like Graham, but souvenirs and other things were for free. He had people from The Family Dog circulating among the crowd, too, and handing out things.

The dance concerts, with their light shows, strobe lights, posters, marijuana, costumes, and all the rest, became tangible symbols of the sixties.

The Grateful Dead, a progenitor of the San Francisco sound, was in the storm center when it started. From June 1965 to September 1967, the founding members were Jerry Garcia, lead guitar and vocals; Bob Weir, rhythm guitar and vocals; Ron "Pigpen" McKernan, keyboard and vocals; Phil Lesh, bass guitar and vocals; and Bill Kreutzmann on drums.

Before being reborn as the Grateful Dead, they were the Warlocks. Phil Lesh was flipping through records and came across a single published by another group by the same name, maybe a Texas band. Since there were at least two, they had to change their name. Speaking tongue-in-cheek, Garcia suggested "Mythical Ethical Icicle Tricycle." They leafed through *Bartlett's Mythology*, but didn't find anything.

Then Garcia opened *Funk and Wagnall's*, pointed a fateful finger and struck pay dirt: Grateful Dead. It was not a macabre expression from a tale by H. P. Lovecraft or Edgar Allan Poe, but a musical term referring to a special kind of ballad about a hero who meets a corpse that is denied proper burial for want of paying a debt. The hero, without expecting anything in return, pays the debt, usually with all the money he has in the world, and thus changes the destiny of the corpse for the better. Not long after his act of compassion and generosity, the hero encounters a traveler who assists him in performing a difficult, if not impossible task. The wayfarer, as it turns out, is none other than the spirit of the deceased person (McNally 101).

The band members were enthralled with this tale imbued with the idea of karma, or an individual's destiny as determined by one's actions, conduct, thoughts and words. The connotations of "Grateful Dead" were mindboggling for the band.

The Dead were well known for their musical improvisations that may have emerged from their worldview, which in turn was influenced or induced by lysergic acid diethylamide. Much of the Dead's music was based on the psychedelic experience. "Deadheads" liked it, seemed to understand it, because their lives had been psychedelicized. Once Garcia had taken acid, there was no turning back–there was no longer any idea of "backness" (McNally 104). Everything became a cosmic river, ever flowing forward and the Dead were the fish in that eternal river.

Owsley "Bear" Stanley III was the band's special chemist, and maybe he was something of an "alchemist" as well. He sponsored the band and freely distributed his latest batches of *newness*. Owsley had money to spend and he spent it freely on new and upgraded equipment for the Dead: tuners, receivers, microphones, amplifiers, instruments, mixers, muters, whatever could be bought. Kreutzmann described their trips as roller-coaster rides without the tracks. Some of the band members said they had telepathic experiences, which was not uncommon when using LSD with people you knew fairly well.

Early on, the band was associated with Ken Kesey and the Merry Pranksters. Prankster Ken Babbs described their relationship by saying the band was the engine for their spaceship. "You're either on the bus, or you're off the bus" was the way Kesey summed up his reality. The "bus" in question was the Prankster bus called "Further," driven by Prankster speed freak Neal Cassidy. The Grateful Dead, in the beginning, was definitely on the bus.

Jerry "Captain Trips" Garcia liked the Acid Tests at first because the musicians could do what they wanted to, there were no specific demands made on them and there was no pressure (Troy 81). If they didn't want to play, they didn't have to. As a result, they had a tremendous amount of freedom to explore themselves as musicians and avoid getting stuck in a mold.

Bob Weir remembers the lights, the speakers, the weird sounds, the pulsating liquid light shows that seemed to have begun with the Acid Tests. It was a colorful extravaganza and an exploration of previously unchartered territory: crazy people with dyed hair wearing rainbow raiment and all out of their minds on acid. Kesey's Acid Tests gave the Grateful

Dead the opportunity to actually become the Grateful Dead by experimenting and improvising.

The Dead used a lot of drugs, except for Pigpen, who was a hard liquor man. In light of the fact that the Acid Tests were all about LSD, this was not too surprising. Bob Weir said the Dead played every Acid Test but one, in Mexico. But as Weir pointed out, they were not trying to escape from reality by taking drugs, but rather use the experiences as "tools" to increase their awareness, to achieve a higher state of consciousness, which does not preclude spiritual awareness.

According to Phil Lesh in *Searching for the Sound*, the Dead had been dropping acid every week for a six-month period, which is quite a lot of acid for anyone. Naturally, their perception of reality changed a lot during that time.

710 Ashbury Street was the Grateful Dead house, or as some have said, Haight-Ashbury's City Hall. "Seven-ten" was a kind of commune and those who lived there contributed to the band. The communards went to bed early as a rule. Jerry Garcia was one of the first to rise in the morning to practice, after downing a cup or two of java.

Unlike a lot of managers at the time, Danny Rifkin, road manager for the band, and Rock Scully, general manager, were not in it for the money. They wanted the band and its music to have an impact on society, and to do that they needed maximum exposure–get as many people as possible interested in the Dead, and get them out to the concerts.

In 1966, the Haight-Ashbury was a safe and friendly neighborhood, and the front door of seven-ten was never locked. This was the case with other communal houses in the

Haight. Michael McClure, the Haight poet, was not afraid to send his young daughter out alone to buy hippie odds and ends at the Psychedelic Shop on Haight Street, the local head shop owned by Ron and Jay Thelin, who had grown up in the neighborhood. Their father managed the Woolworth's store that was right across the street.

Weir stopped taking LSD on August 1, 1966, one year after his first trip, having decided his macrobiotic diet was enough to get him high. Pigpen drank whiskey and cheap wine, sometimes with Janis Joplin, with whom he sang the blues in his room. Janis was not the only guest at 710: Elvin Bishop, John Lee Hooker, Vince Guaraldi, Michael McClure, Emmett Grogan, Peter Berg and others visited the Dead.

The Grateful Dead performed a lot of free concerts, probably more than all the other San Francisco bands, and they often performed in the Panhandle. Their paid concerts were their only real source of income, since they didn't have any albums or singles out yet. During a show at Winterland, the large ballroom at the corner of Post and Steiner Streets that used to be an old ice-skating rink, they had a run-in with the Diggers who were picketing there when the Dead had a gig. The Diggers were opposed to pay concerts, since they believed that everything should be free. But the show went on anyway after some haggling.

The Dead had a fairly busy schedule as far as performances were concerned. In 1966, they played January 6, 8, 13, 15, 16, 28 and 29, at the Matrix; January 14 at the Fillmore; and January 22 and 23 at the Longshoremen's Hall. From February to December 1966, they played at the

Avalon Ballroom, California Hall, Pauley Ballroom at U. C. Berkeley, the Fillmore Auditorium and the Matrix. During that same period, they also gave shows at Veterans Hall, the Harmon Gym, the Northridge Unitarian Church, Rancho Olompali, the University of California Medical Center, the P.N.E. Garden Auditorium and at a place called Afterthought.

Kesey had a Graduation Ceremony scheduled for Winterland on Halloween, October 31, 1966. Many felt this would be his last but also his most outrageous prank. Kesey reportedly planned putting LSD in the water system. Ron Polte, Quicksilver's manager, was one of several people to get in touch with Bill Graham about the prank. Graham had received his dance permit not that long ago, and if anything weird happened at the Ceremony, his permit would have been revoked in short notice, and he would have been washed up as a promoter in San Francisco. Danny Rifkin convinced the Dead to forget about playing at Winterland, and they ended up playing Halloween at California Hall at 625 Polk Street.

Ken Kesey was arrested on October, 20, 1966, and made a surprising public statement: "Taking acid is not the thing that's happening anymore," but added that the Acid Test Graduation would still be held. So what was going to replace LSD? "Leary's supposed to be coming out, and he's supposed to know pieces of it, and Jerry Garcia with his music knows pieces of it," he replied. It is probably safe to say that Kesey told authorities what they wanted to hear. He also said that it was time to move on, and not just get stoned. Kesey was being vague or seemed to be speaking in doublethink.

The day after Halloween, the California Democratic Party was scheduled to hold a political rally at Winterland. For the incumbent governor, Pat Brown, the election against Ronald Reagan was going to be an uphill battle. According to hearsay, Kesey was targeting the governor's rally on November 1, 1966. The Pranksters were supposedly planning on smearing everything with dimethyl sulfoxide (DMSO), a solvent, and mixing it with LSD; that way, if you touched anything, the psychotrope would go right through your skin and get into your system. Everyone at the political rally would be stoned on acid.

The Acid Test Graduation was finally held at the Calliope Company warehouse on Harriet Street, south of Market Street, in a run-down area of the city (Perry 102).

Each of the San Francisco bands had its distinguishing characteristics, but there were also similarities: the folk music origins, the use of improvisation, the merging of styles and long meandering guitar solos, to name a few.

The Grateful Dead was a self-effacing rock band. The band knew Jefferson Airplane, of course, and felt they were a tighter, more professional group of musicians. The Dead tended to see themselves as freaks on a trip. Notwithstanding this diffidence, Jerry Garcia was a respected guitarist in the Haight. He came up with the title to the Airplane's album *Surrealistic Pillow*. After listening to a take Jerry said, "That's as surrealistic as a pillow." It would have been difficult to find a better image.

In November 1966, he reportedly went to Los Angeles to help out, and according to studio logs he played electric lead on "Today" and acoustic guitar on "Plastic Fantastic Lover," "My Best Friend," and "Coming Back to Me." He supposedly arranged "Somebody to Love" (McNally 170). The problem is that Garcia was not given credit for this on the album cover, but reportedly as a joke was listed as "musical and spiritual advisor." One must admit that the wording is peculiar, as though it was a joke. The Airplane may have sneaked him into the recording sessions to circumvent rigid RCA policy.

Unlike some of the other bands in San Francisco, the Dead were not in a hurry to get an album out. They did, however, sign a modest contract with Warner Brothers, making them the company's first rock band (McNally 173). They received a $10,000 advance and eight percent in royalties. Bill Kreutzmann used some of the money to buy a Ford Mustang–definitely not the best vehicle for loading the band's equipment.

The Dead were decidedly not politically outspoken and generally preferred to avoid politics. They played backup to Jon Hendricks on a blues tune entitled "Sons and Daughters," and "Fire in the City" in October 1966, which was used for the soundtrack of the film documentary *Sons and Daughters*, directed by Jerry Stoll and released in April 1967. "Sons and Daughters" and "Fire in the City" were released as a single by Verve Records in Santa Monica, using Jon Hendrick's name.

However, the Grateful Dead did not want their name to appear in the credits. The band was opposed to the War in Vietnam like all psychedelic bands in San Francisco, but they might have been afraid of being harassed by the FBI or other intelligence agencies. This was not just a case of paranoia because Hoover's agents had already stopped by 710 looking for Owsley and other underground celebrities. Apparently, they were well aware of the relationship between the chemist and the band. J. Edgar Hoover was dead set on arresting Bear, the King of LSD, and knew that he was in and out of San Francisco. But there are other reasons for the Dead's apolitical stance: Jerry Garcia wanted the band to be "above life's daily shuffle" and felt their beliefs were far too divergent to use the group's name to advertise it.

The Hell's Angels were regulars in the Haight-Ashbury and the Grateful Dead had a fairly comfortable relationship with them. They performed at the party the Angels gave in the Panhandle for the hippies and Diggers who helped to bail out Chocolate George when he was arrested for living up to the gang's credo–"All on one and one on all"–by helping fellow Angel Hairy Henry Kot when he was arrested for a traffic violation during the Death of Money parade. This is not to say that the Hell's Angels and the hippies were loving brothers; the Angels were unpredictable and liable to fly off the handle at the slightest provocation. What's more, they hated peaceniks and some Angel's liked to exploit and bully hippies.

On Saint Patrick's Day, March 17, 1967, Warner Bros. Records released *The Grateful Dead*. At the time, most agreed the album was inferior to the group's live performances and only a couple of the tracks sounded like the Grateful Dead. The band wanted to record in San Francisco, but for want of an adequate recording studio, it was rushed through recording sessions in Los Angeles in four days, mainly in Studio A. David Hassinger, who had engineered *Surrealistic Pillow*, produced the album. Several of the tracks were cut short at the demand of Warner Bros.

At the same time, San Francisco City Hall was growing ever more hostile to the hippie movement and the police received instructions to stop all unauthorized activity in the Haight. On March 24, 1967, Mayor John Shelley asked the Board of Supervisors to officially declare hippies unwelcome in the city by the Bay. That same day, a rock band was playing in an apartment at the corner of Haight and Ashbury, and a sizeable crowd gathered in the street to listen. The police intervened to stop the impromptu concert, and some people retaliated by cutting the valves of their tires. In all, sixteen people were arrested.

On March 26, 1967, Easter Sunday, a crowd was gathering in Haight Street. The police were present and eager to stop the "illegal rally." The Grateful Dead came to the rescue and helped to avoid another unwanted confrontation by playing for free in the Panhandle. Allen Cohen of the *Oracle* urged everyone within shouting distance to go there and enjoy themselves, rather than pick a fight with the cops.

The Haight Ashbury Legal Organization (HALO) had an office in 710 Ashbury. HALO was a volunteer group of lawyers, basically Brian Rohan and Michael Stepanian, who defended hippies in legal matters such as drug busts. A benefit concert for HALO was held on Tuesday, May 30, 1967, at Winterland, the goal of which was to help pay for Summer of Love expenses that continued to rise. The event was the only time the Dead, the Airplane, the Charlatans, Big Brother and Quicksilver were on the same bill, but there is some doubt whether all five bands showed up, and it seems they did not all perform.

October 2, 1967, was a very bad day for the band, to say the least (Scully 130-31, McNally 225-26, *Dark Star* 101-2). "Hermit" was supposed to be a Prankster. The police reportedly threatened him with an indefinite internment at the Napa State Mental Institution if he failed to cooperate in a number of drug arrests as an informant. Apart from drug use, "Hermit" was also said to be a child molester. In what turned out to be an easy bust, he led the narks to 710, went inside and asked if he could roll a joint from their stash. Mountain Girl gave him a baggie of grass as well. Once outside, he gave the marijuana to the police who went immediately into action. Matthew O'Connor, Chief of the State Narcotics Bureau, Jerry Van Ramm, State agent, and Norbert "the Nark" Currie, head of the SFPD Narcotics Squad, barged through the front door to seize evidence and make arrests. Television crews and reporters were on hand to cover the event, which clearly shows the Dead were targeted. The governor's office, too, had made it known that it was time to clean things up in California. With their cooperative Prankster informant, the San Francisco police busted at least four houses in the Haight-Ashbury that day.

Surprisingly, a brick of marijuana in the cupboard was completely overlooked, but not the hundred dollar bill in an office desk or Pigpen's .32 Baretta pistol, which was legal.

Marilyn Harris, the Grateful Dead's kindly neighbor, kept Captain Trips and Mountain Girl out of jail by telling them to bring up the groceries because she was hungry and wanted to eat. Of course there were no groceries; that was just a ploy to save their necks. She had a front row seat to the raid and was well aware that a couple of narks were still lurking inside the house. Jerry and Mountain Girl, who had come back from Sausalito, went into her apartment and thereby managed to avoid arrest.

Jerry Van Ramm was so happy he was literally kicking his heels at the Hall of Justice. Everyone who was inside the Grateful Dead house at the time was arrested: Bob Weir, Ron Pigpen McKernan, Rock Scully, Danny Rifkin, Bob Matthews, Sue Swanson, Christine Bennett, Toni Kaufman, and others. Their Bail was set at $550 each, a considerable amount at the time.

The 710 bust was fairly indicative of the situation in the Haight-Ashbury just after the Summer of Love. The notion of community had vaporized and you couldn't trust everyone anymore. The police helped to create this situation and took full advantage of it by using informants and harassment. You don't get to be the bully on the block without using your fists and your clubs.

The story of Jefferson Airplane begins with Marty Balin, born Martyn Jerel Buchwald on January 30, 1942, in Cincinnati. He went to Washington High School in San Francisco. In 1962, he changed his name to Marty Balin. Musically speaking, Balin had a folk music background, since he was a member of the folk music group the Town Criers from 1963 to 1964. He said the folk-rock music of the Byrds had a noticeable impact on his style.

Once the pizza parlor was converted into the Matrix, Balin began hunting for musicians to start his band. In retrospect, the name of the club seemed to foreshadow the growth of the San Francisco sound, since "matrix" is defined as a "womb," a place where something originates and develops.

Balin met Paul Kantner at the Drinking Gourd. Kantner, a native San Franciscan who played on the folk music circuit, knew David Crosby, Jerry Garcia and Janis Joplin. He said he was greatly influenced by the Weavers and the Kingston Trio. The Airplane was fueled on high octane psychedelics, as were most San Francisco bands, and Kantner, while residing in Venice Beach in southern California, started dropping acid.

Balin wanted a competent female lead singer for the band and found what he was looking for when he saw Signe Toly Anderson performing at the Drinking Gourd; he simply went up to her and asked her to join the band and she agreed. During the day, Signe, pronounced "sig-nee," worked as a secretary and only sang in the San Francisco folk clubs on weekends or in the evenings. Her strong, melodious voice fit in well, and she could sing the blues to boot, so Balin was sold on her.

The band needed a good lead guitarist and Jorma (pronounced "yor-ma") Kaukonen filled the spot nicely. Jorma learned a lot of guitar from professor Ian Buchanan at Antioch College in Ohio. Buchanan also taught bluesman John Paul Hammond, son of record producer John H. Hammond. From 1964 to 1967, John Hammond Jr. produced six LPs: *Big City Blues*, *Country Blues*, *John Hammond*, *So Many Roads*, *I Can Tell* and *Mirrors*.

After spending two years at Antioch and some time in New York and the Philippines where he studied anthropology, Jorma moved to California where he enrolled at Santa Clara College. While in Santa Clara a friend took him to Santa Cruz where he met Paul Kantner, who was living with some surfers at the time. Jorma met other musicians, too, such as Jerry Garcia, Dino Valente and Billy Roberts. He played guitar with Janis Joplin on several occasions, and quite candidly admitted that she was one of the best blues singers he'd ever heard (Tamarkin 30).

The name of the band is as intriguing today as it was in 1965. According to Kaukonen, the name got started as a kind of joke. Steve Talbot had nicknamed Jorma "Blind Thomas Jefferson Airplane," alluding to Blind Lemon Jefferson, the famous bluesman. Jorma told the rest of the band that if they wanted something really silly, they should try "Jefferson Airplane" (Tamarkin 32).

Bob Harvey was the first bass player. In March 1965, he heard Balin and Kantner talking about music and about creating a band. He asked to join, auditioned and was accepted. It was as simple as that.

Jerry Peloquin, the first drummer, was Jacky Watts' boyfriend. Jacky shared a room with Janet Trice, Marty Balin's girlfriend. Before going to San Francisco where he worked as an optician to pay the rent, Jerry had worked for the Capitol Police Force in Washington.

Marty could see which way the wind was blowing with groups like the Byrds, the Lovin' Spoonful and San Francisco's Beau Brummels, whose first hit single "Laugh, Laugh" was released in December 1964, and by February was number fifteen on the *Billboard* Hot 100 singles chart. The winds of folk-rock were definitely blowing across

America's music scene.

Before the mid-sixties, San Francisco was not a rock 'n' roll city. On the contrary, it was centered firmly around folk music and jazz. There were few places to play rock music and the best recording studios were in Los Angeles.

Friday, August 13, 1965, marked the birth of the Matrix and its first public show. All San Francisco was buzzing about it. Opening night was sold out well in advance, but strangely enough the owners had forgotten to hire any employees to take care of things. That didn't seem to matter, though, and the atmosphere of the club was electric.

Things were moving fast and Jerry Peloquin was soon out of the group, maybe for complaining about the smell of marijuana every time the band practiced. Some of the musicians, like Paul Kantner, thought he wasn't suited for the band's rhythm. Peloquin, who could be tough, says he beat the living shit out of Kantner when he discovered he was interviewing other drummers behind his back (Tamarkin 42).

Marty Balin found a replacement for Peloquin at the Matrix in Skip Spence, born Alexander Lee Spence Jr. Skip, whom Balin said looked like a little Buddha, had played drums in his high school marching band and also for rock bands in junior high, but Spence said he was a guitarist, and not a drummer, and would not be satisfied until he could play the guitar for Moby Grape.

After Peloquin, Bob Harvey, the group's bassist, was replaced by Jack Casady. It was felt that Harvey couldn't keep up with the Airplane's complex rhythm arrangements, but there were possibly other reasons, too. Kaukonen and

Casady knew each other well in Washington D. C., so Jorma made a pitch for his friend to get him in the band. Jack had a difficult childhood because he had been severely handicapped by rheumatic fever when he was seven. Jack and Jorma spent quite a bit of time together and much of that time was spent playing the guitar (Tamarkin 48).

Jack left home when he was eighteen and gave guitar lessons to support himself. Jack and Jorma sometimes saw each other in New York, but Jack hadn't seen Jorma since he moved out west to San Francisco. Then, out of the blue, Jorma called his friend and asked him to come to California to play in a rock 'n' roll band. Jack had in fact stopped playing for some time and might have given up the guitar for good if Jorma hadn't called (Tamarkin 49).

The War in Vietnam was raging and young American men had Uncle Sam to worry about. Casady was in college at that time and dropping out meant he might get a call from his local draft board for a free trip to the jungles of Southeast Asia. Jack thought about it for a while, then packed his bags and went out west in October 1965, when the Airplane had barely been in flight for three months.

The band had some unwritten codes and not everyone liked the way Jack looked. Marty Balin called him "Joe Okie" and Paul Kantner told him to shave off his moustache (Tamarkin 49).

On November 15, 1965, RCA signed two contracts: one with Airplane manager Matthew Katz, and one with Jefferson Airplane. The Airplane received $25,000 in advance, a large sum at the time, plus "good production money" (Tamarkin 58).

Matthew Katz, with whom the band was always quarrelling, had added an addendum to the contract that assured him a percentage of the band's production money. For that reason and others, a long and bitter court battle took place between the band and its manager, which didn't end until 1987.

The band's debut album, *Jefferson Airplane Takes Off*, was released in August 1966. Music censorship was not uncommon at that time and RCA executives thought some of the lyrics were too sexually suggestive. By today's standards the changes seem absurd, but things were different then. In the song "Let Me In," the word "money" was replaced by "funny"; in "Runnin' 'Round this World," "trips" was replaced with a guitar arpeggio; and in "Run Around," the words "lay under me" were changed. The record companies, along with the Federal Communications Commission (FCC), felt they had a role to play in safeguarding American morals.

In the sixties, the FCC banned certain songs that were felt to promote sex or violence, or merely mention the words. Radio stations refused to play a number of songs, too. Some of the ones that were censored on the radio and television included "Unknown Soldier" by the Doors, "How Would You Feel" by Jimi Hendrix, "King Bee" by the Rolling Stones, "My Generation" by the Who, "Eight Miles High" by the Byrds, "Eve of Destruction" by Barry McGuire and "Louie, Louie" by the Kingsmen. These are just a few examples.

Marty Balin did most of the songwriting on the debut album, also collaborating on some songs with Kantner, Spence and Kaukonen. The press paid little attention at the time to the album because the rock press had not yet begun and the mainstream press did not generally cover music releases in this genre.

The Airplane missed The Trips Festival because they went north to Vancouver to perform, in a futile attempt to introduce the band outside of the United States. The Trips Festival was a one-of-a-kind event that had a big impact on Bay Area rock. Moreover, it was widely covered by the local press, both underground and mainstream. Herb Caen covered the festival for the *Chronicle; Life, Look, Newsweek* and *Time* were also there (C. Perry 50).

Rock music started to change after that, and seemed to establish an alliance between the musicians and the audience, straights and hippies, and the media and its public. The Airplane definitely would have profited from the festival.

Jefferson Airplane quickly became one of the house bands at the Fillmore Auditorium in 1966, performing there on February 4 and 19, April 7 and May 6. On April 8, they were at California Hall, May 30 at Winterland, June 4 at Exposition Auditorium, June 22 at the Avalon Ballroom, and June 26 with the Rolling Stones at the Cow Palace. The Airplane was delighted to be part of the San Francisco music scene in the spring of 1966, when Hashbury, as it was familiarly called, was a vibrant, ecstatic village of love, with no one "binding with briars, [your] joys and desires."

As Hunter S. Thompson remarked, San Francisco "was the best place in the world to be," and Haight Street was where it was happening in San Francisco, in the spring of 1966. Marty Balin called it Carnaby Street. But for Skip

Spence, the acid was getting out of hand. In search of a more professional drummer, the band let Skip go and replaced him with Spencer Dryden.

Dryden was actually the nephew of Charlie Chaplin and, as such, had met a few Hollywood film greats, including Boris Karloff, Abbott and Costello and Stan Laurel.

Spencer Dryden worked as a drummer with jazz bands, but made his living playing in Los Angeles strip joints because it was impossible to make a living playing jazz.

While the Airplane was in Chicago playing at Mother Blues to celebrate the August 15 release of their debut album, Signe said she was leaving the band because she couldn't take care of her baby and sing for the Airplane at the same time. Some found her attitude a little hard to understand, but Signe was sincere and did not put her personal career before her family.

After Chicago, the Airplane went to Los Angeles, performing at the well known Whiskey-A-Go-Go on August 24. This was the group's first major engagement in L.A. Not all the reviews were good, but the band did not expect all of them to be good. Pete Johnson of the *Los Angeles Times* wrote a bad review, criticizing Balin's high-pitched twang and the way the band's set was organized.

In the Haight, the Airplane's album sold well, and you could often hear it being played in stores and apartments, but outside of the San Francisco Bay Area, the band was still widely unknown. Donovan (Donovan Philips Leitch, who hails from Glasgow, Scotland), for whom the Airplane was *the* band in San Francisco, alludes to the group in his popular song "Fat Angel," when he sings about Jefferson Airplane flying and getting there on time. Leitch also alludes to drugs in the song.

Grace Slick, born Grace Barnett Wing, of the Great Society, had heard about Jefferson Airplane and went to see them perform at the Matrix.

According to the band members, Signe was asked to leave by Bill Thompson, assistant manager, after the uneventful performance at the Monterey Jazz Festival. But her husband, the Merry Prankster Jerry Anderson, appears to have been the real problem, because of the way he embarrassed some members of the band. Some say he was a loose cannon. Signe, however, said she left on her own, though she never really wanted to go, but since she was devoted to her husband and child, she didn't have much of a choice. The talented singer was idealized in San Francisco, and many were sad to see her go.

Grace Slick's first performance with the Airplane in San Francisco seems to have been at the Fillmore Auditorium on October 9, 1966. They were billed with the Butterfield Blues Band that was making such a sensation at the time with its *East-West* album, released in August 1966. The Grateful Dead was also on the bill. The Airplane gave three more performances at the Fillmore on October 14-16 with Paul Butterfield and Big Mama Thornton.

Signe Toly was a competent singer and performer, no doubt about it. Grace Slick, on the other hand, changed the dimension of the Airplane. The chemistry between her and the other members was stronger and her stage presence was electric. Psychedelic rock was surging in her veins. Signe was more folk-oriented. Grace led the band in different directions musically and vocally. With Grace it was a whole new ballgame.

In late 1966, Bill Graham became the group's manager. The band felt more comfortable with Graham, at least in the beginning, and they had come to hate Matthew Katz because of the insoluble financial problems they had with him.

The Airplane played at the Human Be-In in Golden Gate Park on January 14, 1967. The free concert and happening consolidated the band's reputation and position as a pillar of the emerging San Francisco sound. The Airplane, like the Dead and Big Brother, was officially part of the Haight-Ashbury.

Then in February 1967, the music bomb exploded: *Surrealistic Pillow* was released, emblem of psychedelia and the Summer of Love. The album cover struck one's imagination because of its austerity, except for the ornate lettering which had become emblematic of the sixties. In many ways, it was an eidolon of the counterculture's hopes and aspirations, a metaphor of things that could be, if enough people got together.

The musicians, most of them anyway, are holding instruments they don't play. The cover was finally printed in "bubblegum pink," though Marty Balin said he originally did it in blue (Tamarkin 127). RCA apparently changed the cover without consulting the artist, which was nothing new; in fact, it was common practice among record companies and publishers to make such changes whenever they felt it was necessary.

"Somebody to Love" was the single that sold the best, peaking at number five on the national record charts, but apart from the financial success of the record, the song stood out at the time because it reflected the feeling of the sixties, which in itself embodied a revolutionary spirit and universal ideal of love.

Darby Slick, Grace Slick's brother-in-law and author of the song, returned from India to relish his unforeseen success in the California sun. The lyrics were reportedly composed after his girlfriend left him. That could partly justify the interpretation that the song is a plea for meaningful relationships.

A comparison of the Great Society version and Jefferson Airplane's later version shows how much Grace Slick modified her style. The tone becomes decidedly aggressive and acrimonious in the Airplane's rendition of the song.

The media liked the band and wanted to know more about the members. "Jefferson Airplane Loves You" was the title of the article published by *Look* magazine on May 30, 1967. In early May, the group was on the *Smothers Brothers Comedy Hour*. Naturally, the band performed their two big hits: "White Rabbit" and "Somebody to Love." Tom Smothers introduced "Somebody to Love" by advising the TV viewers to eat a banana to get the most out of it. The "banana" was an obvious allusion to the mellow yellow craze that swept the country, when people smoked banana peels to get high. But of course it didn't work. Grace Slick wrote "White Rabbit," seen as a promotional drug song by many because the lyrics refer to the use of psychotropes such as LSD and hashish.

The Airplane even made it to American Bandstand on June 3, 1967, the popular mainstream music show emceed by the ever youthful Dick Clark. Grace was dressed in black like some haughty, esoteric high priestess. Jack smiled benignly and shook his locks for the fans. Paul, and Jorma did their best to fake it, while poor Marty looked as though he were there by mistake, totally bored with the lip-synched charade.

But the Airplane, with its white, middle class college look, was the darling of the media establishment, which allowed the band to fly the money flag high, since they were getting as much as $15,000 a show (Tamarkin 130). There was good money to be made in hippiedom.

Meanwhile, the Gray Lines "creepy-crawly" sightseeing tours of the Haight-Ashbury had begun: "The only foreign tour within the continental limits of the United States." The peaceful, community ambiance of the neighborhood had been turned into a three ring circus of social voyeurism and "fast-buckism."

Also on 5 April 1967, the creation of the Council for the Summer of Love was announced during a press conference at the old firehouse on Waller Street (C. Perry 171). This was apparently how the expression "Summer of Love" officially originated. The members included the Family Dog, the Diggers, the Straight Theatre, the staff of *The San Francisco Oracle*, the Kiva and others. Saint Francis of Assisi was invoked and City Hall was asked to show compassion. The ostensible goal of the Council was to solve some of the problems created by the arrival of thousands of adolescents. To achieve that end the Council coordinated efforts with the local clergy and the Diggers, helped Dr. David Smith open the Haight-Ashbury Free Clinic on 7 June 1967, supported the work of Reverend Larry Beggs, founder of Huckleberry House, organized a Sweep-In to clean up Haight Street, and produced concerts in the Panhandle to get young people off the street and help them to meet other people.

Publicizing the hippie scene nationally poisoned it. The psychedelic bands were singing about peace and love, drugs and revolution, but did not try to influence city government in favor of more libertarian attitudes towards the hippie counterculture. Though it is true that their songs were a political statement in themselves, the musicians were not activists, they were entertainers, while for city officials and Sacramento, the Haight-Ashbury was simply an eyesore and totally un-American. Some government officials really believed the neighborhood had been overrun with communists.

Jefferson Airplane was riding the crest of the psychedelic wave and wanted to reach more people with their music and their message. Paul Kantner invited "everybody to come to San Francisco." Paul McCartney was drawn there out of curiosity, as was George Harrison. The band showed McCartney around the neighborhood, and then they all went back to their apartment to have a smoke. Paul nonchalantly took out a tape he had brought along to listen to. It was "A Day in the Life."

The Airplane, like the other best known San Francisco bands, was asked to perform at Papa John Phillips and Lou Adler's Monterey Pop Festival. The band was intrigued, but at the same time suspicious.

San Francisco bands were spawned in a music enclave, and the Bay Area music scene was largely ignored by record company executives from Los Angeles because they didn't think it could make money. This indifference did, however, have a positive side, and in the final analysis proved to be an advantage for the bands because it enabled them to develop artistically, without the interference of the record moguls. Soon San Francisco was being compared to Liverpool.

Notwithstanding the mistrust, Monterey Pop did help to promote the careers of some of the bands and some musicians. D.A. Pennebaker's documentary of the festival is interesting as a musical artefact, but it is surprising how technically flawed and mediocre it was at times. "Today" was sung by Marty Balin at Monterey, yet the camera focused exclusively on Grace Slick. This was explained by saying the only lighting was on Grace.

After Monterey, the Airplane played at least two shows at the Fillmore with Jimi Hendrix. They were away from the Haight during the Summer of Love and missed Cream at the Fillmore because they were doing a show for Bill Graham in Bakersfield, of all places.

Chet Helms and Bill Graham, as different as chalk and cheese, had established themselves as the two main rock promoters in San Francisco. Graham could be charming, if it was in his interest, though he never pretended to be a nice guy. Jerry Garcia said doing business with Chet was "like doing business with a hippie." As far as paying the bands was concerned, Bill was a surer bet, he always paid, but with Chet it was different and he sometimes tried to avoid paying or he paid late, or not enough (Graham 199-200).

A thin, bearded, long-haired hippie who wore glasses, sandals and an eager smile, Chet Helms seemed to possess an aura of transcendent love for the Haight-Ashbury and its music scene.

Some may have noticed a foible of being a little pompous at times, but he was sincere, warm-hearted and generous. Personal material gain was not important for Chet, whereas it seemed to be a driving force for Graham, who became truly ecstatic when making money, happy just to feel the crisp greenbacks between his fingers.

Unfortunately, Chet's excessive benevolence would be his undoing. Giving away too many free tickets and letting people in for free meant that he had less money to pay his expenses, which included the bands.

Helms opened a branch of The Family Dog in Denver, Colorado, called the Denver Dog, complete with a four-track recording studio and a spacious dance floor. In fact, he had high hopes of opening several of his "Dogs" in different corners of the world, an ambitious scheme that required solid business acumen and a well organized strategy.

But there were those who were determined to do more than just throw sand into the wheels of the hippie rock revolution; they wanted to nail hippie scalps to the wall. One narcotics agent by the name of John Gray and his associates reportedly harassed customers, management, the band and anyone associated with the Denver Dog. The objective was all too clear, and by 1968, the dance hall was forced to close. They knew that hippies smoked marijuana and didn't support the War in Vietnam. They obviously didn't want that kind of riffraff around their town.

When Helms arrived in San Francisco, he made some money by selling small amounts of grass and helped organize meetings at the Blue Unicorn, at the corner of Hayes and Ashbury, for a group called LEMAR, which stood for "Legalize Marijuana." Later, Helms organized jam sessions at the Albin Rooming House at 1090 Page Street.

Rodney Albin had been running the large Victorian as a rooming house since 1964 (Selvin 48). Rodney and his brother Peter, both bluegrass musicians and students at San Francisco State, rented rooms to students, freaks and artists. The Albin brothers knew a lot of musicians and soon 1090 Page became a hangout for people into music.

Out of Helms' famous jam sessions a band was formed: Sam Andrew on guitar, Chuck Jones on drums, Peter Albin on bass and Paul Beck on guitar (Echols 123). A casual, carefree atmosphere reigned at 1090, and quite a bit of good grass, too, as they jammed songs on the Rolling Stones' albums. Paul Beck was soon replaced by James Gurley, and Chet Helms became its manager, looking after the band on a full time basis.

The band's name, Big Brother and the Holding Company, has got to be one of the most evocative names in the history of rock 'n' roll. It was hit upon during a stoned rap session about capitalism and George Orwell's sinister, dystopian novel *Nineteen Eighty-Four*.

The members of the band started out as acoustic musicians. Peter Albin had the most experience at the time, having played in some folk clubs around San Mateo. Sam Andrew, whose father was in the air force, had travelled around quite a bit and had lived overseas. He studied at the Sorbonne in Paris from 1963 to 1964, and after arriving in the Haight-Ashbury planned on studying linguistics at U. C.

Berkeley (Echols 123).

James Gurley hailed from Detroit and came from a totally different background. He spent four years at the Catholic Brothers of the Holy Cross with the intention of becoming a monk (Echols 124). He met Felice Reisman (Nancy Gurley) at The Cup of Socrates, a local coffee house, and she soon became his wife.

As a boy, James had an experience that few could boast about. With his father, a professional stunt car driver, they put on a show in which James was strapped to the hood of the car that crashed through a flaming wooden wall. Their extremely popular act was billed "The Human Battering Ram." Unfortunately, during one of their spectacular crashes, James lost his front teeth and his hair was very badly burned; so bad, in fact, that he had to shave his head bald. People called him "weird Jim Gurley" because of his shaved head, but when he was with Big Brother, he let his hair grow.

James and Nancy went west to California in 1960 and ended up in San Francisco. James Gurley and Sam Andrew spent a lot of time together in the Haight-Ashbury, strolling up and down the street, hanging out in coffee shops and playing guitar in the Panhandle. Bob Seidemann took what would become a famous photograph of James as a cowboy, or frontiersman, with a feather tied to his hair and a string of hippie beads around his neck. The photograph became an iconic symbol of hippiedom after it was used on the poster for the second annual Tribal Stomp at the Avalon Ballroom on 17, 18 February 1967.

Seidemann knew Nancy Gurley, described as

"supersexual" and "superhip," and met James through her. This was the Haight-Ashbury, so they could be friends who had sex together.

James and Nancy were probably among the very first people to drop acid in the Haight. They also spent time in Mexico eating hallucinogenic mushrooms with the local Indians, something that was thought to be very exotic for young Americans. Nancy Gurley was no slouch, either. She was a *magna cum laude* student from Wayne University, where she graduated with a master's degree in English literature.

Big Brother and the Holding Company's first gig was apparently at Berkeley's Open Theatre in December 1965. Their set was mostly improvised and instrumental. A film of the band playing at 1090 Page Street was projected during their performance. They played two important gigs in the beginning of the New Year. On January 21, 1966, they played at the Trips Festival, and on February 12 they did a benefit for Democratic congressional candidates and the Vietnam Study Group at the Fillmore Auditorium.

One of the things that made James Gurley stand out musically was his use of finger picks. This helped him to play guitar faster than many musicians. Peter Albin did most of the singing before Janis came long, and Dave Getz soon replaced Chuck Jones on drums. After graduating from Cooper Union in New York, Getz relocated to San Francisco to study at the Art Institute. He received his master's degree in fine arts in 1964, and then went to Europe on a Fulbright scholarship. Having played drums in the Catskills and toured Europe with a Dixieland band, Getz had some valuable performance experience, but it was nothing compared to the apprenticeship he would receive in the Haight-Ashbury. After drifting away from music for a while to devote his time to painting, suddenly, in 1965, something went "click" in his head and he was back in the swing of things, even trying to form a group with Victor Moscoso, the poster artist, and others at the Art Institute where he taught. Not surprisingly, Getz felt out of place and at odds with those who taught there and did not want to get trapped in their closed circle of routine and narrow mind-sets. Dave Getz met Peter Albin completely by chance in a café just below his studio.

Albin spoke enthusiastically about his band and the upcoming concert on February 12, 1966, at the Fillmore Auditorium with The Great Society, Wildflower, Quicksilver Messenger Service and Big Brother and the Holding Company. After listening to Big Brother and taking in the atmosphere of the Fillmore, Dave's sole ambition was to become a member of the band. Shortly thereafter, he played informally with the other musicians and was accepted as a member in March. Big Brother performed at the Fire House on Sacramento Street on March 19, 1966; maybe it was there that Getz did his first gig with Big Brother.

Improvisation, experimentation, high decibels and long solos were a part of the San Francisco sound and style— sometimes to the detriment of technique and accuracy. Before Janis came along, Big Brother's approach was anything but linear.

Gurley was a big fan of John William Coltrane ("Trane"), the exuberant jazz musician and composer, and sought to adapt Coltrane's style to the guitar, an extremely ambitious task one must admit. Gurley had a following in San Francisco, and many felt he epitomized the Big Brother sound, as some called it, though his playing was not always very clean or in tune. He loved to embark on some of the most outrageous guitar solos imaginable, some of which lasted for more than forty minutes, but with no apparent direction. Psychedelic rock musicians of the mid-sixties were often criticized for playing instruments that were out of tune; this was often due to the fact that they were too stoned to tune their instruments correctly.

Big Brother knew it needed a competent female vocalist to make it big. They had auditioned a few local singers before Chet Helms mentioned his good friend Janis Joplin. James Gurley and Peter Albin had heard her sing in North Beach and it seems they were not totally sold on the idea of having her as a lead singer, fearing that her bold, raucous style would be a dish too hard for the band to digest. Chet went ahead anyway and brought his Port Arthur friend out west again.

Back in Texas, Janis was wondering how she was going to get out. The only answer she came up with was: sing! Port Arthur was a sure overdose, so she went to Austin to pursue her on again, off again career as a folksinger. It turned out to be a crossroads in her life.

The 13th Floor Elevators, "pioneers of the psychedelic sound," went to Austin to perform at the Methodist Student Center on March 12, 1966. The occasion was the Teodor Jackson benefit. This was the only time Janis appeared with them on the same stage, though they did not perform together (Drummond 125-26). Janis is said to have been stunned by the band's deafening performance and supposedly approached them to see what they thought about having her as a vocalist. Janis was influenced by Roky, said Tary Owens, but her singing style was different from his, and she was singing Bessie Smith, not psychedelic rock. Jim Langdon, on the other hand, does not see any of Roky Erickson's influence in her singing, apart from the fact that they could both scream like banshees (Drummond 126).

Travis Rivers, manager of the Print Mint in the Haight and an old friend of Janis' from Texas, was supposedly sent by Chet Helms to bring her back to San Francisco. Joplin's own version of the anecdote is too funny for words and says a lot about the lustful image she liked to project of herself. According to Janis, she didn't really want to leave Texas, but Travis was such a remarkable lover that she couldn't refuse. Janis wasn't motivated by agape, she wanted hard love with a man. Her numerous relationships with young, androgynous women were of a different sort.

On June 6, 1966, she got around to writing her parents from California. It seems they never knew about her leaving. She spoke about Chet Helms and what a big shot he was as a promoter and that she would soon be famous. To reassure her parents, Janis said she could always go back to Texas and her university courses if things didn't work out as planned. She also apologized for disappointing them. It is hard to believe that she really considered going back there, because she was overjoyed with life in the Haight-Ashbury and happy to be part of the rock revolution that was burgeoning there.

Big Brother and the Holding Company had established

itself as an important rock band by the time Janis arrived. Feelings in the group towards Janis varied. Sam Andrew felt they were doing her a favor. The band respected her and recognized her talent but was not in awe of her singing. Janis had a lot of potential, but she also had to pick up a few tricks of the trade, one of which was learning to sing with electric guitars that liked to play really loud. Up to that time, she had only sung with acoustic guitars. Of course the band had to change, too. From a very experimental type of electric sound the band would become more conventional and also more popular in the psychedelic counterculture.

Peter Albin has a different story to relate. He claims that Big Brother didn't really audition Janis at all. According to him, he and Gurley persuaded the rest of the band to bring her to California because they knew she would work out just fine.

The problem was that the fans that had supported the band from the beginning were not very happy with the change. For them, taking on a female vocalist would result in the band's losing its natural craziness and becoming too much like all the others. For them, Janis was an albatross around Big Brother's neck, and they strongly urged the band to drop her.

As far as the concerts were concerned, Big Brother played regularly at the Fillmore and the other main ballrooms. They played at the Love Pageant Rally on October 6, 1966, to protest the prohibition of LSD. They reportedly played during some Hell's Angels parties, too.

On January 29, 1967, two weeks after the Human Be-In, a musical event called the Mantra Rock Dance took place at the Avalon Ballroom. It was a fundraising effort organized by the International Society for Krishna Consciousness (ISKCON) to support their new center on Frederick Street, right next door to the Diggers. The Grateful Dead along with Moby Grape, a rising star in the area, also appeared on the bill. The musicians played for free with the proceeds going to the Hare Krishna Temple. The religious group even flew in its guru from India, Swami Prabhupada, to attend the rock dance. Allen Ginsberg greeted him at the airport with a group of worshippers, chanting madly and playing his small cymbals. Timothy Leary and Owsley Stanley III also participated in the Mantra Rock Dance, where being righteously stoned was a necessity. It was another example of the Haight's interest in Eastern spirituality, though not everybody was willing to shave their head, sell sticks of incense, meander about the city begging for alms and live on rice.

The San Francisco Oracle ran an advert for the concert in its "Human Be-In" issue and spoke about the religious leader, the science of God and the courses on the *Bhagavad Gita* to be taught at the temple. The article, written by Mukundah Das Adhikary, asserted that if one wanted to increase one's spirituality, it was better to chant and dance than get stoned on acid and put Ali Akbar Khan on the turntable, or trip out at a mixed media rock dance.

The theme was a crowd drawer, and some three thousand people attended the fund raiser, with admission set at $2.50. It was a traditional style dance for San Francisco at the time with strobe lights, a light show, Hell's Angels backstage for "security," and thick fumes of marijuana spiraling lazily above the audience.

People were brightly dressed, gaily dressed one would say at the time, in the East Indian and South American fashion. The audience brought its own instruments to make noise. The Hell's Angels were the anomalous element in the crowd, dressed as usual in their leather boots, denim jackets, German crosses, helmets, and chains.

Group chanting by Swami Prabhupada reportedly lasted nearly two hours. He was followed by Big Brother with Janis who sang "The House of the Rising Sun" and "Ball 'n' Chain." Moby Grape gave one of its early performances which helped it to get gigs at the Avalon and Winterland, and ultimately land a record contract with Columbia Records.

In June, Janis, backed by Big Brother, gave a memorable performance at the Monterey Pop Festival. The critics eulogized her Saturday afternoon show.

After Monterey, Big Brother played at the Fillmore with the Jimi Hendrix Experience on June 25, 1967, and gave an inspired performance. On July 4-9 they played with Bo Diddley, born Ellas Otha Bates, the Chicago blues performer who had such a tremendous influence on so many great groups, including the Rolling Stones and the Beatles. In February and March 1968, Big Brother was in New York, where they played for the first time on February 17, 1968. On March 8, 1968, they played at Bill Graham's Fillmore East.

Considering the number of rock bands that performed in San Francisco and the Bay Area, it is obvious that there were many that could be considered part of the San Francisco sound. It's a question of deciding exactly what geographic area one is talking about, how far one wants to go from San Francisco and what types of bands one is willing to include. Apart from the three most popular bands–Jefferson Airplane, the Grateful Dead and Big Brother and the Holding Company–one must add the obvious Country Joe and the Fish, Moby Grape, Quicksilver and the Charlatans. There were also numerous other bands that played a role in creating the San Francisco sound prior to the Summer of Love: Santana, Sly and the Family Stone, Blue Cheer, The Beau Brummels, The Great Society, The Mystery Trend, The Vejtables, The Chocolate Watch Band, The Syndicate of Sound, The Loading Zone, and probably others.

Brought together musically in mid-1965, Country Joe McDonald and Barry "the Fish" Melton performed as a duo. They were influenced by folk music and especially Woody Guthrie. McDonald was politically active and took part in the Free Speech Movement on the Berkeley campus in 1964-1965. Other musicians were soon added: Bruce Barthol on bass, Paul Armstrong on guitar, David Cohen on guitar and John Francis-Gunning on drums. The latter would be replaced by Gary "Chicken" Hirsch. David Cohen switched to organ. The band learned to play as a group at The Jabberwock, a small club at the corner of Telegraph Avenue and Sussel Street in Berkeley. Their ballroom debut was apparently on August 26, 1966, when they played at the Fillmore after replacing 13th Floor Elevators. They were billed there with Sopwith Camel. Other performances included: 15 October 1965, at the San Francisco State Vietnam Day Committee Teach-In; 23 October 1966, at the Fillmore Auditorium with the Yardbirds; 17 December 1966, a benefit for LEMAR; and 14 April 1967, a free performance in the Panhandle on the eve of the peace march.

The group signed with Vanguard Records in December 1966. On May 11, 1967, they were at the Fillmore for the Vanguard Records party.

The band's debut album was *Country Joe and the Fish: Electric Music for the Mind and Body*. The album was released on May 11, 1967, in time for the Summer of Love. Recorded in Berkeley at Sierra Sound Laboratories, it was an immediate hit as one of the first psychedelic albums, with nearly half a million copies sold. The freaky side of the band is demonstrated in "Section 43" and also "Bass Strings," with its eerie, East Asian tonalities. The album is a mixture of politics and psychedelia. "Not So Sweet Martha Lorraine" was the only single that charted.

Moby Grape was another noteworthy band of the sixties. The group was comprised of Skip Spence on guitar, Jerry Miller on lead guitar, Bob Mosley on bass, Peter Lewis on guitar, and Don Stevenson on drums. Their eponymous album was released on June 6, 1967, just in time for Monterey Pop. Ten of the thirteen songs on the album were released on five singles the very same day; probably not the best marketing strategy because they couldn't all sell. Only "Omaha" and "Hey Grandma" charted.

The album, which constituted a nexus between various musical genres and psychedelia, sold well, reaching number twenty-four on the *Billboard* chart list. Skip Spence, former drummer for the Airplane, played rhythm guitar. He wrote "Omaha" and "Indifference" and collaborated on "Someday." The group seemed to exude a popular form of rebelliousness that the Haight hippies could identify with.

A huge promotional gala was organized at the Avalon Ballroom with Columbia Record executives, hippies, the San Francisco elite and about two thousand people raving in the audience. Janis Joplin was on hand to perform two numbers with the band, Hawaiian orchids were strewn everywhere and Moby Grape wine was flowing freely.

Later that evening, Skip Spence, Peter Lewis and Jerry Miller went to a club called the Ark where they picked up three minors from San Mateo. They took off for Mount Tamalpais in Marin, and a well known spot for local teens at the end of a forest trail. But the local police knew about the party spot, too. Spence was fooling around with his pants off when the cops pulled up, and to make matters worse, Miller forgot to get rid of the roach he was holding in his pocket. The three musicians were arrested for contributing to the delinquency of a minor; Miller was booked with the additional charge of possessing narcotics. The mainstream press made a big deal out of it, though nothing serious really happened, and radio stations began pulling their songs from the programming. The album sold well, nonetheless, probably because of the bad publicity, selling over 200,000 copies.

Some talented and imaginative people left Texas and made a name for themselves in San Francisco: Janis Joplin, Chet Helms, Doug Sahn of the Sir Douglas Quintet and Roky Erickson and the 13th Floor Elevators. The Haight-Ashbury was a home away from home for the psychedelic rockers from Austin, who performed throughout the spring and summer of 1966 at the Fillmore. The group also played at the Avalon on November 13, 1966, and September 30, 1967. Their most popular psychedelic rock songs included "Hair Like Sunshine," "Pride of Man," "Got My Mojo Working," and of course "Dino's Song."

The Haight-Ashbury marveled at the new albums that were aired on KMPX (106.9 FM), where Larry Miller and Tom Donahue promoted freeform rock radio. Freeform radio meant that the disc jockey was free to choose the records he wanted to play, no matter what the radio station's commercial motivations were. Naturally, the vast majority of stations imposed a strict programming format on its DJs, so KMPX was all the rage with the counterculture.

Larry Miller started broadcasting rock music for the station on 12 February 1967. Tom Donahue started on 7 April of the same year. KMPX was original in that it played a lot of album cuts that weren't released as singles, plus artists that were less well known. Sometimes they might play the entire side of an album without interruption. In the spring and summer of 1967, the most popular albums aired on the station were *Surrealistic Pillow*, *Are You Experienced*, *The Doors*, *Sgt. Pepper's Lonely Hearts Club Band*, *Electronic Music for the Mind and the Body* and *Freak Out*.

The San Francisco sound of the sixties was directly related to the hippie movement, psychedelia and the counterculture. This nascent genre of rock was developed in and around San Francisco from 1965 to 1967. Ralph Gleason referred to it as "the Liverpool of the U.S."

The San Francisco sound was loud, community based music that was often played at benefits and special events. It involved improvisation, strong tonalities, a "roving" style, a larger role for the bass guitar, long guitar solos and the melding of genres. Innovative chord progressions also gave it an unusual sound. All the instruments played a prominent role in the music, but brass and reed instruments were not used, or very rarely so.

This genre of rock clearly broke away from the fifties style of rock 'n' roll. Folk, jazz, blues and country music had a strong influence on the San Francisco sound. The lyrics seemed to change overnight, becoming much wider in scope as they sought to encompass politics, universal love, war, racism, imperialism, freedom, compassion, expanded consciousness, drugs, you name it. Bob Dylan, the Beatles and other British bands also had a noticeable impact on the genre. With the longer tracks on LPs, the music that originated in San Francisco and the Bay Area took off in directions that were blatantly antithetical to AM radio.

11

Lysergic Acid Diethylamide

The story of lysergic acid diethylamide ($C_{20}H_{25}N_3O$), more commonly known as LSD-25, LSD, or simply acid, began with its discovery by the Swiss chemist Albert Hofmann, born on January 11, 1906, in Baden, Switzerland. He became the unwitting hero of the psychedelic counterculture by synthesizing and consuming LSD. The father of LSD worked for Sandoz Laboratories that has since become a subsidiary of Novartis, in Basel. Hofmann is the author of several books, including *LSD: My Problem Child*.

On November 16, 1938, Hofmann synthesized LSD, the goal of which was to develop a respiratory and circulatory stimulant. But he forgot about his synthesis until April 16, 1943, at which time he accidentally ingested an uncertain amount and soon realized how tremendously powerful the drug was. His perception was greatly affected, and he beheld fantastic visions and sumptuous, vibrating colors he had never dreamed of.

On April 19, 1943, World War II was raging in Europe. Hofmann decided to take 250 micrograms of lysergic acid diethylamide to see what would happen. His usually banal bicycle ride home would be the strangest he had ever known as he was plunged into "Is-ness," which is to say the inherent quality of existence.

Albert Hofmann was always candid about his "problem child," and throughout his life he often praised the psychotrope because of the "inner joy" it made him feel. He referred to it as "medicine for the soul," but at the same time he felt it had been misused by some who lacked a feeling of responsibility.

From the very beginning the CIA was obsessed with the drug. The Agency became interested in LSD when it started looking for a way to covertly alter a person's behavior with a mind control drug, something that might even be used to modify a person's sense of loyalty (Lee 13). The minute quantities that had such a powerful effect on people seemed well suited to their peculiar needs, plus the fact that the drug was colorless and odorless, so it couldn't be detected. LSD, much more so than cocaine, mescaline or marijuana, modified a person's perception of reality.

Ergot is a natural source of lysergic acid. In China and other parts of the Far East, the rye fungus, like numerous other plants, is used in medicine. It may have been used in ancient Greece during the frenzied ecstasy of the Dionysian Mysteries. Sandoz became interested in it because of its well documented history.

Dr. Max Rinkel, in 1949, was the first person to bring the drug to the United States. He gave it to his partner, Dr.

Robert Hyde, who reportedly took the first acid trip on American soil. Very little research existed at that time on hallucinogenic drugs, but that changed abruptly when generous grants became available like manna from heaven and highly regarded scientists initiated research at reputable institutes: Robert Hyde at the Boston Psychopathic Institute, Harold Abramson at Mount Sinai Hospital and Columbia University in New York, Carl Pfeiffer at the University of Illinois Medical School, Harris Isbell at the Addiction Research Center in Lexington, Kentucky, Louis Jolyon West at the University of Oklahoma and Harold Lodge at the University of Rochester. There were probably others.

The seminal research was prompted by the rampant paranoia endemic to the Cold War between the United States and the Soviet Union. The Korean War was fought from 25 June 1950 to 27 July 1953, but by 1948, already, Korea was divided into two separate regions, each with its own separate government: the Americans in the South, the communists in the North. There was fear in the upper echelons of the CIA that the Soviets and Communist China would get access to the drug, and in 1951 there were reports that the Russians had acquired fifty million doses from Sandoz (Marks 48). This information was later found to be erroneous. It seems the military attaché in Switzerland made the wrong calculations because he mixed up a kilogram and a milligram. The common fantasy at the time was that it might be put into America's drinking water–Ken Kesey's dream come true!–so they asked Dr. Nick Bercel in Los Angeles what would happen (Lee 21). "Nothing," he said.

MK-ULTRA was an illegal CIA program conducted in

the United States. It began on April 13, 1953, when Allen Dulles, as director of the Agency, officially authorized it. The program, headed by Sidney Gottlieb, was proposed by Richard Helms, who would become director in June 1966. MK-ULTRA, a top secret mind control project, was run by an extremely small group within the Agency called the Technical Services Staff (TSS); few knew about the program or had access to information about it.

Several secret operations were organized as experiments. One of the most widely publicized was Operation Midnight Climax. In San Francisco in 1955, prostitutes were paid to pick up clients and bring them back to a brothel where they would be drugged unknowingly. A certain George Hunter White watched the couple behind a two-way mirror. These "experiments" continued until 1963. According to Gottlieb, who commented on the program after his retirement, it was a waste of time.

The CIA had some strange psychiatrists on its payroll, and Dr. Ewen Cameron, president of the World Psychiatric Association, was perhaps one of the strangest. He believed that mental illness was like a contagious disease and that government institutions must fight the spread of these diseases. He conducted experiments, which amounted to nothing less than total brainwashing, in an effort to find a cure for schizophrenia. First the test subject's memories were erased, then the person's psyche was reprogrammed.

The CIA paid Cameron $69,000 from 1957 to 1964 to conduct experiments at the Allan Memorial Institute in Montreal and gave him *carte blanche* to wield absolute authority when using LSD, paralytic drugs and electroshock at as much as forty times the normal power, putting his victims into drug-induced comas for weeks and with one subject for three months. This in itself is terrifying, but it becomes monstrous when one considers the fact that Cameron did his aberrant experiments on patients with minor problems. After the psychiatrist's "treatment," many were permanently debilitated; some no longer could even talk, while others couldn't remember their name. In her book *The Shock Doctrine*, Naomi Klein refers to Cameron's research as torture. In other experiments, Dr. Harris Isbell kept inmates, mostly black patients, on LSD continuously for seventy-five days at the federal drug hospital/penitentiary in Lexington, Kentucky. Similarly, Dr. Carl Pfeiffer used prison inmates at the federal prison in Atlanta and the Bordentown Reformatory in New Jersey, to conduct his tests.

On May 26, 1954, the CIA ordered its field offices to keep track of all research involving LSD. In 1953, Sandoz shipped its product directly to the Federal Drug Administration (FDA), which supervised distribution in the United States, thus assisting the CIA-funded experiments. Moreover, Sandoz kept the American government well informed of its production and shipment and reassured it that the communist bloc would not be able to procure the drug (Marks 48). Not being one to take risks, the CIA bought ten kilos of LSD from Sandoz–one hundred million doses–so it couldn't fall into the hands of countries behind the Iron Curtain. One wonders what became of it.

The United States Army also showed an interest in LSD and envisioned using it in combat. Tests were conducted at different camps. One group of tests was conducted at Fort Bragg in North Carolina to see how soldiers reacted on the drug during military exercises (Lee 38). Experiments were also run at the Aberdeen Proving Ground in Maryland, Fort Benning in Georgia, Fort Leavenworth in Kansas, Dugway Proving Ground in Utah and at various military stations worldwide. Tests were also conducted with LSD as an interrogation drug.

By the mid-sixties, about fifteen hundred military personnel had been used in LSD experiments conducted by the U.S. Army Chemical Corps (Lee 40), but it would be abandoned for more powerful chemicals such as 3-Quinuclidinyl benzilate, or BZ, an incapacitating agent invented in 1951 by Hoffman-La Roche, a Swiss firm.

Captain Alfred Matthew Hubbard, "Cappy" for his friends, was also referred to as the "Johnny Apple Seed of LSD," because he turned so many people on. Photographs depict him as a roly-poly man with a crew cut and a peculiar albeit jovial sort of smile. He worked for the Office of Strategic Services (OSS) during World War II, and became a millionaire by dealing in uranium. In the early fifties he was scientific director of the Uranium Corporation of Vancouver. He owned his own airplane, yacht and Dayman Island off the coast of British Columbia. He is credited with being the first person to promote and distribute LSD.

Hubbard met Dr. Humphry Osmond in 1953. The British psychiatrist was doing research with Dr. John Smythies at Weyburn Hospital in Saskatchewan, Canada, on schizophrenia and mescaline. Osmond was responsible for coining the term "psychedelic" in 1957, a fusion of the

Greek words *psyche* (mind) and *delos* (manifest). Hubbard, described by Osmond as "powerfully built," "genial," and "an excellent host," had contacted the British psychiatrist to procure a quantity of mescaline, which was perfectly legal at the time. According to Abram Hoffer, Hubbard showed him and Osmond how to enhance LSD experiences.

Hubbard paid a visit to Dr. Timothy Leary in 1963 in Cambridge, Massachusetts. Leary admitted he was impressed by Hubbard's military uniform and the Colt .45 in his holster. Hubbard reportedly brought some LSD with him and gave it to Leary in exchange for psilocybin.

Hubbard's origins were extremely humble, having grown up in poverty in Kentucky, one of the poorest states in the country at the time. He lacked schooling, but he had "visions" that supposedly guided him throughout his life in the sense that they helped him to make crucial decisions.

One day in the woods near Spokane, Washington, Hubbard had a strange vision which evoked, in nebulous terms, his mission to spread the use of LSD. While leafing through *The Hibberd Journal* (1951), he ran across an article about laboratory rats being given LSD. Intuitively, he knew he had to investigate. He got in touch with the scientist that was conducting the research and was given some LSD that he consumed. From then on, he revered the psychotrope as a sacrament.

Hubbard had an intriguing work record that included the Canadian Special Services, the United States Justice Department, and the Bureau of Alcohol, Tobacco and Firearms. Many have surmised that he was involved in the MK-ULTRA project and the CIA. This will probably never be known because the head of the program, Sidney Gottlieb, destroyed compromising documents in 1973, on direct orders from director Richard Helms.

Hubbard had vast connections, due in part to his work in the area of uranium. According to Todd Fahey in "The Original Captain Trips," he dosed more than six thousand people before LSD became illegal on October 6, 1966. He gave it to people of rank in the Catholic Church in the United States, Bill Wilson of Alcoholics Anonymous, and psychiatrists in Beverly Hills who prescribed it to celebrities such as Stanley Kubrick, Cary Grant, James Coburn, Jack Nicholson and Anaïs Nin.

Like Timothy Leary and Richard Alpert, he dreamed of creating clinics where serious research could be carried out on the hallucinogen. To be sure he had enough of the drug to work with, he bought a gram in Switzerland, which is roughly enough for ten thousand doses, and put it in a safe-deposit box at the Zurich airport. But his stash was discovered and he was arrested and deported. Later, he travelled to Czechoslovakia where he put LSD in tablet form so it would be easier to use.

Al Hubbard was a very resourceful individual and had adopted the axiom of those who have struggled to succeed: "Never say never." He solved the problem of not having necessary scientific credentials by simply buying a Ph.D. in biopsychology from Taylor University for $25 so he could be hired as a clinical therapist.

In 1957 he met Ross MacLean, medical superintendent of Hollywood Hospital in New Westminster, Canada, and from that time on a large part of the hospital was used for the psychedelic therapy of chronic alcoholics. The Food and Drug Administration gave Hubbard "IND#1," a drug permit that allowed him to experiment with LSD in the United States. Needless to say, these permits were not easy to acquire.

Hubbard, with Abram Hoffer and Humphry Osmond, achieved an unprecedented recovery rate in their treatment of alcoholics, which was sometimes as high as 60% to 70%. After ingesting LSD, patients gained insight into their self-destructive behavior and wanted to change. Alcoholics Anonymous had a much lower rate of success with its chronic patients.

Despite his achievements, Hubbard and Ross MacLean had divergent views on how to best use the drug. MacLean, who was charging the exorbitant price of $1,000 a dose, was making money on his patients' suffering. Hubbard refused to get rich off LSD and felt MacLean's callous attitude was inimical to achieving his therapeutic goals, so he resigned.

After leaving New Westminster, Hubbard moved on to Palo Alto, California, and the Stanford Research Institute (SRI), where he was promptly hired by Willis Harman.

But things suddenly changed. In a short period of time, the American government's perception of LSD changed radically, particularly after Richard Helms was appointed Director of the Central Intelligence (DCI) in June 1966. He was sworn in during an elaborate ceremony in the White House, with members of Congress and even a marine band. Few people would be able to imagine the enormous power of the DCI. With Helms at the head of the CIA, LSD soon became illegal in California. With the mass media in the government's pocket, it wasn't surprizing to see articles in the mainstream press purposely designed to frighten and intimidate the public, though they were generally based on jejune fantasies rather than fact. *Life* magazine published a long article entitled "LSD: The Exploding Threat of the Mind Drug that Got Out of Control." According to *Life*, you could go crazy by taking the drug. In the next few years, there was an outbreak of ridiculous films foreshadowing the demise of the nation. *Wild in the Streets*, released on May 29, 1968, described how American youth take over the government and the entire country with LSD, after which they enslave their parents and the older generation they despise.

In March 1966, President Lyndon Johnson signed the Drug Abuse Control Amendment, thus making the mere possession of LSD a felony, punishable by fifteen years in prison. The police and the FBI went wild raiding hospitals and doctors' offices in a frenzy to seize the illegal psychotrope.

To escape persecution and protect his property, it was rumored that Al Hubbard buried his acid in Death Valley, California, though that is not a tale told by the Old Ranger from *Death Valley Days*.

After the government anathematized LSD, Hubbard lived the rest of his life in relative poverty, knowing his acid dreams would never be consummated. He died on August 31, 1982, at the age of eighty-one. As far as is known, he did not go insane from ingesting lysergic acid diethylamide.

There is no evidence that he was a CIA agent, though his involvement in psychedelic drugs must have brought him into direct contact with the Agency. Sandoz and the FDA informed the CIA of all sales and shipments of the drug, so they had to know what he was doing and where he was doing it.

Al Hubbard was, admittedly, a mysterious character and the complete story about him will probably never be known since so many classified documents have been shredded. He believed that LSD could change the world, as did Timothy Leary, Ken Kesey and a lot of hippies in the Haight-Ashbury, with whom "Cappy" could not empathize. That in itself is perhaps a little amazing.

Augustus Owsley Stanley III was born on January 19, 1935, in Kentucky. His grandfather, who had the same name, had been governor of the state, senator and a representative who had staunchly opposed prohibition. Owsley got along well with his grandfather, a lot better in fact than with his father.

Owsley, also known as "Bear" because he was a hairy-chested adolescent, dropped out of the University of Virginia, and in 1963 he dropped out of U. C. Berkeley after his first semester. He was an eclectic individual who thrived on living in the present: he studied ballet in Los Angeles and worked for a while as a professional dancer, and he served one year in the U.S. Air Force, but it was in Berkeley that he found his true calling in life when he set up his first small laboratory and began producing his special brand of LSD.

On February 21, 1965, the local police, rivaling the buffoonery of the Keystone Cops, raided his apartment after being tipped off. They were hoping to find methamphetamine, but only confiscated Owsley's last batch of acid, legal at the time. Not to be intimidated, he sued the police to recover his equipment, since that was the only way to get it back. It was at this time that his LSD began appearing on Haight Street. Bear was turning San Francisco and the suburbs on to the purest and most reliable acid since Sandoz, and it was a lot easier to get.

Owsley said he heard the Grateful Dead for the first time on December 10, 1965. The band was playing at the Fillmore Auditorium, the second benefit for the San Francisco Mime Troupe; Jefferson Airplane, the Great Society and Mystery Trend also performed before a packed house. In what must have been a weird trip, Owsley said he was terrified of Jerry Garcia's guitar. It was power, thought, emotion all rolled into one, a veritable tribal experience for him.

Owsley sponsored the Grateful Dead financially and he also worked as their sound engineer. He even conceived of the band's logo, the highly emblematic skull and lightning bolt that he and Bob Thomas drafted on paper together. It adorned the group's amplifiers and speakers so they wouldn't get mixed up with another band's equipment.

In the spring of 1966, Owsley, Melissa Cargill, his girlfriend, and Tim Scully moved to Point Richmond in Richmond, California, to set up shop in a neighborhood near the Richmond-San Rafael Bridge. The petroleum refinery was not far off, with the familiar orange storage tanks on the opposing hill. There, Owsley turned out his famous "White Lightning" mix. As far as anyone knows, he was the first freelance manufacturer of acid in the country and perhaps the entire world. Many baby boomers revered and worshipped Bear and spoke of him in hushed tones, as if dealing with the stuff of legend.

It is difficult to know for certain how much he produced. Owsley claimed he made less than five hundred grams of lysergic acid diethylamide, and because the doses were high, a little more than one million doses (Forte 276). Those who are interested in etymology and neologisms will be pleased to know that Owsley has the rare distinction of having his name in the Oxford Dictionary, because "Owsley" refers to quality LSD.

Unlike Timothy Leary or Ken Kesey, his objectives were a lot less grandiose. He said he made it so that he and his friends knew exactly what they were taking, but, in fact, he was turning on thousands of people, including Kesey's crowd.

Bear had a strange diet that was unusually limited: just meat and milk. He reportedly began eating this way after reading an article about Eskimos, and was convinced their diet was healthier than most.

In February of 1966, Owsley and the Dead moved to Los Angeles and lived in a middle class neighborhood of Watts, off Western Avenue. Everyone was on a diet of meat, fried chicken, milk and LSD. Owsley claimed he wanted the band to eat meat because it was cheaper (*Dark Star* 81). Though the musicians and their girlfriends did not particularly care for Bear's Eskimo diet, they knew there was no point in arguing with him about it. The place they were living in was primitive, to say the least. It didn't have a stick of furniture: no chairs, no table, no lamps, nothing but foam mattresses and army blankets that served as beds. There weren't any plates or spoons in the kitchen, either, just forks and knives.

The meat had to be eaten right out of the frying pan (Scully 38-39).

It is perhaps less well known that Owsley developed sophisticated public address systems for the Grateful Dead, beginning in 1966, and he taped live sessions of the Dead and other bands, including Jefferson Airplane, Big Brother and the Holding Company, Santana, Jimi Hendrix, Blue Cheer, Taj Mahal, Quicksilver Messenger Service and others. Owsley plugged the tape recorder directly into the sound board to get the best recording possible.

On December 20, 1967, Owsley's laboratory in Orinda was raided and LSD was found. This helps to explain why there was so much *bad* acid in the Haight-Ashbury at the end of the year. His acid had always been considered a guarantee of purity and authenticity, but after the Summer of Love, a lot of adulterated hallucinogens were circulating freely in the neighborhood, along with speed and heroin, and that sealed the fate of the once peaceful Haight.

From 1970 to 1972, he was sent to Terminal Island Federal Prison, which was a medium-security prison in San Pedro. It is interesting to note that he sincerely felt he ended up doing time in jail for something he should normally have been rewarded for. Owsley never doubted for one minute that he was an upstanding member of society, or that the authorities punished him to set an example. He felt it was a political maneuver and in many ways one would have to agree with him.

There are few photographs of Owsley from the sixties because he was always just one step ahead of the law, and he didn't want to help the authorities by having his picture taken everywhere, but also because he wasn't interested in becoming a celebrity. Despite his bravado and his dauntless personality, he was not interested in publicity or notoriety. As he himself pointed out to those who knew him, celebrity is a dangerous thing that destroys people.

Owsley's first acid trip was reportedly in April of 1964. After having received a gift of Sandoz LSD from a lawyer, he and Melissa Cargill, a U. C. Berkeley undergraduate enrolled in chemistry, decided to make their own; hopefully as good as the acid manufactured by Sandoz, in Switzerland. They found the formula in the *Journal of Organic Chemistry* in the library of the University of California. Clark Kerr was totally unaware of the enormous contribution "Cal" had made to the counterculture and the growth of the knowledge industry.

It was about this time that Owsley supposedly discovered *The Kybalion*, first published in 1908 by "the three Initiates" who claimed it was based on Hermeticism. The seven "principles" provide the key to this specialized esoteric work: mentalism, correspondence, vibration, polarity, rhythm, cause and effect, and gender.

These principles took on deeper meaning during an acid trip when it was easier to perceive the interconnected relationship of everything and the unity of all existence. In this sense it may be said that we are "reflections" of a far greater consciousness.

Owsley created the Bear Research Group in order to receive lysergic monohydrate, the chemical needed to make LSD. One's state of mind was an important consideration when producing the drug, since it could be reflected in the final product. At least that is what the underground chemist believed.

Bear reportedly first gave Kesey LSD in the fall of 1965 at Kesey's home in La Honda. Although at first skeptical of the gift, he soon recognized the quality of the donation. Kesey liked to take four hundred micrograms of LSD, said Owsley, which is about twice the normal dosage, and difficult for many to control.

It seems safe to say that without Owsley, the Acid Tests would never have occurred.

During the Muir Beach Acid Test on December 11, 1965, Owsley freaked out and admittedly experienced ego death. He castigated Kesey and the Pranksters for provoking people and playing with their minds while they were on the drug. The Pranksters responded by sniggering and laughing up their sleeves.

Owsley was a reliable supplier for the important psychedelic events in California and the San Francisco Bay Area. He gave White Lightning for the Be-In, and if he had prepared several hundred thousand doses, as was claimed, it was a lot more than was actually needed, since between twenty and twenty-five thousand people attended the happening. He supplied the Monterey Pop Festival with Owsley Purple and he probably supplied other significant happenings like the Love Pageant Rally.

It may seem surprising, but Owsley was extremely critical of Timothy Leary. What he did, said Owsley, was of "minimal value" to the hippie counterculture. Above all, he criticized what he felt was Leary's "fuck you" approach. Bear's point of view was that the former Harvard professor was only interested in the publicity LSD gave him and didn't seem to care about the harm he was doing with his provocative statements. His antagonisms and brash attitude brought about the laws against psychedelics, said Owsley. Ram Dass, formerly Richard Alpert, was probably closer to the mark when he said that the polarization between the establishment and the counterculture was bound to happen. Things could have been done "more politically and coolly," but the polarization and the conservative backlash were inevitable. Johnson and Reagan had declared a war on drugs, and Richard Helms was organizing national strategy as DCI.

In the final analysis, one can always blame a scapegoat for everything that went wrong, but Timothy Leary was not acting alone and he had always cautioned users to respect the notions of set and setting to avoid bad psychological trips.

Kenneth Elton Kesey was born on September 17, 1935, in La Junta, Colorado. He is undoubtedly best known for his first novel, *One Flew over the Cuckoo's Nest*, published in 1962. The book was a huge success and had a strong impact on American society, both mainstream and underground.

Kesey received a Bachelor of Arts degree in speech and communication from the University of Oregon in 1957. In 1959, he received a Woodrow Wilson Fellowship which allowed him to enroll in the creative writing program at Stanford University, in Palo Alto.

But things did not always go smoothly for Kesey at Stanford. He clashed openly with Wallace Stegner, the director of the department, who already held Kesey in low esteem, and who probably had something to do with his application for a Stegner fellowship being rejected. Kesey did, however, manage to receive a Harper-Saxton fellowship for *Zoo*, a novel in progress, which remained unpublished.

At the time, Kesey and his wife were renting a cottage at 9 Perry Lane–bohemia in Palo Alto–between Vine Street and Leland Avenue. Extramarital sex between neighbors seemed to be habit-forming there, according to numerous accounts, and the Keseys sometimes indulged themselves.

Vic Lovell, one of Kesey's neighbors, heard that Veterans Hospital in Menlo Park, next to Palo Alto, was paying volunteers to take psychedelic drugs during scientific experiments. Lovell, who supposedly turned on Richard Alpert to marijuana, persuaded his friend Kesey to enroll in the program with him (P. Perry 11).

Neither Lovell nor Kesey were aware that it was a secret project financed by the CIA to study behavior modification. For several weeks Kesey took a variety of drugs: psilocybin, mescaline, lysergic acid diethylamide, Ditran, IT-290. Some made him sick, some made him feel good, some shook his imagination and some opened the doors of perception. Kesey said he was grateful for the experience because it showed him new "scenes" (P. Perry 21).

After the experiments, Kesey wanted to pursue his drug experiences on a more personal basis, so he got a summer job in 1962 at the same hospital, working the graveyard shift as a psychiatric aide: cleaning up, mopping the floors and opening drug cabinets to see what he could pilfer. He was like a child in a candy shop, and Leo Hollister's drug cabinet was particularly rewarding. Though he had apparently stopped the experiments, he still had sizeable quantities of LSD-25 in stock. Kesey, always resourceful, brought his typewriter to the nurses' station and worked on his novel when his work on the graveyard shift was done (P. Perry 12).

Kesey delineated his characters by studying the patients and nurses at the hospital. Many of his observations were made when he was under the influence of LSD. Chief Bromden, on the other hand, was imagined after taking eight peyote buttons. Bromden, often called "Chief Broom" by the black orderlies, is the Native American in the novel and the narrator who pretends to be deaf and dumb so people will ignore him. Making Bromden the narrator gave an unusual twist to the story, since he is a mental patient whose narration often shifts from fantasy to fact and back again. The book is a critique of American society because the mental institution–a microcosm of the United States–is in reality a lot sicker than its patients.

For at least ten months, Kesey typed furiously, often at night, the most productive time for him; during the day he read excerpts from his manuscript in class. Happily for Kesey, Malcolm Cowley was often his writing professor that semester. They got along well and Cowley gave encouraging advice to his student and sent enthusiastic reports to Viking Press to help his student get published.

Cowley was a well established literary figure and editorial consultant who helped Jack Kerouac publish *On the Road* at Viking Press and who edited such literary monuments as Ernest Hemingway and William Faulkner. Cowley's approach to teaching and creative writing was commendable in that he always sought to create an atmosphere that cultivated creativity. Needless to say, it was exactly the sort of atmosphere Kesey needed to develop his writing skills and talent.

Back at 9 Perry Lane, things were evolving, too. Ken and his wife Faye were throwing some pretty wild parties. Malcolm Cowley described one that he went to, attended by students from the advanced writing course, Vic Lovell and other friends. One thing that stood out in Cowley's mind was the very large punch bowl full of green "Kool-Aid," with a devilish mist swirling above the bowl because Kesey put dry ice in it. Cowley, mistrustful of the strange green brew, felt it was safer to take a few swigs of bootleg whiskey that Ken's grandma brought all the way from the backwoods of Arkansas.

The publication of *One Flew over the Cuckoo's Nest* catapulted Kesey into literary stardom. The majority of the book reviews were eulogistic. *The New York Times* praised it as "a glittering parable of good and evil." The unexpected encomiums brought the devoted minions that soon became known as the Merry Pranksters. To embellish and exalt their psychedelic fantasies, the Pranksters used pseudonyms. This highly unusual group of acidheads included Neal Cassady (Sir Speed Limit), whom Jack Kerouac used as a model for Dean Moriarty in *On the Road*, Ken Babbs (the Intrepid Traveler), Mike Hagen (Mal Function), George Walker (Hardly Visible), John Babbs (Sometimes Missing), Chuck Kesey (Brother Charlie), Dale Kesey (Highly Charged), Paula Sundsten (Gretchen Fetchin'), Ron Bervirt (Hassler), Steve Lambrecht (Zonker), Jane Burton (Generally Famished), Sandy Lehman-Haupt (Dis-mount), Carolyn Adams (Mountain Girl), and Denise Kaufman (Mary Microgram) (P. Perry 44-45).

With the money from his book royalties, Kesey bought a house and property in La Honda, California, a short drive from San Francisco, and finished his second novel there entitled *Sometimes a Great Notion*. La Honda, a sparsely populated town in the sixties, is nestled in the Santa Cruz Mountains. Kesey's house was about a mile west of Apple Jack's Inn. Today it has become known for its Cabernet Sauvignon, a grape of French origin that gained notoriety because of the fine Bordeaux wines it was used in.

The publication of Kesey's second novel required him to be in New York; that explains why he bought the 1939 International Harvester school bus, had it painted in Day-Glo and rigged for the legendary trip east.

On June 14, 1964, the archetypal voyage began. It would become a metaphor for the hopes and dreams of the psychedelic counterculture. Neal Cassady, Kerouac's hero, was on the road again, sometimes driving on LSD, but without getting in accidents because he said he drove the bus through his hallucinations (*Dark Star* 60).

When they arrived in New York, Cassady took the obligatory detour to visit Allen Ginsberg and Jack Kerouac. Ginsberg didn't seem to mind the antics of the Pranksters, but Kerouac wondered if they might be communists, and their freaky madness annoyed him.

Ginsberg got on the bus to visit Leary in Millbrook and was probably the person who suggested they go there.

Kesey's bus "Further" roared up to the Millbrook estate amidst billows of thick green smoke from the smoke bombs they set off to announce their unexpected arrival in the morning hours, making as much noise as their whistles, flutes and larynxes would allow.

Apparently Kesey's band had some idea that it would be a meeting of the minds and acid tribes. The Pranksters wanted to party, use dope and decide the fate of the psychedelic counterculture; not so the acolytes of Millbrook. Kesey's group was disappointed and felt rejected. Leary was lovesick and had the flu, so he went to bed. He didn't have the feeling history was being bypassed.

In fact, apart from the fact they took LSD, the two groups were poles apart. Kesey was probably closer to the Hell's Angels than he was to Leary. They had different approaches, different perceptions of reality and different reasons for using drugs. It's not that they were antagonistic, they were just not kindred spirits. The Pranksters' goal was to blow minds, see how people were conditioned and then "prank them," in other words, do outrageous things to disrupt their social conditioning. For blowing people's minds it was effective–less so for changing people's attitudes. Maybe that's why the federal authorities feared Timothy Leary more than Ken Kesey.

Once back in California, the Acid Tests began. Kesey, a man with a mission, like Timothy Leary or Alfred Hubbard, sought to raise people's consciousness with LSD, but each had a different modus operandi for achieving that goal. For Kesey it meant throwing crazy parties and giving LSD for free in psychedelicized Kool-Aid. In the beginning, the parties were at Kesey's place in La Honda. The dates can be listed as follows: First Acid Test: 27 November 1965, at Ken Babbs' house in Soquel, California, near Santa Cruz. This was probably more of a private party than anything else.

Second Acid Test: 4 December 1965, in San Jose, with the first appearance of the Grateful Dead, known as the Warlocks at the time. Third Acid Test: 11 December 1965, at Muir Beach, California. Fourth Acid Test: 18 December 1965, in Palo Alto, California. Fifth Acid Test: 24 December 1965, in Portland, Oregon. Sixth Acid Test: 8 January 1966, at the Fillmore Auditorium in San Francisco. Seventh Acid Test: 15 January 1966, in Portland, Oregon. Eighth Acid Test: 21-23 January 1966, "Trips Festival," at the Longshoremen's Hall, San Francisco. Ninth Acid Test: 29 January 1966, Sound City Studios, San Francisco. Tenth Acid Test: 5 February 1966, in Los Angeles, at the Northridge Unitarian Church. Eleventh Acid Test: 12 February 1966, at the Youth Opportunities Center in Watts, Los Angeles. Twelfth Acid Test: 25 February 1966, at the Cinema Theatre, 1122 Western Avenue, Hollywood. Thirteenth Acid Test: 12 March 1966, at the Danish Center, Los Angeles. Fourteenth Acid Test: 19 March 1966, at Carthay Studios, 5907 West Pico Boulevard, at the corner of Fairfax. Fifteenth Acid Test: 25 March 1966, at Troupers Club, Sunset Strip, Los Angeles. Sixteenth Acid Test: 30 September to 2 October 1966, San Francisco State. Seventeenth Acid Test: 31 October 1966, scheduled at Winterland, but transferred to a warehouse on Harriet Street, San Francisco. Eighteenth and last Acid Test: Brown College and Rice University, Texas, organized by Kesey's friend Larry McMurtry (see postertrip.com, "The Acid Test Chronicles"). Ken Kesey did not attend the Acid Tests in Los Angeles. This probably explains why they were different from the others.

The Acid Tests were in part an experiment in group psychology. The Pranksters were supposedly trying to develop hidden powers of the mind similar to those used in telepathy; powers they could use as a group, rather than as individuals.

What Kesey liked about the Acid Tests when they began in La Honda was that they weren't "a closed circle." In other words, no one was sure where they might lead. An element of uncertainty was present, as was an element of danger. Some liked living on the razor's edge where things could get out of control.

On May 5, 1965, which was Mother's Day, Kenneth Anger and a group of diabolists from San Francisco were invited. The Pranksters sacrificed a chicken for them in a rather gruesome manner, but Anger's group did not appreciate the theatrics and left before it was over.

On August 7, 1965, the Hell's Angels were invited to a party at Kesey's La Honda home. This was a bold move on his part. Hunter S. Thompson, who wrote a book on the notorious motorcycle gang, strongly advised Kesey against it, because the Angels were well known for their spontaneous and uncontrollable violence. Although the party was praised for being peaceful, there was an episode of sexual violence, namely the alleged gang rape of a twenty-five-year-old woman. The incident is described in Tom Wolfe's *The Electric Kool-Aid Acid Test* and Hunter S. Thompson's *Hell's Angels*. It has been claimed that the girl involved was Neal Cassady's girlfriend and that she was jealous of Allen Ginsberg. It has also been said that she actually consented to the gang bang and that she did it to get some sort of revenge against Cassady. A lot of game playing was going on in La Honda.

Jerry Garcia did not like all the craziness, despite the fact that the band was at most of the gatherings. At the same time, it's true that the Grateful Dead coalesced as a group at the Acid Tests because they were free form, allowing the band to do a lot of experimentation with their music.

The Acid Tests were about getting high, and part of the getting high was about recognizing the spurious nature of society and the pseudo-reality we are forced to exist in. Marijuana and LSD had always been part of the Acid Tests because they had a "spiritual purity" to them, said Kesey. He also felt the drug problem would have been a lot less serious if grass had been legalized. "There've been a lot more people hurt on astro-turf than grass," Kesey joked.

Timothy Francis Leary was born on October 22, 1920. Those who were deeply involved in the LSD phenomenon had their lives transformed in many ways, and such was the case with Leary.

There were traumatic events in Timothy Leary's life that seem to have determined important aspects of his character, some of which would stay with him his entire life. Leary's father, who had the same first and middle names as his son, abandoned the family when Timothy was thirteen. He was in fact raised by two women, his mother and aunt, who were devout Catholics. It is probably not surprising then that religion, albeit of a very different sort, should play such a significant role in his LSD sessions that were supposed to be a quest for absolute truth.

While a cadet at West Point Military Academy, he was

found drunk. When he was questioned about it, he lied, making his offense much worse, since that constituted a serious breach of the honor code. As a result, he was asked to resign. When he refused, he was "silenced"–the other cadets totally ignored him in an effort to force him to leave. This almost lasted for a year before he finally said goodbye to his incipient military career and received an honorable discharge.

After West Point, he enrolled at the University of Alabama in 1941, in the Reserve Officers Training Corps (ROTC)–the target of numerous student protests in the sixties–but the following year he was expelled for spending the night in the female dormitory. He was then drafted into the U.S. Army and did his basic training at Fort Eustis in 1943. After that, he was assigned to Deshon General Hospital in Butler, Pennsylvania, and stayed in the clinic for the deaf where he met Marianne Busch, who became his first wife in April 1945. Leary was discharged in January 1946.

Eager to return to an academic setting, he finished his degree at the University of Alabama in the summer of 1945 by taking correspondence courses, and received an M.S. in psychology in 1946 from Washington State. Timothy Leary received his Ph.D. in clinical psychology in 1950 from U. C. Berkeley.

It was at Kaiser Hospital in Oakland that Tim met Mary Della Cioppa. They soon started having an affair and his wife Marianne found out about it. She was profoundly depressed as a result and exhibited suicidal tendencies. The drama occurred on Tim's thirty-fifth birthday. He woke up to find a suicide note on his wife's pillow. She got into the front seat of the family car, started the engine and killed herself by carbon monoxide poisoning. But she took the time to bake Tim a birthday cake before she left.

1959 was Leary's big year. He was hired as a lecturer in clinical psychology at Harvard University in Cambridge, Massachusetts. No doubt he was happy to leave California behind after the tragic death of his wife.

In August 1960, Leary travelled to Cuernavaca, Mexico, and on August 9, 1960, he consumed hallucinogenic mushrooms containing psilocybin with Lothar Knauth, an East German refugee, two young women, and another couple. After eating seven of the moldy mushrooms, everything suddenly became very different as the psilocybin began to take effect. The effects vary from one person to the next but can involve heightened sensory awareness, synesthesia, altered perception of space and time, out of body experiences, a feeling of oneness and other unusual experiences. The drug sometimes induces an adverse reaction involving panic, depression, confusion or paranoia. It depends on a person's state of mind.

The following day, they were joined by Richard Alpert. When asked about his experience, Tim made his often quoted remark: "I learned more in the six or seven hours of this experience than in all my years as a psychologist." But an even greater high was awaiting Dr. Leary the day he was given a dose of LSD by the Executive Secretary for the Institute of British-American Cultural Exchange, Michael Hollingshead.

After eating LSD in cake icing, Hollingshead got in touch with Aldous Huxley, who suggested he contact Dr.

Leary at Harvard to see how the psychotrope might best be used.

Hollingshead wasted no time in meeting Leary and over lunch at the Faculty Club, he spoke about the amazing effects of lysergic acid diethylamide. He also said he was broke and depressed and needed a place to stay. Leary invited him to his house, saying he could sleep in the attic.

Leary was hesitant and did not want to take the drug at first because it had been produced in a laboratory, unlike peyote or sacred mushrooms which were natural. He also admitted that he was a little scared. But in December 1961, Leary was finally persuaded to try it, stating afterwards that it was a "shattering experience." Because of it, he seemed awed by Hollingshead, though not everyone had the same opinion. Richard Alpert called him "a paranoid nut."

Research for the Harvard Psilocybin Project had apparently begun in October 1960. Aldous Huxley attended research group meetings on a regular basis in October and November, but Leary was concerned that there was too much talk and not enough hard research using the drug. Sandoz resolved that dilemma by sending him pillboxes with two milligram doses of psilocybin (Greenfield 119). He continued receiving the small pink pills for the next seven months.

The Good Friday Experiment, so called because it took place on Good Friday, 20 April 1962, was conducted by Walter Pahnke, under the supervision of his principle academic advisor Timothy Leary, with students from Andover-Newton Theological School participating as test subjects. Ten students were given psilocybin and ten were given a placebo. The results were dramatic: nine out of ten students given the drug said they had religious or mystical experiences, whereas only one out of ten in the control group had a religious experience. Walter Pahnke, a medical doctor from the Midwest and an ordained minister preparing his Ph.D. in the history of religion, did not use psilocybin himself during the experiment in order to remain as objective as possible and not be accused of bias.

Like Captain Al Hubbard, Leary liked to play Johnny Appleseed. Leary gave LSD to the attractive Mary Pinchot–wife of Cord Meyer, a top CIA official–who said she wanted to share the drug with "a very important man." She was undoubtedly referring to President Kennedy since they were having an affair and had smoked marijuana together in a bedroom of the White House (Lee 86). According to the *National Enquirer*, 2 March 1976, Mary was taken to the White House in a limousine driven by a Secret Service agent. They met regularly in this fashion until the president was assassinated on 22 November 1963. Mary was shot to death on October 12, 1964, less than a year after the assassination of John F. Kennedy, and just three weeks after publication of the Warren Commission Report. Mary, like many others, rejected the official version. She kept a diary of her relationship with the president that the CIA sought energetically to recover. Toni Bradlee, Pinchot's sister, supposedly found the diary and gave it to James Jesus Angleton, who reportedly burned it at CIA bureau offices. What actually happened has been a source of debate ever since. In any case, the Agency had been watching Leary and Pinchot and must have known that she gave LSD to president Kennedy and the effects it would have on him.

Timothy Leary said Mary phoned him after the assassination and was distraught, talking about how they couldn't control him anymore because he was changing too fast. She added that *they* (i.e. the United States government) had covered everything up (*Flashbacks* 194).

The CIA was keeping a close watch on Leary's research and reading his articles. "What to Do When the Vietcong Drops LSD in Our Water Supply" was published in the *Bulletin of Atomic Science* in the spring of 1962. In it, Leary advised dumping acid in the water supply so people would know what to expect from the drug.

Meanwhile, pressure was starting to mount on Leary's research group on campus. Dr. Max Rinkel, reportedly involved in the MK-ULTRA project, fustigated Leary in the Harvard Alumni Review. Dr. Robert Heath, a CIA employee, did likewise (Lee 86). The CIA disliked anyone outside the Agency's sphere of influence working with psychedelic drugs, nor did it like the idea of using them for therapeutic purposes, or seeing some wannabee Prometheus distributing doses of divine fire to the general public. With its solid links inside and around the university, it would not have been difficult to get Leary and Alpert removed.

In March 1962, the psilocybin project came under serious attack during a large faculty meeting. Dr. Herbert Kelman, who had received a grant from the Human Ecology Fund, reportedly linked to the CIA, questioned whether Leary's research project was an "intellectual endeavor," or rather a utopian quest, a panacea for society's ills (Lee 87).

It wasn't long before the U.S. Food and Drug

Administration, known for patronizing the Agency's drug research, got involved, too. This came about as a result of an article in the *Boston Herald*, a Hearst tabloid, published on 16 March 1962: "Hallucination Drug Fought at Harvard–350 Students Take Pills." In order to make the title hit closer to home, the paper substituted "students" for "subjects."

Key players at the university and in the local community anathematized the Psilocybin Project. Some of Leary and Alpert's colleagues were extremely jealous because they were losing a lot of research assistants who preferred the exhilaration of drug research. Graduate research is a key aspect of university prestige, particularly at a university like Harvard. The chairman of the department, David McClelland, played the role of Cassandra, vociferating about the pernicious consequences of drugs and solemnly announced that students who took part in Leary's drug research would be dropped from Harvard's Ph.D. program (Forte 186). This threat made it clear to the students that they had no alternative but to abandon the Psilocybin Project.

A growing number of people even thought Leary was a pusher, though no one dared to publicly accuse him. In the closed, aseptic world of the New England university, Leary and Alpert became the subject of professional and private scrutiny. A modern witch hunt was in full sway.

In May 1963, Richard Alpert was fired for giving psilocybin to an undergraduate. In his biography of Timothy Leary, Robert Greenfield says Alpert gave the student LSD (197), but in *Look* magazine Andrew Weil says it was psilocybin. Maybe it was both. A memorandum dated 6 May 1963, at a meeting of the university president and fellows of

Harvard stated that Dr. Timothy Leary was dismissed because "he failed to keep his classroom appointments" and was absent "without permission." His salary had already been terminated on 30 April 1963.

Leary and his team of researchers had decided to separate research from Harvard, supposedly to take the pressure off himself and his associates by establishing the International Federation for Internal Freedom (IFIF), with offices in Cambridge. Their strategy was to supply drugs to research groups in the United States. IFIF was immediately flooded with requests.

The third draft of the organization's statement of purpose, dated 3 November 1962, is rife with the abstruse imagery that became Leary's trademark. The Board of Directors included Timothy Leary, Richard Alpert, Ralph Metzner, George Litwin, Madison Parnell, Huston Smith and Gunther Weil. Soon there were three thousand paying members. Their credo was that everyone should have the right to use hallucinogenic chemicals if they wanted to, because of their "internal freedom." Their goal was to promote "new social forms," whatever that was supposed to mean, and Leary optimistically predicted that soon twenty to thirty million Americans would be using LSD on a regular basis. The Office of Security, a bureau within the CIA that was keeping a close eye on Alpert and Leary, wanted any information about the use of LSD reported immediately (Lee 85).

IFIF, not surprizingly, immediately ran into obstacles. Because Harvard had confiscated their psilocybin, Leary and Alpert ordered one million doses from Sandoz for $10,000.

Sandoz, however, asked permission from Harvard, which disapproved. Moreover, the ten thousand dollar check was not covered by sufficient funds.

There were basically two suppliers of the drug in the United States: psychiatric hospitals and the underground, and it was virtually impossible to get it from hospitals.

Soon, there were no structures in industrialized societies to conduct research with psychedelics to see how they could benefit humanity. The last hospital to engage in the use of psychedelics for therapy was Spring Grove Hospital in Baltimore, Maryland, and it was closed in the seventies.

IFIF headquarters in Zihuatanejo, Mexico, did not work out, but Peggy Hitchcock was director in New York, and her family was filthy rich. They had this "old house" in Dutchess County, New York–a sixty-four room mansion in Millbrook–which Billy Hitchcock generously made available. Leary was set, for a while at least.

Once settled in Millbrook, IFIF was terminated and a new organization took its place: the Castalia Foundation, which took its name from the colony in Herman Hesse's novel *The Glass Bead Game* (*Das Glasperlenspiel*), for which he won the Nobel Prize for literature in 1946.

It was his last novel and his most complex work. The plot is set in the distant future. The protagonist, Joseph Knecht, grew up in Castalia, a remote utopia reserved for the intellectual elite. His quest was to master the Glass Bead Game, a combination of aesthetics and scientific arts.

The Castalia Foundation created its own journal, *The Psychedelic Review*, to promote research and spread its ideas. Unlike the remote utopia in Hesse's novel,

Millbrook's Castalia would interact with society as an active, didactic force, and a model for others to emulate to achieve higher states of consciousness. That is how Leary and the board of directors envisioned their purpose, in any case.

Millbrook was like a tale by Charles Perrault or Hans Christian Andersen, and like their tales, there was a darker side to the seemingly endless euphoria. That side would express itself in overindulgence.

The Tibetan Book of the Dead was quoted by Aldous Huxley in *The Doors of Perception*. It was used by Leary, Alpert and Metzner to write *The Psychedelic Experience* (1964), a book that was written to help people deal with manifestations of ego death during a psychedelic trip. Turning on became a ritualistic initiation into a religious order, a psychedelic sect. Kesey and the Pranksters sought to control the experience, too, albeit by pushing users in directions that could cause them to freak out.

Both Kesey and Leary used the media to promote their agendas that resembled carefully packaged products. "I'm a charlatan," Leary quipped, bating the public that the mass media was bombarding with a litany of psychedelic swizzle. The messianic enthusiasm and dime store slogans–"You have to go out of your mind to use your head"–turned some people off, particularly those in academe, but as his former wife Rosemary Woodruff pointed out, Leary was a show-off who loved playing to the gallery, and so the quest for fame became even more important than the quest for higher consciousness.

After Timothy Leary's appearance at the Senate Hearings on psychedelic drugs, he met the media icon

Marshall McLuhan for lunch at the Plaza Hotel. McLuhan, who was director of the Center for Culture and Technology at the University of Toronto, told Leary that he was selling a product, that he needed to think more seriously about advertising, and that he needed to associate LSD with positive things such as "beauty," "fun," "intelligence," and so on. He also advised Leary to get his rock music friends to compose catchy jingles for him. One other important thing he told Tim was to always wear a smile and never be peevish (*Flashbacks* 251-53). Leary took note of McLuhan's scholarly advice and spent a few days ransacking his forty billion neurons for an appealing package for the psychedelic revolution. Suddenly, while taking a shower, he had a brainstorm that would transform psychedelia: "Turn on, tune in, drop out!" It seems that the dictum came from an article entitled "Drugs on Campus: Turned On and Tune Out," by Merv Freedman and Harvey Powelson, published on 31 January 1966, in *The Nation*.

Yet one problem with slogans is that with time they tend to become vague and meaningless, if they are not already vague and meaningless to begin with. And then the inevitable occurred: Leary's catchy jingle was coopted by the advertising industry. A soft drink brand told consumers to "turn on to flavor, tune into sparkle, and drop out of the cola rut." Billy Graham, the evangelizer and close friend of Richard Nixon, exhorted his flock to "Turn on Christ, tune in to the Bible, and drop out of sin." The September 22-28, 1967, *Berkeley Barb* ironized Tim's wisdom on its cover with a seemingly psychedelicized LBJ wearing hippie beads, long hair, a Captain Trips hat and a clerical collar, pointing a threatening finger with the title below: "Turn Off, Tune Out, Drop In."

Like Kesey, Leary understood what the media wanted, and that prompted him to provoke and test people's preconceived ideas. The television networks wanted stories that were newsworthy, and the more sensational they were the better. Leary gave them more than they had bargained for. The important thing was to be talked about, whether it was good or bad. "The medium is the message," said McLuhan, and Leary understood the message very well.

But Leary and Millbrook were being closely watched and police informants had easy access to the mansion. Authorities were waiting for a chance to make a well publicized bust. In December 1965, Leary and his family were caught at the Mexican border with a small amount of marijuana. On March 11, 1966, he was found guilty and Judge Ben Connally, brother of Texas governor John Bowden Connally, sentenced him to thirty years in prison and a $30,000 fine. Leary was also ordered to be committed to a hospital for the criminally insane for psychiatric observation for a period of three months. By comparison, the three men convicted of killing Malcolm X were sentenced to twenty-six years in prison.

Leary went back to Millbrook while his legal team appealed the verdict.

Dutchess County prosecutor G. Gordon Liddy, well known for his role in the Watergate burglary, was itching to raid the mansion, and on April 17, 1966, he got his chance. Leary, Frederick Swain, his wife Nancy, and Barry Kaplan were arrested in a two a.m. raid that involved twenty-two officers from the Dutchess County Sheriff's Office. A Grand Jury indicted them on May 11, 1966, for possession of marijuana.

But on September 23, 1966, Judge Raymond C. Baratta dismissed all charges because Liddy and the Sheriff had failed to inform the occupants of their legal rights.

Soon the League for Spiritual Discovery replaced the Castalia Foundation. It sponsored a psychedelic, religious celebration called "Death of the Mind" on September 20, 1966, at the Village Theatre.

The show was roughly based on Hermann Hesse's novel *Steppenwolf*. "Death of the Mind" was described as a "coming-out party" for East Coast hippies who had recently learned about the wonders of LSD (Greenfield 285). It was a way for Leary to proselytize, make money and transform himself into a performing artist. Eleanor Lester of *The New York Times*, in an article dated 4 December 1966, praised it as a huge off-Broadway event, although Tim never received an Obie for his showmanship.

Leary performed a number of these shows on the east and west coasts to help pay for his legal expenses which were increasing by leaps and bounds, but also because he wanted to stay in the countercultural spotlight.

In September 1966, a Leary interview was published in *Playboy* magazine. When he was asked what LSD was like, Tim replied that it was the strongest aphrodisiac known to man, fully aware of what the magazine's readers wanted to hear. And making love when you were high on LSD was as if your billions of cells were making love to her billions of cells. He stressed the point that people took LSD to achieve sexual ecstasy. Marshall McLuhan would have enjoyed the advertisement, even though it was assuredly false, and Leary probably didn't believe it either, but he had the interviewer where he wanted him, and so he took him for a little ride, or shall we say "trip."

On December 12, 1966, Leary held a press conference at the ritzy Fairmont Hotel in San Francisco to promote his psychedelic celebrations. There were two shows during the third week of January 1967 at the Berkeley Community Theatre and at Winterland. Timothy was the darling of *The San Francisco Oracle*, and his Death of the Mind celebration was advertised in issue number five. It was described as "a re-enactment of a great religious myth using psychedelic methods: sensory meditation, symbol-overload, media-mix, molecular and cellular phrasing, pantomime, dance, sound-light and lecture-sermon gospel." Tickets were on sale from $2.25 to $4.75.

On January 5, 1967, Leary gave a press conference at the Playboy Mansion in Chicago for two psychedelic celebrations at the Arie Crown Theatre. Then it was back to San Francisco for the Human Be-In on January 14, in Golden Gate Park.

"We bombed in San Francisco," said Rosemary Woodruff, referring to the "Death of the Mind" shows. Assuredly, the Trips Festival and the dance concerts at the Avalon Ballroom and the Fillmore Auditorium were tough acts to follow, and Leary's light show was second rate, as critic Ralph Gleason noted.

Apart from his psychedelic extravaganzas, Leary lectured at any college or university that was willing to pay his $1,000 a night fee–a considerable amount in 1967.

In July 1967, while the Summer of Love cauldron was boiling over in the Haight-Ashbury, forty people were arrested while leaving or entering the Millbrook estate on trumped up charges. But the police harassment turned out to be effective in destroying the commune, although it was a violation of Leary's legal rights.

He knew it was time to pack up his bags. Leary flew the coop in Billy Hitchcock's plane and visited hippie communes: Drop City, outside Trinidad, Colorado, and New Buffalo near Taos, New Mexico. On returning to Millbrook, it was decided that the estate could not be defended, and so it was closed for the rest of the summer.

Timothy Leary knew what was happening in the Haight-Ashbury during the Summer of Love, but he was not directly involved in it, one way or the other.

The Haight-Ashbury in the mid-sixties was about LSD. It could not have become what it did without the drug. The CIA, always on the lookout for LSD, wanted to know who was using it, for whatever reasons. Many have wondered what they were so concerned about. The Agency was not worried about the safety of Americans because it had used them as guinea pigs in illegal experiments. Some have conjectured that the Agency was afraid that a sector of the population might begin to see things for what they really were, namely that our social existence was based on illusion, deception and fraud; or worse yet, that large numbers of people might have extraordinary experiences–religious, philosophical or other–and begin to question what they were doing with their lives and want to break with the past. They might also start to question the motivations of those who governed the masses and realize that society was inherently unjust and needed to be changed to make it more egalitarian, democratic and human. If that were the case, the next logical step would be to question the country's role in foreign affairs, particularly in Southeast Asia and South America. Those in positions of authority would feel threatened by groups promoting profound social transformation and would seek ways to bolster the State's authority while undermining an adverse grassroots movement that was believed by many to be communist inspired. There is no question whatsoever that the government used the intelligence community to subvert groups and social movements that were antagonistic to the establishment.

12

Poster Art

A revolution was taking place in the mid-sixties, and the nucleus for that vibrant activity was the Haight-Ashbury in San Francisco. Rock music was part of that revolution, with Chet Helms and Bill Graham promoting dance-concerts at the Avalon Ballroom, Fillmore Auditorium, Winterland and the Matrix. Since the Haight-Ashbury gained international importance because of lysergic acid diethylamide, and because this trend influenced rock music, a synergistic effect developed between the acid, the music, the light shows, the people and the posters, with the latter seeking to enhance or extend the trip. Of course on a basic level the posters were used to advertise the events in the ballrooms, but they meant a great deal more to the people who attended the dance-concerts. Perhaps not all the artists caught up in the zeitgeist knew that their posters were revolutionary, because they were too busy trying to meet the short deadlines to get them drawn and printed, but promoter Bill Graham could not ignore the tremendous financial possibilities of the artwork, and began saving copies and selling as many as he could. Art history was in the making.

Offset lithography was the primary method used to print the San Francisco rock posters. Small offset shops printed runs of posters cheaply and quickly, while establishing a friendly atmosphere that was conducive to creativity.

These posters quickly became emblematic of the countercultural revolution. Clearly, a very specific social group was targeted. The lettering, which in some cases is purposely illegible, was not meant for the straights and squares that were in too much of a hurry to stop and try and decipher what was written.

Today, posters from this unique era in American history are sought by collectors and investors, because those in mint condition are rare. For example, Wes Wilson's fourteen by twenty inch poster for the Quicksilver Messenger Service and Sopwith Camel dance-concert on 22-23 July 1966, sells for $1,650; the handbill for the same event goes for nearly $900. The well-known Zig-Zag handbill for the Family Dog sells for $1,000. A first printing of the poster is virtually impossible to find. Many of the artists still living today wish they had stashed a few for a rainy day.

The posters, postcards and handbills to advertise the shows were distributed in head shops, record stores, universities, or poster shops, and the posters were stapled to walls or taped to windows, thus explaining why it was often difficult to find original copies in perfect or nearly perfect condition. Museums such as the Louvre in Paris and the

Smithsonian in Washington D. C. have collections, and the Haight Street Art Center at 215 Haight Street is a good place to see them.

Wes Wilson, Alton Kelley, Stanley "Mouse" Miller, Rick Griffin, Victor Moscoso and Bonnie MacLean produced most of the posters for Graham and Helms between 1965 and 1967. The poster artists broke the canons of design, thereby reflecting the liberated spirit of the neighborhood and the sixties, and that is why they are famous today. They often represented altered states of consciousness and a desire to go beyond the establishment's reality.

The bulk of the most well-known posters were produced for the two main promoters, both are numbered series. The series for Bill Graham, the "BG" series, includes about three hundred posters from 1966 to 1973, two years after the closing of Fillmore West on 4 July 1971, when the famous music venue yielded the floor to Japanese automobiles. The Family Dog series, or "FD" series, goes from 1966 to 1968, when the Avalon Ballroom was closed because City Hall refused to renew the dance-concert permit, citing complaints from residents about noise and dirty hippies. In reality, political pressure had been coming from San Francisco, Sacramento and Washington to clean up the Haight-Ashbury.

The posters were printed with postcards, handbills and tickets with the same artwork, though sometimes the colors were changed. When a person arrived for the show, they would buy their ticket, and sometimes were given a free poster or handbill.

Posters from the San Francisco music venues in the mid-sixties had definite characteristics. The three qualities that stand out most are the color, the imagery and the lettering. The artists boldly explored the use of color, often combining contrasting colors on the color wheel, such as red and green, blue and orange, or yellow and violet with varying shades, thus creating an illusion of depth that was emphasized under a black light. The imagery was often fantastic or surrealistic, depending on the artist. Themes from the Old West, particularly the use of American Indians or cowboys, were popular, as were graceful female forms, motifs and philosophical symbols such as the yin and yang. The lettering, often rounded and squeezed into various shapes, or highly stylized as a form of calligraphy, became an art in itself. The form, like the semantic content of the poster, was the message, too. Moreover, the poster sheet was completely covered, and the work was done by hand.

Robert Wesley Wilson was the first poster artist to work with Bill Graham on a regular basis. He was born on 15 July 1937, in Sacramento, California. His first years were spent near Placerville, in El Dorado County, at the foot of the Sierra Nevada Mountains. He was raised by his mother, a school teacher, who taught in different places in Northern California. As a boy he spent long hours out of doors, a fact which helped to forge a creative temperament. As a teenager he lived in Auburn and other rural towns in the Sierra foothills.

After graduating from high school, where he took courses in mechanical and architectural drawing, he did his obligatory military service at the age of sixteen, which involved six months active duty. The year was 1953, and the Korean War officially ended on 27 July 1953. Later, he was a part-time junior college student for four years, concentrating on philosophy. In the summer of 1959 he worked in an architect's office, and the following year he enrolled at San Francisco State College, where he met his first wife. Wilson, who was attracted to Buddhism and the teachings of Alan Watts and D.T. Suzuki, eagerly attended related courses at the Vedanta Society.

Having decided to become an artist, Wes dropped out of San Francisco State in the spring of 1963 before finishing his Bachelor of Arts degree, and enrolled for courses in painting and life drawing at the San Francisco Academy of Art in 1964. Because he had three daughters, he needed to support his family by working fulltime. Domestic conflicts forced him and his wife to separate, and they later got a divorce.

Wes entered the world of poster art indirectly. He was living at the Wently, a hotel on the corner of Polk and Sutter known for its cheap rooms, and spending time at Foster's, an all-night café on the street below. Kent Chapman, with whom Wes would discuss Buddhism and art, urged him to see Bob Carr, a guy who studied eastern religions and philosophies, psychology and higher states of consciousness. Bob, as cofounder of The Center for Integration in Seattle, Washington, was interested in developing human potential, part of which was helping people to develop a sense of awareness. With the help of psychologists, in 1956 he was able to acquire some lysergic acid diethylamide from Sandoz laboratories, which he used in personal growth experiences.

Around 1960 he closed the center and relocated in San Francisco.

Bob Carr's apartment was known as a place for socializing, and Wes and his future wife Eva, a ballet student, spent time there. Having already used lysergic acid diethylamide, which was legal at the time, he believed it could help Wes to achieve greater potential as an artist. Consequently, Wes took his first acid trip at Carr's apartment. As they became close friends, Bob asked Wes to go into business with him and open a small printing shop. Wes accepted, probably because it was the best opportunity at the time, and the two became business associates.

Contact Printing started business in the spring of 1964. It was a very small shop in the basement of Bob's apartment building. Wes worked in the shop, doing the jobs on the "funky" seventeen by twenty-two inch press, and Bob sought paying clients. Most of the work they did was rather ordinary: stationary, sales announcements, business forms, and so on, but they did print programs for the Trips Festival, a seminal event, after meeting Stewart Brand, and also for the San Francisco Mime Troupe, managed at the time by Bill Graham. The Trips Festival flyers were designed and printed by Wes on that press. This "transformative" event, organized from 21 to 23 January 1966, brought him into contact with a number of people in the counterculture, including Ken Kesey and the Merry Pranksters. It paved the way for the dance-concerts that were associated with the counterculture.

Contact Printing lasted for a couple of years before it was sold when Bob Carr inherited some money, which he used to travel to India.

Wes was not interested in running the business by himself since he was planning to become a freelance poster artist. Prior to the selling of Contact Printing, he had been doing poster work. His customers liked the fact that he could produce them quicker and cheaper than others. He did his first rock posters on their old seventeen by twenty-two inch press when Bob left for India. The first Family Dog posters were done on that "funky" machine (Marks).

Yet, even before the Trips Festival, something else had assisted Wes Wilson while on the road to becoming an artist, and that was a political poster he designed and published in 1965 called "Are We Next?" That was the year that LBJ significantly escalated the War in Vietnam.

Wes Wilson is proud of his American heritage and his ancestor Charles Thomson, member of the Continental Congress, but he was aware of the abuses of power and the motivations behind the Bay of Pigs invasion and the War in Vietnam, in which the United States supported puppet dictators rather than adhere to the will of the Vietnamese people.

"Are We Next" depicts the Stars and Stripes, but the stars are on a swastika with a blue background, suggesting that a totalitarian form of government could take control in the United States. Sinclair Lewis warned of the same thing in his novel *It Can't Happen Here*, and of course there was George Orwell's *1984*.

When Wes showed his poster to Ivor Powell at West Coast Litho, the only words on it were "Be Aware." Powell rightfully felt that the artist's message was too vague and that he needed to add the important question: "Are We

Next?" In any event, that is how the wording came about on the poster (Marks). It got plenty of attention at an antiwar demonstration across the bay in Berkeley, though Allen Ginsberg felt it was a little "too paranoid." But that was way back in 1965. Strangely enough, the Anti-Defamation League sent representatives to Wes's residence because they were concerned it might be anti-Semitic [sic]. Wes assured them that it was not, that his wife was Jewish, and that her father, a screenwriter, had been blacklisted in Hollywood.

Chet Helms of the Family Dog liked the poster a lot, so "Are We Next" got Wes doing posters for him and his shows at the Avalon Ballroom. Chet was a very nice person, but not well-organized like his arch-rival Bill Graham. Helms paid about sixty dollars for each poster, which included printing, artwork, delivery and anything else. Three hundred copies of each poster were printed. Helms gave him the photograph of an American Indian wearing a top hat and smoking a long pipe that he had taken from the *American Heritage Book of Indians*. This was used to create the Family Dog logo, together with the phrase "May the baby Jesus shut your mouth and open your mind." The poster for the Paul Butterfield Blues Band and Quicksilver Messenger Service dance-concert at Fillmore Auditorium on March 25-27, is one of the most interesting posters he did for Chet Helms, said Wilson. Letters fill the empty space, and a man with a naked torso holding one hand on his head occupies the center. The viewer can only guess why he is in this unusual position. It turns out that the picture was taken from a book by Bernarr MacFadden on "how to live the happy life," surely a subject of interest for the flower children of the

Haight-Ashbury.

The poster he did for the Beatles' concert at Candlestick Park further consolidated Wilson's reputation. The celebrated disk jockey from radio station KYA, Tom Donahue, got in touch with Wes to do the poster, a fact which confirms his notoriety as a poster artist. It was entitled "Here Come the Beatles." The yin and yang with the British and American flags overlaid testifies to an interest in mysticism.

Working with the charismatic promoter Bill Graham was not an ordinary experience. Wes enjoyed working for Graham because he had greater freedom, and Bill knew he could count on Wilson to produce a quality poster on short notice; so they got along for a while. But, not surprisingly, they got in a heated argument over money.

They were working on a legal contract because Wilson wanted the copyright for his artwork and be able to receive royalties for those that were sold. They had, in fact, worked out a deal together and signed the draft to their contract, which Graham's attorney was supposed to clean up and print a presentable copy that both men would sign. Wilson says he was supposed to receive six percent in royalties, which, at the time, was not a bad deal for a graphic artist. But then *Time* magazine published an article stating Graham had sold some one hundred thousand posters. Consequently, Wilson asked for his fare share of royalties, saying Graham owed him $6,000, according to the article in *Time*. Graham started raising his voice and got on the defensive and before you knew it, their "friendship" was a thing of the past. Probably suspecting some mismanagement, Wilson went to check up on Graham's accounting with some friends. But tempers flared and both were in a fighting mood, and actually agreed to settle their differences outside in the street. Everybody got up and walked down the stairs to go outside, but as Wilson and his friends went out the door, Bill quickly locked it behind them so they could not get back in. The deal was over. Wilson says their agreement was not honored from that day on. Unfortunately for him, Graham had the only copy of the contract, and, so, from a legal standpoint, he could not prove anything. Unfortunately for Wilson, too, he lost the copyright on the posters he had done for Graham. "Bill had shown himself to be a lying crook rather than an honest person," said Wilson (Marks).

The work schedule for producing the posters was hectic, to say the least, since he had to produce them in a week or sometimes just three or four days. The whole process depended on scheduling the bands, and they were impossible to schedule several weeks in advance. It was extremely rare for Graham to have a band signed up for a show more than a week ahead of time. So the posters had to be printed quickly. Wilson went to see Marty Balin from Jefferson Airplane, because his dad was a printer, but he needed two weeks to do the job.

In the nascent dance-concert scene, people did not expect a lot of money. In the beginning, tickets at the Fillmore and the Avalon sold for $2.00; that price went up later to $2.50 and $3.00, which was cheap, though not everyone had it. It was not easy to balance everything out because there were three bands on the bill that had to be paid, plus extra musicians, the people who did the light show, and the poster artist. But those who were part of the scene were just glad to be part of it and have a good time.

When Wes first started doing posters for Graham, he had to work with small printers, because the big ones charged too much, but, eventually, he got more money out of Graham and they could do more complicated things like expanding the color bleeds and printing handbills, tickets and different posters at a time.

The business expanded very quickly. The print run budget for the first shows was about sixty dollars for three hundred posters, a ridiculous price by today's standards, but later the first printing was multiplied by ten and the budget shot up to about nine hundred dollars, with Wilson getting a hundred dollars more. Young people were collecting the posters from the start to decorate their rooms, though they were not always in mint condition. Off-set lithography production in the San Francisco Bay Area soared by the end of 1967.

"The Flames" poster is a watershed in Wilson's evolution as a poster artist. It was printed for the dance-concert on Friday and Saturday, 22-23 July 1966, The Association, Quick Silver Messenger Service, Sopwith Camel and Grassroots were on the bill. Ivor Powel at West Coast Litho did the printing. It was an artistically frenzied time for Wilson who was producing several posters a week. His wife filled it in for him in the middle of the night.

Wilson's sources of inspiration were varied: French Art Nouveau, the Viennese Secessionists, and the Jugendstil artists who celebrated the female form, symbolizing Mother Earth, motherhood and love.

As far as bands were concerned, Wes especially liked the early Jefferson Airplane with their first female vocalist, Signe Toly Anderson. He remembers the first time he heard "Get Together" by Dino Valenti, performed at California Hall. For him it was the anthem of the countercultural movement.

Although he liked Jerry Garcia, one of the shining stars of San Francisco, he admits not being a Grateful Dead fan. Quicksilver Messenger Service, he recalls, was a good band, and Big Brother and the Holding Company, managed by Chet Helms, and, naturally, the Jimi Hendrix Experience. But the band that made the biggest impression on Wilson was not a San Francisco band, but the iconic group of musicians from Los Angeles: The Doors.

There was a sense of community in the Haight-Ashbury in the mid-sixties, which was exemplified by a number of music benefits to raise money for friends in distress. This was the case when a fire burned up Alton Kelley's apartment and when Bob Fried, poster artist, died at the age of thirty-seven, leaving a widow and two children behind. The benefit in his honor at Winterland raised $8,000 dollars for his wife Penelope.

After the Summer of Love, Wes and his family were forced to vacate a house they were renting in Marin County. Tired of having to move so often, they started looking for a place to buy. Sometime in 1968, Wes received a $5,000 check from the National Endowment for "contributions to American Art", which enabled them to purchase a house in Lagunitas (Medeiros).

In 1976, he was able to make a lifelong dream come true

by buying a large farm in Missouri, in the Ozark Mountains. Before the family moved in, his second son was born. Wes used the property to begin a cattle farm, taking care to respect Mother Nature by implementing natural, organic methods (Medeiros).

Alton Kelley was born on 17 June 1940 in Houlton, Maine, a town on the Canadian-American border in northeast Maine. The family moved to Connecticut to work in the armament industry during World War Two. After graduating from high school, Alton studied industrial design in college. He worked for two years as an aircraft mechanic, but quit in hopes of finding greener pastures. He hitchhiked to California in 1964, arriving in Southern California and Los Angeles where he repaired motorcycles and raced them on weekends.

When Alton got fed up with the smog in Los Angeles, he took a trip north to San Francisco, ending up in North Beach, the Italian and bohemian district of the city. By late 1965 he had joined the group of poets, artists and political activists known as the Family Dog, living in the Victorian at 2111 Pine Street, between Webster and Buchanan Streets. The house was known as the "Dog House" in the psychedelic counterculture.

Kelley had a bedroom in the spacious Victorian where the rent was cheap, and he covered it with day-glo paint and numerous collages. He also painted a lightning bolt that stretched across the floor and went across a chair without stopping.

Although lacking in experience, he was not lacking in

artistic enthusiasm and he did the drafting and lettering for a number of dance-concerts organized by the Family Dog. When some of the original members left the collective, Alton continued to collaborate with Chet Helms, and in 1964 he met a guy from the Motor City who would be a future collaborator: Stanley Mouse.

Stanley George Miller was born on 10 October 1940, in Fresno, California, but he grew up in Detroit, Michigan. In grammar school he was nicknamed "Mouse" because of the many sketches of mice he had done in his notebooks (Lemke 91). Miller never liked grammar school or high school, and when he stopped trying to play the game, he was expelled. He found art much more gratifying because he could see the immediate results. To improve his craft, he enrolled in the School for the Society of Arts and Crafts in Detroit, but he did go back to high school, a different one, and received his diploma in 1959 and a reputation for being a talented cartoonist (Grushkin 74-75). He tried college, like many young people at the time, but he soon realized he was not made for that sort of learning. From eighteen to twenty-five, 1958 to 1965, he traveled around "airbrushing hot rod designs on T-shirts" (Grushkin 74). Unlike many young people of his generation, he got along with his parents, who helped with his small business called Mouse Studios. Stanley took care of the decals, posters and T-shirts, his father served as manager, while his mother handled the mail-orders. One of the marks of his success is that Monogram Models used some of his designs for their production of model car kits, a popular pastime at the time.

In 1964 Miller drove his Porsche to California and began

living in a windmill on Telegraph Avenue in Berkeley, the main street leading to the university campus. 1964 was the year the Free Speech Movement began on the campus. It was not long before he drove across the Bay Bridge to San Francisco where he met people in the Family Dog at 2111 Pine Street, and he distinctly remembers seeing Alton Kelley sitting on a "pile of trash" and talking the leg off a table.

In 1965 he received his "greetings" from his local draft board informing him to report to his induction center on short notice. Miller did not waste any time driving back to Detroit so he could avoid induction.

Having succeeded in obtaining a classification that would exempt him from military duty, Miller wanted to return to the West Coast and San Francisco. He went to a drive-away service, in other words a business that has cars that need to be driven to different locations. He was given a hearse which he loved (Grushkin 75). It was perfect for him because it had plenty of room for all his stuff. To celebrate being out of the draft, he put a sticker on the back window that said: "Make Love, Not War" (Lemke 92) and drove to California with his girlfriend Suzi and a dog named Cigar.

On 21 January 1966, he arrived in front of Longshoremen's Hall, at 400 North Point Street, San Francisco. There were a lot of people there that evening because it was the first night of the celebrated Trips Festival, sponsored in part by Ken Kesey and the Merry Pranksters.

Miller was living on 17th Street in the Mission district when he ran into Alton Kelley again, probably at 2111 Pine Street, a natural place to hang out and smoke. Miller was easily recognizable with his long frizzy hair, beard, Zorro hat, metal-rimmed glasses and black apparel, the everyday accouterments of a Haight-Ashbury freak. Kelley was ecstatic when he affirmed that there were five thousand people just as crazy as they were in the city, meaning the stoners and freaks of the counterculture.

Miller noticed a change in San Francisco in 1966: the psychedelic dance-concert posters had become very trendy. Alton Kelley, George Hunter and Michael Ferguson were handling the posters and handbills for the Family Dog, and they were having a ball doing it. That was clearly a niche Miller could fit into.

The Captain Beefheart poster–misspelled on the poster– was his first work, before Miller and Kelley began collaborating (Grushkin 75). The duo was inspired when they produced the poster for the Big Brother and the Holding Company and Quicksilver Messenger Service show at the Avalon Ballroom on 24-25 June 1966 (FD 14). Miller calls it "Zig Zag Man." Both he and Kelley were afraid they might get hassled by the police, since Zig-Zag was the mark of rolling papers used by most heads in the Haight-Ashbury, and the logo was synonymous with marijuana, an illicit drug at the time.

Kelley and Miller pursued their collaboration for the Family Dog and produced what are considered classic psychedelic posters. "Skull and Roses" was done for the Grateful Dead concert at the Avalon (FD 26), "The Girl with Green Hair" (FD 29) was printed for the Jim Kweskin Jug Band, Big Brother and the Holding Company, Electric Train dance-concert, with the image of the young lady being taken from a poster by Alphonse Mucha. "The Dollar Bill" (FD

19), a spoof on American capitalism and its currency was done for the Bo Diddley, Sons of Adam, Oxford Circle, Big Brother and the Holding Company dance-concert on 5-6 August 1966.

During their collaborations, Kelley and Miller would often work on the same sheet at the same time, one working on the left-hand side and the other on the right-hand side. Kelley was good at layout and Miller was better at drawing and lettering.

Walter Medeiros, rock poster historian, says that essentially all the posters signed "Mouse Studios" were a joint effort by the two artists (Grushkin 76). They used images from a "graphic flea market," in other words popular images or pictures that may have been well-known, or that could be found in books. Alton Kelley said that there was "no real direction" at the outset, but once they began a project, things seemed to naturally fall into place. In many ways their work was a synthesis of what they had seen and what was going on at the time. Their poster art inspired another artist, Rick Griffin, to leave Southern California and move to San Francisco to become part of the artistic scene.

Richard Alden Griffin was born on 18 June 1944, near Rancho Palos Verdes, in Los Angeles County, California. As a boy, Rick would accompany his father, an engineer and "amateur archeologist," to Indian sites in quest of Native American artifacts. He learned to surf when he was fourteen with his friend Randy Nauert.

Like Stanley "Mouse" Miller, Rick began drawing at an early age, copying pictures from his favorite magazines and exploring his obsessive theme, namely surfing. He created "Murphy" in 1961, the surfer character who shouted "cowabunga," a term borrowed by surfers from television's "The Howdy Doody Show." The "perma-stoked gremmie" became an international success via T-shirts and paraphernalia. After graduating from high school, Rick worked for *Surfer Magazine*, which he left in 1964 because he was getting bored.

Rick hitched a ride north with the intention of going to San Francisco, but was awakened by the lunatic laughing of a driver gone berserk and the veering of a vehicle dangerously out of control. Before everything went black he remembered being thrown from the car onto the road and seeing his cheap suitcase being smashed to smithereens. When he opened his eyes he could faintly hear someone reading Psalm 23, which is read to someone you think is dying: "Yea, though I walk through the valley of the shadow of death, I will fear no evil: for thou art with me; thy rod and thy staff they comfort me." This traumatic experience may have resulted in Rick's conversion to Christianity. His face was scared from hitting the pavement and his left eye was dislocated, which is maybe what the flying eyeball in his artwork unconsciously alludes to. Friends noticed a dramatic change in both his lifestyle and his art after the accident.

At the Chouinard Art Institute, which later became Cal Arts, he met Ida Pfefferle, who would later become his wife and the mother of his four children. He also became associated with the Jook Savages, a group of artists and musicians who led a bohemian existence in Southern California.

Rick Griffin and the Jook Savages took part in the Watts Acid Test. There were at least five acid tests organized in Los Angeles by the Merry Pranksters. The one in Watts was organized at the Youth Opportunities Center on Saturday, 12 February 1966. "Really crazy. Totally crazed," commented Griffin. After this psychedelic experience, he wanted to go north to San Francisco, so he traveled there with the Jook Savages. Apparently, he had already seen the Charlatans at the Red Dog Saloon in 1965, but by 1966 things had changed in a spectacular way.

Rick and the Jook Savages performed a few intimate concerts and met a lot of people from the Haight-Ashbury. Ron and Jay Thelin, the brothers who ran the Psychedelic Shop, invited him to do an art exhibition, and that resulted in his first poster. He also met the organizers of the Human Be-In and did his second major poster that brought him immediate notoriety. An Indian on horseback with a guitar and holding a blanket in his right hand is the central figure. "Pow-wow, a gathering of the tribes" is written at the top in capital letters. The names of the "celebrities" at the Be-In form two columns, with Timothy Leary and Allen Ginsberg at the top. Chet Helms was so enthusiastic about those two posters that he urged Rick to do some for the Family Dog, and he quickly agreed.

As Rick admitted, his art school courses in Los Angeles did not get into the pen and ink drawing that he liked so much. Basically, he learned a lot more by doing posters. Admittedly, that period was a time of experimentation for Rick Griffin. Although his first posters were black and white, he was soon experimenting with color, learning something new with every poster he did, progressing from two colors to four. At the same time, he was learning different aspects of print colors: mixing, gearing the overlays, using tones, and so on.

Rick was blessed with a playful sense of irony and jocosity, a characteristic that was highlighted by an extremely serious sense of execution. No one could match his meticulously executed pieces. A good example of this is FD 79, a poster he did for the Opening of the Denver Family Dog on 8-9 September 1967, at 1601 West Evans Street, Denver, Colorado. The graphics in this poster are done with the care of a resolute perfectionist. He meticulously incorporated icons from advertising such as Elsie the cow, the Zig-Zag Man, the Quaker Oats man, the Sunmaid Raisin girl, the Cream of Wheat man, *et al*, without forgetting the peyote buttons, the hallucinogenic mushrooms, and the Family Dog Indian. His posters for the New Improved Psychedelic Shop and the Jook Savage Art Show were produced with the same sense of perfection. The popular theme of Native Americans was reiterated with cameos on the top, a figure standing dressed as an Indian, and a group of wild Indians on horseback, brandishing their rifles as though they had just galloped out of a movie by John Ford. Griffin knew how to get the viewer's attention, whatever the subject was.

When the peace and love turned sour in the Haight, Rick left Northern California to resettle in San Clemente around 1969. He did work for film maker John Severson, *Surfer Magazine* and also worked on the *Man from Utopia* comix. In the next decade he devoted himself to his faith, doing graphics for the Christian music scene, *The Illustrated Book of Saint John*, and the Calvary Chapel in Costa Mesa.

In 1976, he went to Europe with Gordon McClelland as part of an exhibition spanning several cities including Amsterdam, London and Sunderland. They also found time to go surfing on the Atlantic coasts of France and Spain. When they returned to Southern California, they wrote and published Rick's illustrated biography. In 1985 Rick returned to *Zap Comix* after a ten year absence to produce "Arthur PEN Dragron" [*sic*]. The last time he drew his celebrated Murphy was in 1987.

On 15 August 1991, after being told Robert Beerbohm's gallery had sold a painting for $1,800, tragedy befell the gifted artist. On his way back home to Stadler Lane in Petaluma, riding his Harley-Davidson motorcycle, a van apparently forced him off the road when he tried to pass it. He was not wearing a helmet and received fatal head injuries. He died on 18 August 1991 at the age of forty-seven. One of his last pieces was published in *San Francisco Magazine* just prior to his untimely death. It depicted a man at Heaven's Gate, holding his drawing tools.

Victor Moscoso was born on 28 July 1936 in Oleiros, Galicia, Spain, and arrived in Brooklyn in March of 1940. Growing up in a borough of New York influenced his attitudes and had a definite impact on shaping his character. The Spanish civil war was fought between 1936 and 1939, and beginning in 1937, thousands of children were evacuated from the war-torn nation.

Images from Brooklyn in the forties were embedded in

his memory: the development of the boroughs, Canarsie, the different ethnic groups, the soccer games, the dance halls, picnics in Queens, dancing on the waxed floors, the gangs, which he did his best to avoid, and the violence. Victor enjoyed running in competition, specializing in the mile, and playing basketball. He was president of the student body in high school, but soon realized he was merely participating in a masquerade, an establishment ritual devoid of any real substance. Life in Brooklyn taught him the hard realities of social Darwinism and undoubtedly helped him to survive in a competitive world. "If it doesn't kill you, it makes you stronger," said Moscoso. We can assume that he got stronger.

He studied at the High School of Industrial Art, although his first choice was the High School of Music and Art. His curriculum was a balance of technical skills and humanities. In retrospect, he was not disappointed with the school because he met some very interesting people and, more importantly, he learned a craft.

Moscoso says he became interested in art at a very early age. Drawing was a great source of gratification and he was jubilant at the prospect of being paid for what he *liked* to do, especially if that meant "drawing naked ladies." To this very day he vividly remembers tracing Sheena the Queen of the Jungle without any clothes on, and the exhilaration he felt when undressing her. *Dick Tracy* and *Steve Canyon* were among his favorite comic strips.

When he was sixteen he worked part time as a printer for Graphic Industries Inc., on East 20th Street, in the heart of the garment district; after graduation he began working full time there. But the job was painfully boring and made him realize how much he wanted to get out and learn new techniques. College seemed like a good idea, though his mother failed to understand, like many parents of that generation who felt that the goal in life was to make money. As a result, he was one of two thousand applicants to take the college entrance examination and was one of the ninety fortunate applicants to be accepted.

Moscoso says that most of the craft he learned was at Cooper Union Art School, such as Josef Albers' color theory, vibrating colors. Later, when he was in San Francisco in 1966 and saw Wes Wilson's "Association" poster, he understood at a glance: the green and red lettering were "vibrating." In other words, when two opposite colors on the color wheel are of equal intensity and value, the eye cannot determine "which one is in front of the other." Albers referred to this phenomenon as "simultaneous contrast."

After leaving Cooper Union, Victor went to the Yale Art School, which was actually his second choice, because he wanted to attend U.C. Berkeley, in California, and study with David Park. The problem with Berkeley is that they wanted him to take undergraduate courses such as history and mathematics, the kinds of courses that Moscoso hated with a passion. All he really wanted to do was practice his craft, "paint all day and all night," and so the choice was easily made. Moreover, many of his friends were going to New Haven to study, so that helped him, too. To pay his way through college he worked as a waiter, a good-paying job compared to many because of the tips.

The psychedelic posters, with the undecipherable

lettering and the vibrating colors, gained importance, becoming an art and a form of entertainment. Of course posters were used to advertise the dance-concerts, and with the handbills they were the primary form of advertisement. Such was also the case with the posters for the Moulin Rouge by Henri de Toulouse-Lautrec. Moscoso said he identified with the French artist born in Albi.

Moscoso had more training than the other poster artists working in San Francisco, but, paradoxically, he had to take a step back and reconsider his approach, to "rewire and change the circuits" that he had previously assimilated. Lysergic acid diethylamide helped him to do that. Not that he could draw on acid. That would be like trying to draw when you are falling down the stairs (Groth). So he looked at what the others were doing: Wes Wilson, Alton Kelley and Stanley Mouse. Wilson often made the foreground indistinguishable from the background; and the lettering was on the same plane as the foreground. Stanley Mouse and Kelley taught him that the Zig-Zag papers are more than what they appear to be. By reversing, so to speak, what he had learned, Moscoso was able to produce effective poster art. He did posters for the Family Dog, but never worked directly for Bill Graham, although he did work with Rick Griffin who was doing a poster for Fillmore Bill. He did album covers for bands later on: Herbie Hancock, Steve Miller Band, Manfred Mann, Jerry Garcia, David Grisman, Willie McBlind, *et al*. The Matrix posters he did were for Neon Rose, Moscoso's own company.

The posters for the dance-concerts were historical events. Since they represented dated events at specific locations that could be placed in a chronology, they became historical. Posters merely depicting a specific theme or image would not have, *à priori*, the same historical significance. Moscoso was aware of this, and he drew a parallel between Henri de Toulouse-Lautrec and the posters produced for the dance halls.

Moscoso admitted that "Stone Façade," his first poster, was not a success, but (FD 38) entitled "Top Hat" and called "The Man with the Spiral Eyes" was very effective as a psychedelic poster. It was produced for the Avalon Ballroom's 9-10 December 1966, dance-concert. The iconic Family Dog Indian, the logo for the collective, is depicted wearing spiral glasses. The background has the same psychedelic pattern, thus creating some confusion. Are the glasses letting the background come through, or is the Indian wearing the same pattern as the background?

Victor Moscoso began doing posters for the dance-concerts in 1966. According to the Family Dog numbered series, Victor's first poster for Chet Helms was FD 32, the "Rooster," produced for the Quicksilver Messenger Service and Sons of Champlain concert at the Avalon Ballroom on the 28-29 October 1966. "Sunflowers," produced for the 25-26 November 1966, show for Quicksilver and Big Brother and the Holding Company, would be a more effective piece.

It was in the spring of 1967 that he met Rick Griffin. Moscoso remembers his first impression of the surfing artist. It was at the house on Gough Street. There were several artists with their portfolios waiting to see Chet Helms. When he set his eyes on Rick he said to himself, "Jesus Christ! There he is" (Groth). Later, they met again and became good friends. Griffin went to see Moscoso at his place one day and they started talking about art and a poster for a Chuck Berry show that Rick was working on, and he asked Victor what he might use for the central image. Victor suggested doing a portrait of Rick, whose moustache was transformed into a peacock and whose face became a butterfly. Rick finished the left-hand side, and Victor did the right-hand side, so it was a collaboration.

Moscoso, an industrious artist, created his own company called Neon Rose, and that gave him total control of the production process. It was formed after the "Top Hat" poster in December of 1966, which was so successful that he was given credit from Bernie Moss, a well-known printer in Sausalito, a small town just north of the Golden Gate Bridge, about four miles north of San Francisco. He did his "Junior Wells" poster for the 27 December 1966 to 8 January 1967 show at the Matrix. Victor did everything himself because the ballroom did not have the money to commission the work. Wanting to do event posters, he decided to solicit the ballroom by making a deal they could not refuse. He agreed to give them two hundred free posters and he would run off as many as he could afford, selling those himself. It was profitable for both Moscoso and the Matrix.

Royalties are the share of proceeds received for the sale of artistic creations, in this case rock posters. This was a problem with the two major promoters, Bill Graham and Chet Helms, who were reticent about sharing benefits. In some cases, artists even lost the copyright for the posters they had made. When the poster shops began making sizeable profits on posters, it became clear to the artists that they needed to defend themselves. Wes Wilson got in touch with Victor Moscoso to say that the artists for the Family Dog–Wilson, Kelley, Mouse and Moscoso–needed to confront Helms about this important issue. In short, they said they wanted to receive royalties for the posters that were sold. Helms refused, so they threatened to boycott the Family Dog. Chet was no fool, so he agreed to give them twenty percent of the amount received for the sale of posters (Groth). They continued to receive one hundred dollars for the original. Today that amount seems like a paltry sum considering the amount of work that went into their creations, but it was a respectable amount in 1966, when you could rent a room in the Haight for fifty dollars a month, or less. It was after the threatened boycott that Moscoso decided to print the posters himself and give them to the ballroom for free, thereby circumventing the dilemma of royalties.

Almost overnight, then, posters became a lucrative business that many wanted to be part of. Poster shops usually sold other items, too. Poster shops were also head shops, or specialty shops that sold paraphernalia for smoking hashish and marijuana. When underground comix became a mass market medium, they were sold in the head shops with the posters; and after the decline of the poster fad, comix continued to be sold in the head shops, affirms Moscoso. Comix such as *Zap Comix*, published by Donald Donahue under Apex Novelties, became a source of revenue for poster artists, but the first printing of *Zap* was in February of 1968, after the Summer of Love.

Moscoso's growing up in New York was probably partly

responsible for his business acumen, which not all the artists possessed. He had his own company and was making and selling the posters himself. But he also needed a network of regular clients and distributors. One solution to that problem was Berkeley Bonaparte, a distribution company in the East Bay, cofounded by Cummings Walker.

He and Louis Rappaport had always wanted to start something together, some sort of avant-garde trip like a coffee shop or a bookstore. In December of 1966, Louis got in touch to say he had a great idea: it was going to be posters, and so a collective was formed in Berkeley, a traditionally radical enclave in Northern California (Grushkin 84). It started out as a mail-order business selling photographic posters of people like Lenin and Trotsky, which definitely set the tone. The name, Berkeley Bonaparte, was apparently chosen on the spare of the moment because the post office required a name. The first "non-political" poster they did was one by Rick Griffin entitled "In God We Trust," a sort of pseudo one dollar bill with cannabis and psychedelic mushrooms growing around the base of the pyramid topped with an all-seeing eye. In fact, the poster *is* political, though its orientation is implied. At the time, Rick and his wife Ida were living in their Volkswagen bus and doing their best to scrape up nickels and dimes. Berkeley Bonaparte was eager to help Rick out, especially after they had seen how talented he was. They were not getting rich by any means, but people there got about fifty bucks a week and all the grass they could smoke, so at least they stayed stoned (Grushkin 84).

Naturally, they were into the ballroom scene and knew

what was happening at the Fillmore and the Avalon, but they were also somewhat against the "establishment" in the Haight-Ashbury, in other words Bill Graham and the Family Dog, and did what they could to help starving artists. They distributed some pieces by Bob Fried, Stanley Mouse and Alton Kelley, and later Victor Moscoso. Like many of the artists themselves, Cummings and Louis were learning about printing as they went along. After the Summer of Love, Cummings published *Art Eureka*, a book that could serve as a reference work on posters up to that time. It proved to be a bestseller because they sold about twenty-five thousand copies. Rick Griffin generously did the cover with his habitual professionalism, and even gave him the original signed work, "To Snick from Rick" (Grushkin 83-85).

Victor Moscoso described Rick as "a very quiet fellow," but adding that at times he could become very open and "verbal" in private (Groth). He knew Rick well because they collaborated on several posters. Victor's respect for Rick is apparent, because of his accomplishments, and Rick was already a legend because of his eponymous character Murphy.

Like others in the counterculture, Victor Moscoso realized that "popularity destroys," that waves of young people going to the Haight-Ashbury would destroy the feeling of community that existed in 1966. "If there was a Summer of Love, it was 1966," he said (Groth). He also compared the Haight-Ashbury to "a goldfish pond," where before long "the sharks showed up" to devour the goldfish. When the accouterments of the psychedelic counterculture became too commercial, greed took over and what was once rare, unusual and communal became the prevailing current of thought.

Apart from his psychedelic posters for the Matrix and the Family Dog, Victor Moscoso did work for *Zap Comix*, *Rolling Stone*, along with his record album art, original art, modern posters and some work in animation. Together with Wilson, Kelley, Miller and Griffin, he was one of the pillars of psychedelic poster art in San Francisco up to the watershed Summer of Love.

Bonnie MacLean was born in Philadelphia, Pennsylvania in 1939, but she grew up in Trenton, New Jersey. She studied French at Pennsylvania State University and after graduation she moved to New York in 1960 (Lemke 71) and worked at the Pratt Institute, a private university whose main campus was in Brooklyn. At the same time, she was going to night school, taking a course in figurative drawing; but New York was not to her liking, so in 1963 she left for San Francisco. Bill Graham interviewed her for a secretarial job at Allis Chalmers in 1964, the large corporation that manufactures machinery for a wide variety of industries. Although Bonnie was pleased with her interview, Graham did not hire her because he did not like her "awful turquoise coat" (Grushkin 73). When Bonnie complained, he interviewed her a second time and she got the job. Some time later they began dating. They got married on 11 June 1967, had a son, David Graham in 1968, and got divorced in 1975 after a fairly long separation. Bonnie went back to Pennsylvania in 1972 and married the painter and sculptor Jacques Fabert. She lives in Pennsylvania today.

Apart from her figurative drawing classes, Bonnie had no other training as an artist. When Bill Graham began running Fillmore Auditorium, she was doing pretty much everything to make the dancehall run smoothly, like passing out handbills, taking tickets, or writing the names of the bands on the chalkboard upstairs.

Unlike most of the poster artists at the time, she was not into drugs, and though she said she did not feel like she really fit in, that did not seem to matter to her. In a sense, she was in the counterculture without ever really being part of it. Of course working at the Fillmore meant that she saw the most popular bands of the sixties. Donovan, the Mothers of Invention and Janis Joplin of Big Brother and the Holding Company were her favorites.

Bill Graham liked to have her working with him because she was "critical, and she was creative." Bonnie did chalk art on the billboards in a way that was informative, decorative and funny. One billboard was used to indicate the bands for the current show, another was used to promote the upcoming show (Grushkin 74).

When Bill Graham and Wes Wilson had their falling out, he urgently needed someone to do the weekly posters, a major element in the dance-concerts. Because of the way she did the chalkboards, he was sure she could do the rock posters. So Bonnie stepped in at a critical time to keep the printing presses running.

Her first poster was for the Jefferson Airplane, Pauper show on 12-14 May 1967, when young people from across the country were migrating to the Haight-Ashbury. Bonnie is listed as the artist for twenty-eight posters in the Bill Graham

Presents numbered series, a fact which attests to her importance in this artistic medium.

Having seen the posters that were produced by Wes Wilson, she learned from them, and she also developed her own personal style. One can sense the enthusiasm she exuded in the execution of her craft. Basically, she followed the general trends for poster art at the time: the artwork covered the entire sheet, a central figure or motif was used, lettering fit into shapes, and contrasting, or near contrasting colors were chosen. She also experimented with forms to find the most effective way of covering the sheet. Bonnie was mostly interested in the human face, so it became important as a vehicle for emotions suggested by subtleties of expression that evoked attitudes of the time and the place (Lemke 72). She also explored the use of motifs such as Indian totems, the dove and peace symbol (the logo for the Campaign for Nuclear Disarmament, created by Gerald Holtom), so relevant in the sixties when demonstrations protested the war. Bonnie was glad to have been part of that special time, when "emotions were real" and people knew how to live in the present. Her poster artwork is exhibited in the Fine Arts Museums of San Francisco, the San Francisco Museum of Modern Art and the Brooklyn Museum.

Although divorced, Bill Graham and Bonnie MacLean remained friends, and the Christmas before his tragic death, he gave her a very special gift: all her "original black and white Fillmore poster drawings," which she had not seen since she left (Lemke 73). Naturally, she was deeply touched.

"The posters were the branding of the counterculture," said Stanley "Mouse" Miller, "a shot heard around the world" (Lemke 91). This seems very true. They signaled a revolution, a cultural revolution that many hoped could grow and flourish. But that era in American history was fragile, and short-lived. Although the flower children wanted to make love not war–love, but not necessarily sex–the domineering parent of the establishment wanted to promote war, not love. Today, we realize how ephemeral the time was. And that aspect is reflected in and by the artwork of the posters.

Conclusion

During the summer of 1967, something very special was happening in the Haight-Ashbury district of San Francisco; and more than fifty years later it still evokes various and sundry feelings on the part of those who experienced it first hand, as well as many who have experienced the original thrill vicariously, proof that it somehow strikes an emotional chord.

Flower power was the stuff that psychedelic dreams were made of. Fantasies can be illuminating, especially when they are set side by side with reality, though reality is often more difficult to identify and understand. When trying to unscramble a movement as complex as the Summer of Love, we need to overcome the urge to believe that the things that thrilled us the most were true.

There are rare occasions when time seems to stand still, when a singular event outstrips the imagination. Dropping out became a national fantasy in the spring and summer of 1967, and all across the nation many young Americans began a pilgrimage west in quest of peace and love.

As the gurus of the counterculture well knew, dropping out was no easy task. For some it could be a spiritual act. Gautama Buddha dropped out sometime between 558 and 491 BCE. He was in his late twenties, so it is said, when he left his palace on Kanthaka, his trusty steed, to lead the life of a mendicant. But Siddhartha Gautama was unique because he attained enlightenment.

Timothy Leary gave new meaning to the expression with his catchy mantra, which was in fact an assertive political act, for it represented a *de facto* rejection of American values and a lifestyle that millions had resigned themselves to accept, though they could not bring themselves to wholly believe in it. Dr. Leary was well aware of the political nature of his dictum when he announced: "We are absolved from all allegiance to the United States government and all governments controlled by the menopausal" in his "Declaration of Evolution." It could be argued, of course, that most governments have always been controlled by the menopausal, or even perhaps that governments by their very nature are menopausal.

Although Leary's axiom became inane in the mouths of many, it was nevertheless a war dance for those who uttered the magic syllables to give voice to their defiance. The younger generation rejected a system based on exploitation, just as they rejected the Protestant work ethic, seen by many as a manipulatory scam designed to enslave a population that strangely resembled the Oceanians of George Orwell's dystopian epic *Nineteen Eighty-Four*.

As far as work was concerned, what the counterculture

rejected was its meaninglessness. Hippies wanted to enjoy what they did, but most establishment jobs were simply debilitating or downright ridiculous. Apart from selling grass, LSD and other drugs, there weren't too many ways of making a living in the Haight, so many maintained some economic ties with the system to pay the rent.

Dropping out could be dangerous, too. The characters portrayed by Dennis Hopper and Peter Fonda in *Easy Rider* dropped out, but not for long since southern rednecks, caricatures of the establishment, murdered them in cold blood after humiliating them in a greasy spoon café in Morganza, Louisiana, that was later torn down. College males risked being drafted if they dropped out of school and could be sent to fight and die in the jungles of Vietnam, where 58,217 American soldiers lost their lives for no good reason. It did not make the world or the United States safer for "democracy," a strangely ghost-like term that is often overused by our leaders, though it is as illusory today as it has ever been.

The hippie ethos was antipodal to the establishment in many ways as regards materialism, imperialism, hedonism, work, personal appearance and ecology. Of course just being in the Haight-Ashbury during the much ballyhooed hippie blast was symbolic of one's rejection of the establishment and its exploitative economic system. It was the first time anything like that had ever happened in the land of apple pie and baseball.

The hippies revered "all nature equally," and revering nature was included in the ten commandments of the counterculture. The snag was that ecology came into conflict with mass consumer society that was founded on colossal waste. The negative aspects of consumerism, among which were the distorted values of consumers and the manipulatory practices of Madison Avenue, were thoroughly analyzed by Vance Packard in his bestseller *The Waste Makers*.

Before Packard, marketing analyst Victor Lebow voiced a very different attitude in the *Journal of Retailing* in 1955 when he said "we need things to be consumed, burned up, worn out and discarded at an ever increasing pace." Much to our regret today that is exactly what happened in the fifties, sixties and beyond. An elite class got filthy rich by despoiling the planet.

For their part, modern industrialists misinterpreted Francis Bacon's idea of dominion over nature to suit their commercial and technological interests. Yet as Charles A. Reich observed, technology was a "mindless instrument" that pulverized everything that got in its way (Reich 5). This explained in part why the counterculture idealized the American Indians who lived in harmony with their environment, and why they rejected the establishment. But the war against nature in the sixties was also about ordinary, everyday greed–those who love money never have enough and those that desire wealth are never satisfied.

The Summer of 1967 was about love, too, of course. Love was all you needed! The peace and love generation liked to believe that love would be enough, but when a word becomes a cornerstone for a social movement, you need to have a clearer perception of what you mean and what you plan to do. The Diggers, as anarchists and revolutionaries, had given some thought to this and came up with the Trip without a Ticket, Free Food in the Panhandle and crash pads. But unlike many ingenuous hippies, the Diggers knew the score–that the law of the jungle always prevails in capitalist society where the haves oppress the have-nots.

Some hippies believed in an idealistic form of love similar to Saint Paul's, as expressed in his First Epistle to the Corinthians 13: 4-8: "Love is patient, love is kind; love is not jealous or boastful; it is not arrogant or rude. Love does not insist on its own way; it is not irritable or resentful; it does not rejoice at wrong, but rejoices in the right. Love bears all things, believes all things, hopes all things, endures all things. Love is eternal." But idealistic love never helped anyone to succeed in a competitive world.

For many young people, the system was the primary cause for the loss of meaning and self. This was not something that happened spontaneously for no good reason. It was built into a corrupt society that devoured your dreams, your spontaneity and your joy (Reich 7-8). The older generation no longer even tried to conceal its contempt for life, spending billions and billions of dollars to develop more efficient ways of killing, though almost nothing for joy.

Some wanted the mass media to shoulder the blame for the imbroglio of the Summer of Love. It is true that the media advertised the event considerably, both the mainstream and the underground, while rock musicians were exhorting their fans to go to San Francisco with flowers in their hair, and songwriters were imagining idyllic refrains based on the shadowy notions of peace and love. Quite naturally, many were taken in by the hype and wanted to see what was happening in hippiedom, particularly if they came from boring, colorless towns that had nothing to offer. Everybody was talking about the Summer of Love, so it's unfair to pin all the blame on a convenient scapegoat, though the media were in part responsible.

The sad fact of the matter is that there was a concerted effort to destroy the Haight-Ashbury, where Hate won the final battle with Love, a battle that was omnipresent and omnitemporal. Violence was rampant in the Haight in the fall of 1967: rape, assault, robbery, police brutality, harassment, arrests. Add to that the fact that community services were virtually inexistent and it is easy to understand why the slough of despond had gotten worse. Death of Hippie aptly depicted the scene. The feeling of community that had existed to some extent up to the Human Be-In was eroded. It was symbolic, too, that Ernesto Che Guevara was executed on 9 October 1967, with the approval of the CIA and the American government.

The *coup de grâce* in the Haight was brought about by hard drugs, essentially heroin and amphetamine. The marijuana market seemed to have dried up and the quality of LSD left something to be desired after Owsley's arrest in December 1967.

There was a noticeable surge in rural communalism as significant numbers of hippies abandoned the Haight. Those that could went to live in the country, far from the insoluble urban problems of surviving in a hostile environment. Three years later, the Weathermen abandoned formal protest and declared war on the United States.

A lot of water has gone under the Golden Gate Bridge since the summer of 1967, and the hippies from the sixties would have trouble recognizing the Haight-Ashbury today. The once modest neighborhood has become a tourist trap that excels in exploiting the legend created by the Summer of Love. You won't find Diggers dishing up stew in the Panhandle, but numerous restaurants serve everything from tandoori to veggie burritos. You won't find crash pads either, but there are hotel rooms at $130 a night.

Weekends in the Haight-Ashbury are crowded with tourists, shoppers and panhandlers. The Upper Haight, from Stanyan to Masonic, has been declared a "shopping zone," where you can buy anything from a snowboard to a two thousand dollar gown.

Every year, thousands undertake a pilgrimage to the Haight-Ashbury, often because of the original Summer of Love. But what does the expression mean today? What ghosts from the past are still haunting Haight Street?

Many early immigrants to America sought to build utopian communities, but most got sidetracked somewhere along the way and their labor remained unfinished. The psychedelic counterculture gave new verve to the utopian vision in the mid-sixties, but by the time the Summer of Love rolled around, the milk of human kindness had turned sour in the land of milk and honey.

Today, words like *utopia* conjure up wild imagery for some and a whole string of isms like fanaticism, totalitarianism, authoritarianism and so on, plus evil things like gulags and cancer. But the map is not the territory, nor is the word the thing.

We can thank Sir Thomas More for this mysterious word that means "nowhere" or "some ideal place," which, by the way, is imaginary. That need not stop us, however, from eliminating at least some suffering, hate and ignorance by showing more compassion and love, which sounds a lot like a hippie cliché. There is nothing wrong with making the world more egalitarian, with more equality in justice, government and economics. There are no utopias in our world anyway, that at least should be apparent to everyone.

There could not possibly be any harm in promoting life rather than promoting death, and making life simpler and better for most people, and not just on the other side of the world, but right here at home. Maybe we have fooled ourselves into thinking we can share in corruption without becoming corrupt ourselves, and maybe we have forgotten we are all strangers and pilgrims on the earth.

ॐ

Bibliography

Amburn, Ellis. *Pearl: The Obsessions and Passions of Janis Joplin*. New York: Time Warner, 1992.

Anthony, Gene. *The Summer of Love*. Millbrae, California: Celestial Arts, 1980.

Barber, John F. *Richard Brautigan. Essays on the Writings and Life*. Jefferson, North Carolina: McFarland, 2007.

Berkeley Barb, November 4, 1966; November 25, 1966; January 6, 1967; June 30 - July 6, 1967; July 14-20, 1967.

Blackstock, Nelson. *COINTELPRO. The FBI's Secret War on Political Freedom*. New York: Pathfinder, 2011.

Braunstein, Peter and Michael Doyle, eds. *Imagine Nation. The American Counterculture of the 1960s and '70s*. New York: Routledge, 2002.

Carlson, Evan E. *Outrageous Pamphleteers. A History of the Communication Company, 1966-1967*. Master's thesis, San Jose State University, August 2012.

Cohen, Allen, ed. *The San Francisco Oracle*, Facsimile Edition. Berkeley, California: Regent Press, 1991.

Coyote, Peter. *Sleeping Where I Fall*. Washington D.C.:

Counterpoint, 1998.

Christensen, Mark. *Acid Christ. Ken Kesey, LSD, and the Politics of Ecstasy*. Tucson, Arizona: Schaffner Press, 2010.

Demaris, Ovid. *The Last Mafioso*. New York: Bantam, 1985.

Drummond, Paul. *The Saga of Roky Erickson and the 13th Floor Elevators, the Pioneers of Psychedelic Sound*. Los Angeles: Process Media, 2007.

Echols, Alice. *Scars of Sweet Paradise. The Life and Times of Janis Joplin*. London: Virago Press, 2001.

Fahey, Todd B. "The Original Captain Trips," *High Times*, Nov. 1991, pp. 38-48, 64-65.

Fiegel, Eddi. *Dream a Little Dream of Me. The Life of 'Mama' Cass Elliot*. London: Sidgwick & Jackson, 2005.

Forte, Robert, ed. *Timothy Leary. Outside Looking In.* Rochester Vermont: Park Street Press, 1999.

Friedlander, Paul. *Rock and Roll. A Social History*. Boulder, Colorado: Westview Press, 1996.

Furlong, Monica. *Zen Effects. The Life of Alan Watts*. London: Houghton Mifflin, 1986.

Gaskin, Stephen. *Amazing Dope Tales. And Haight Street Flashbacks*. Summertown, Tenn.: The Book Publishing Co., 1980.

Ginsberg, Allen. "The Great Marijuana Hoax," *Atlantic Monthly* 218, No. 5, November 1966, pp. 104 ff.

Gitlin, Todd. *The Sixties. Years of Hope, Days of Rage*. New York: Bantam, 1987.

Graham, Bill and Robert Greenfield. *Bill Graham Presents.* New York: Doubleday, 1992.

Greenfield, Robert. "Owsley Stanley: the King of LSD," *Rolling Stone*, 14 March 2011.

– *Dark Star. An Oral Biography of Jerry Garcia.* New York William Morrow, 1996.

– *Timothy Leary.* New York: James H. Silberman, 2006.

Grogan, Emmett. *Ringolevio.* Frogmore, St. Albans: Panther, 1976.

Groth, Gary. "An Interview with Victor Moscoso," *The Comics Journal* 246, 2002.

Grushkin, Paul D. *The Art of Rock. Posters from Presley to Punk*, 2nd ed. New York, London: Abbeville Press, 2015.

Henke, James with Parke Puterbaugh, eds. *I Want to Take You Higher. The Psychedelic Era 1965-1969.* San Francisco: Chronicle Books, 1997.

Higgs, John. *I Have America Surrounded. The Life of Timothy Leary.* Fort Lee, New Jersey: Barricade Books, 2006.

Hjortsberg, William. *Jubilee Hitchhiker. The Life and Times of Richard Brautigan.* Berkeley, California: Counterpoint, 2012.

Jim Keith, *Mind Control, World Control.* Adventures Unlimited Press, September 1997.Laing, R.D. *The*

Politics of Experience. New York: Ballantine, 1974.

Lancelot, Michel. *Je veux regarder dieu en face*. Paris: J'ai Lu, 1975.

Lattin, Don. *The Harvard Psychedelic Club*. New York: HarperCollins, 2010.

Leamer, Laurence. *The Paper Revolutionaries. The Rise of the Underground Press*. New York: Simon and Shuster, 1972.

Leary, Timothy. *Flashbacks*. New York: Putnam, 1990.

Lee, Martin A. and Bruce Shlain. *Acid Dreams*. London: Pan Books, 2001.

Marks, Ben. "Psychedelic Poster Pioneer Wes Wilson on the Beatles, Doors, and Bill Graham," Collectors Weekly, 19 September 2011.

Marks, John. *The Search for the Manchurian Candidate*. New York: Viking, 1979.

McClelland, Gordon. *The Art of Rick Griffin*. San Francisco: Last Gasp of San Francisco, 25 February 2015; previously published by Paper Tiger, 1980, 2002.

McMillian, John. *Smoking Typewriters*. New York: Oxford University Press, 2011.

McNally, Dennis. *A Long Strange Trip. The Inside History of the Grateful Dead*. New York: Broadway Books, 2002.

Medeiros, Walter, "Robert Wesley Wilson," wes-wilson.com, 2005.

Miller, Timothy. *The 60s Communes. Hippies and Beyond*. New York: Syracuse University Press, 1999.

- *The Hippies and American Values*. Knoxville, Tenn.: University of Tennessee, 1991.

Pahnke, Walter N. *Drugs and Mysticism*. Ph.D. dissertation, Harvard University, June 1963.

Peck, Abe. *Uncovering the Sixties. The Life and Times of the Underground Press*. New York: Pantheon, 1985.

Perry, Charles. *The Haight-Ashbury: A History*. New York: Vintage Books, 1985.

Perry, Helen S. *The Human Be-In*. New York: Basic Books, 1970.

Perry, Paul and Ken Babbs. *On the Bus*. London: Plexus Publishing, 1991.

Phillips, John with Jim Jerome. *Papa John*. New York: Dell, 1986.

Psychedelic Review, Vol. I, No. 1, June 1963; No. 2, Fall 1963; No. 3, 1964; No. 5, 1965; No. 6, 1965; No. 7, 1966; No. 8, 1966; No. 9, 1967.

Reich, Charles A. *The Greening of America*. New York: Bantam, 1971.

Riggenbach, Jeff. "Timothy Leary's New Trip: A Reason Interveiw," *Reason*, April 1977.

Roszak, Theodore. *The Making of the Counter Culture*. New York: Doubleday, 1969.

Santelli, Robert. *Aquarius Rising. The Rock Festival Years*. New York: Delta, 1980.

Schnabel, William. *Les Années 60*, third edition. Brixey: Le Diable Ermite, March 2015.

Schou, Nicolas. *Orange Sunshine*. New York: Thomas Dunne, March 2010.

Sculatti, Gene and Davin Seay. *San Francisco Nights. The Psychedelic Music Trip 1965-1968*. London: Sidgwick and Jackson, 1985.

Scully, Rock with David Dalton. *Living with the Dead.* New York: Little, Brown & Co., 1996.

Selvin, Joel. *The Musical History Tour*. San Francisco: Chronicle Books, 1996.

Slater, Philip N. *The Pursuit of Loneliness*. Boston: Beacon, 1970.

Slick, Grace with Andrea Cagan. *Grace Slick. Somebody to Love*. New York: Time Warner, 1998.

Tamarkin, Jeff. *Got a Revolution! The Turbulent Flight of the Jefferson Airplane*. New York: Atria, 2005.

Time, "The Hippies," Vol. 90, No. 1, July 7, 1967.

Torgoff, Martin. *Can't Find My Way Home. America in the Great Stoned Age, 1945-2000*. New York: Simon & Schuster, 2004.

Troy, Sandy. *Captain Trips. A Biography of Jerry Garcia*. New York: Thunder's Mouth Press, 1994.

Watts, Alan. *The Book on the Taboo against Knowing Who You Are*. New York: Vintage, 1989.

Weil, Andrew T. "The Strange Case of the Harvard Drug Scandal," *Look*. 5 November 1963.

Yablonsky, Lewis. *The Hippie Trip*. New York: Pegasus, 1969.

Index

A

A Declaration from the Poor Oppressed People of England, 126
Abramson, Harold, 263
Acid Tests, 218, 223, 224, 276, 282, 284, 285
    dates, 282–83
Adler, Lou, 90, 91, 92, 116, 119, 244
Affirming Humanness, 168
Albers, Josef, 323
Albin Rooming House, 24, 247
Albin, Peter, 24, 25, 247, 249, 250, 251, 253
Albin, Rodney, 247
Alioto, Joseph, 195, 203
All Watched Over by Machines of Loving Grace, 156
Alpert, Richard, 32, 33, 39, 49, 55, 56, 167, 198, 268, 277, 278, 288, 292
    fired from Harvard, 291
And God Created Woman, 32
Anderson, Chester, 84, 151, 158
    rock music, 178
Anderson, Signe Ann (Toly)
    departure, 240
Andrew, Sam, 247, 248, 253
Anger, Kenneth, 182
Any Fool on the Street, 138
Artists Liberation Front, 77, 82, 128
Ashbury, Munroe, 20
Ashton, Dangerfield, 177

B

Babbs, Ken, 219, 223, 280, 282
Balin, Marty, 206, 232, 233, 234, 235, 236, 237, 238, 239, 241, 245, 310
    songwriting, 237
Bardo Thodol, 186
Bassant, Maurice, 173
Beatles, 90, 96, 106, 108, 111, 116, 165, 186, 255, 260
Beausoleil, Robert ("Bobby"), 182
Beauty and the Beast, 32
Berg, Peter, 79, 84, 92, 126, 127, 128, 137, 139, 148, 211, 225
Berkeley Barb, 47, 48, 57, 113, 130, 140, 143, 157, 189, 295, 343
    Monterey Pop, 119
Berkeley Bonaparte, 328
Bernofsky, Gene, 196
Bhaktivedanta Swami, 176
Big Brother and the Holding Company, 247–55
    after Monterey, 255
    first gig, 249
    members of the band, 247
    Monterey Pop, 99, 100
    name, 247
Big Sur, 43
bodhih, 182
Book of Revelation, 26
Booker T. and the M.G.'s, 109

Bowen, Michael, 24, 26, 32, 33, 34, 36, 38, 39, 40, 167, 169, 171, 174, 175
Branaman, Bob, 188, 189
Brautigan, Richard, 156
Brave New World, 42, 67
Brown, Edmund "Pat", 129
Brown, Jerry, 57
Brownton, Page, 188
Bruce, Lenny, 212
Buddhism, 34, 60, 65, 171, 188
Buffalo Springfield, 91, 112, 113
Burden, Eric, 96, 97
Burroughs, William, 190
　drugs, 190
Busick, Armando, 184
Butcher, Brooks, 139
BZ, 266

C

Cameron, Ewen, 264
　electroshock, 264
Canned Heat, 98
Cargill, Melissa, 272, 275
Carr, Bob, 190, 305, 306
Carter, John ("Shob"), 187
Casady, Jack, 235
　college, 236
Cassady, Neal, 280, 281, 284
Castell, Luria, 213, 214
Castillo, Elias, 18
Cheap Thrills, 99
Chief Joseph, 183
Chinmayananda, 191
chromosomal damage, 191
Cipollina, John, 104
City Lights Books, 58, 167, 173, 184
classified ads, 200
Cleaver, Eldrige, 57, 150
Cochran, Eddie, 113
Cocteau, Jean, 32

Cohen, Allen, 24, 26, 29, 32, 33, 36, 37, 163, 168, 170, 171, 173, 181, 184, 187, 192, 195, 230
COINTELPRO, 202
Colaianni, James, 150
Cold War, 263
Collier, John, 184
Coltrane, John, 250
Commedia dell'Arte, 127
Communication Company, 84, 130, 147, 152, 178, 343
conch shell, 40
Contact Printing, 306, 307
Cooke, John Starr, 34
Council for the Summer of Love, 243
Country Joe and the Fish, 45, 103, 170, 207, 256, 257
　Vanguard Records, 257
Coyote, Peter, 77, 79, 85, 92, 123, 126, 128, 148, 155
Crawdaddy, 158
Crick, Francis, 25
Crosby, David, 107, 108, 113, 233

D

Dahlstrom, Eric, 187
Davis, Clive, 95
Davis, Ronnie, 127, 128
　Fillmore, 209
Death of Hippie, 142
Demaris, Ovid, 203
Dick, Philip K., 159
Digger Do, 137
Diggers, 123–45
　Mime Troupe and, 128
　names of, 126
　responsibility, 144
dimethyl sulfoxide, 227
Dionysian Mysteries, 262
Disobey the Fascist Curfew, 169
Doherty, Denny
　Monterey Pop, 118

Donahue, Tom, 205, 259, 309
Donovan, 111
Dostoyevsky, Fyodor, 145
Drogstore Café, 24
Drop City, 72, 196, 299
Drug Abuse Control
  Amendment, 270
Dryden, John, 71
Dryden, Spencer
  Charlie Chaplin and, 239
  jazz, 239
Duncan, Gary, 104

E

East Village Other, 157
Electric Music for the Mind and Body, 257
Elliot, "Mama" Cass
  Monterey Pop, 117
Elmore, Greg, 104
English Diggers, 124, 126
Erickson, Roky, 252
Esalen Institute, 197
Everard, William, 125

F

Fabert, Jacques, 330
Fallon, Michael, 22
Faryar, Cyrus, 113
Federal Communications
  Commission
  banning songs, 237
Federal Drug Administration, 265
Ferlinghetti, Lawrence, 39, 45, 58, 174
  Fuclock, 192
Fifth Estate, 157
Fillmore Auditorium, 208
First Amendment, 173
Flashbacks, 44, 295
Food is God, 194
Foster, Paul, 218
Free Speech Movement, 165
Freiberg, David, 104

Fritsch, Bill ("Sweet William"), 92, 126, 148
Full Moon Public Celebration
  of Halloween, 138
Fuller, Buckminster, 193

G

Garcia, Jerry, 25, 114, 115, 116, 219, 221, 222, 224, 226, 227, 229, 233, 234, 245, 272, 285, 345, 348
  Acid Tests, 223
Garfunkel, Art, 97
Gavin, Arthur, 37, 38, 177
Gestefax, 152
Getz, Dave, 249, 250
Ghost Tantra, 176
Gilbert, Jack, 173
Ginsberg, Allen, 33, 39, 40, 43, 45, 52, 58, 59, 60, 61, 176, 181, 190, 216, 254, 281, 284
  biography, 247–55
Gleason, Patrick, 173
Gleason, Ralph, 93, 122, 208, 209, 259, 298
Glide Memorial Church, 78, 79, 85, 87
Golden Sardine, 184
Gottlieb, Sidney, 264, 268
Graham, Bill, 64, 93, 94, 95, 209, 211, 212, 217, 219, 226, 241, 245, 246, 303
  black performers, 212
  political protest, 212
  theatre, 211
Gray Lines, 243
Greenwich Village Trilogy, 151
Griffin, Rick, 36, 38, 177, 182, 197, 303, 317–21
Grogan, Emmett, 50, 77, 78, 79, 80, 83, 84, 86, 92, 123, 126, 128, 136, 138, 139, 144, 148, 154, 158, 169, 225
Grossman, Albert, 96, 101
Grouès, Henri, 74
Guevara, Ernesto Che, 150

Gurley, James, 247, 248, 249, 250, 251, 253

H

Haight Independent Proprietors, 77, 132
Haight Street Art Center, 303
Haight-Ashbury, 20
Hari om namah shivaya, 41
Harmon, Ellen, 213
Harrison, George, 165
Harvey, Bob, 235
Hayward, Claude, 84, 149, 150, 155, 158
Helbing, Carl, 174
Hell's Angels, 46, 85, 140, 142, 218, 229, 253, 254, 255, 282, 284
Helms, Chet, 24, 91, 98, 99, 119, 199, 209, 215, 219, 220, 221, 245, 246, 247, 251, 252, 258, 269, 277, 301, 303, 308, 312, 314, 319, 325, 326, 327
    association with Graham, 220
    concerts, 219
    The Family Dog, 246
Helms, Richard, 264, 268
Helter Skelter, 182
Hendricks, George, 141
Hendricks, Jon
    Sons and Daughters, 228
Hinckle, Warren, 149
Hite, Bob ("Bear"), 98
Hodges, Dave, 81
Hoffer, Abram, 267, 269
Hoffman, Abbie, 131
Hofmann, Albert, 43, 261, 262
    synthesized LSD, 261
Hollingsworth, Ambrose, 37, 38, 177
Holtom, Gerald, 197, 332
Honigman, Richard, 192
Hoover, J. Edgar, 202
Howl and Other Poems, 59

Hubbard, Alfred, 43, 266, 267, 268, 270, 271, 289
    biography, 266–71
Hubbard, L. Ron, 34
Huxley, Aldous, 42, 44, 287, 288, 294
Hyde, Robert, 263

I

In Search of a Frame, 130
Isaiah, 126
Isbell, Harris, 263
ISKCON, 254

J

Jagger, Mick, 97
Jefferson Airplane, 241
    American Bandstand, 242
    contacts, 236
    debut album, 237
    Fillmore Auditorium, 238
    Look magazine, 242
    Los Angeles, 239
    Monterey Pop, 109, 244
    Somebody to Love, 241
    Surrealistic Pillow, 227, 241
Johnson, Matthew, 129
Jones, Chuck, 249
Jook Savages, 318, 319
Joplin, Janis, 99, 100, 101, 112, 119, 219, 220, 225, 233, 234, 249, 251, 252, 253, 255, 258
    Monterey Pop, 99
    starting with Big Brother, 253
    Texas, 251

K

Kali, 189
Kandel, Lenore, 39, 42, 43, 79, 84, 126, 136, 172, 173
    In Transit, 180
Kantner, Paul, 109, 233, 234, 235, 236, 237, 244

Karpen, Julius, 100, 101
Katz, Gabe, 171
Katz, Matthew, 106, 236, 237, 241
    court battle with band, 237
Kaufman, Bob, 184
Kaukonen, Jorma
    Casady and, 236
Kelley, Alton, 36, 198, 213, 303, 312, 313, 315, 316, 317, 324, 327, 329, 330
Kennedy, John F., 107, 289
Kerouac, Jack, 43, 58, 59, 60, 190, 279, 280, 281
Kesey, Ken, 171, 216, 223
    arrest, 226
    biography, 277–85
    Chief Bromden, 279
    La Honda, 281
    Malcolm Cowley and, 279
    One Flew over the Cuckoo's Nest, 280
    The Trips Festival, 218
    Vic Lovell and, 278
Klein, Naomi, 265
KMPX, 259
Kolburg, Andy, 112
Kooper, Al, 103
Kot, Henry, 140
Krassner, Paul, 178
Kreutzmann, Bill
    Monterey Pop, 115
Kutner, Beverly, 96
KYA, 214

L

La Morticella, Robert, 139
Lane, Mark, 107
Las Sergas de Esplandián, 19
League of Spiritual Discovery, 172
Leary, Timothy, 171, 185
    Be-In, 43
    biography, 55–58, 285–99
    Castalia Foundation, 293
    chromosome damage, 190
    Cuernavaca, 287
    Death of Mind, 297
    dismissed from Harvard, 292
    Good Friday Experiment, 288
    Gordon Liddy and, 296
    Harvard Psilocybin Project, 288, 291
    Hollingshead and, 288
    Houseboat Summit, 55, 66, 67, 73
    IFIF, 292
    Marshall McLuhan and, 295
    Mary Pinchot and, 289
    The Psychedelic Experience, 294
LEMAR, 247
Lennon, John, 186
Lesh, Phil, 114
    Monterey Pop, 116
Levine, Steve
    Notes from the San Andreas Fault, 180
Lieberson, Goddard, 96
Linenthal, Mark, 173
Los Angeles Free Press, 157
Love Pageant Rally, 23, 24, 26, 27, 30, 33, 149, 168, 253, 276
Lucifer Rising, 182
lysergic acid diethylamide, 25, 48, 165, 191, 222, 261, 262, 270, 273, 278, 288
    CIA, 262
    experiments, 266

M

MacLean, Bonnie, 303, 330, 331, 332
MacLean, Ross, 268, 269
Mahakali, 189
Maha-lila, 70
Maitreya, 42, 43
Majestic Hall, 208
Manson, Charles, 31, 73, 182
Mantra Rock Dance, 253

Marinello, Frank, 98, 119
Marshall, James W., 19
Martha and the Vandellas, 119
Masekela, Hugh, 106, 110
McCartney, Paul, 91, 96, 107, 108, 244
McClure, Michael, 32, 39, 45, 48, 60, 84, 86, 142, 156, 168, 173, 176, 187, 225
McDonald, Country Joe, 256
McDonald, Joseph ("Country Joe"), 103
McGee, Hetty, 183
McGuinn, Jim (Roger), 107, 108
McKenzie, Scott, 94, 95, 111, 112, 118, 200
McKernan, Ron ("Pigpen"), 86
   Monterey, 115
   whiskey, 225
McLuhan, Marshall, 151, 201
McMasters, John, 35
Melody Maker, 118
Melton, Barry ("the Fish"), 256
Merry Pranksters
   goals, 282, 284
   members, 280
Metesky, George Peter, 148
Metevsky, George, 148
Metzner, Ralph, 185
Miller, Stanley Mouse, 36, 82, 314, 317, 324, 327, 329, 333
Minault, Kent, 79, 84, 126, 128, 139, 148
MK-ULTRA, 263, 267, 290
MOBE, 192
Moby Grape, 106, 207, 254, 255, 256, 257, 258
Monck, Chip, 91
Money Is an Unnecessary Evil, 130, 155
Monterey Pop Festival, 89–122
   board of directors, 91
   Diggers and, 92
   gate receipts disappear, 121
   Hell's Angels and, 98
   ticket prices, 95
Moon, Keith, 114
Morning Star Ranch, 72
Moscoso, Victor, 36, 81, 82, 83, 220, 250, 303, 321, 322, 323, 324, 325, 326, 327, 329, 330, 345
Mother's, 205
Mouse, Stanley, 36, 39, 197
Murcott, Billy, 135

N

Naropa Institute, 59
Neon Rose, 324, 326
Noble Savage, 71, 72
Nyro, Laura, 106, 108, 109

O

Ohlone, 18
On programing the Psychedelic Experience, 185
Operation Midnight Climax, 264
Orlovsky, Peter, 58
Osmond, Humphry, 266, 269
Ostin, Mo, 95

P

P.O. Frisco, 167
Pariser, Alan, 89, 90, 91
Paul Butterfield Blues, 101, 104, 105
peace symbol, 197
Peloquin, Jerry, 235
Pennebaker, Donn Alan, 93, 94, 101, 112, 245
Pentagon Rising, 192
Perry, Charles, 86
Pfefferle, Ida, 318
Pfeiffer, Carl, 263
Phillips, Jim, 180
Phillips, John, 90, 91, 94, 98, 101, 114, 117, 160, 244
Pilafian, Peter, 91

Index

Pinchot, Mary, 289
Polte, Ron, 101, 226
Powell, Ivor, 307
pradakshina, 41
Prajna Paramita Hridaya sutra, 181
Prophesy of a Declaration of Independence, 169
Puckett Academy of Dance, 220

Q

Quicksilver Messenger Service, 25, 45, 94, 101, 104, 207, 250, 274

R

Radha-Krishna Temple, 138
Ramparts, 149, 150
Rappaport, Louis, 328
Rawls, Lou, 96, 110, 111
Reagan, Ronald, 172
Red House, 144
Redding, Otis, 106, 110, 116, 212
Resnikoff, H'lane, 151, 155
Revelation of Saint John, 194
Rifkin, Danny, 92, 94, 115, 122, 224, 226
Rig Veda, 34
Ringolevio, 123
Rinkel, Max, 262
Rivers, Johnny, 90, 91, 96, 97
Rivers, Travis, 252
Robinson, Smokey, 91
Ross, Jerry, 95
Rossman, Michael, 165
Rousseau, Jean-Jacques, 71
Rubber Soul, 111
Rubin, Jerry, 34, 39, 44, 49, 131, 192
Rudhyar, Dane, 188
Rush to Judgment, 107
Ryder, Japhy, 60

S

S.S. *Vallejo*, 51
sadhu, 39, 47, 61, 175
Saint Francis, 183
San Francisco Mime Troupe
    first benefit, 209, 210
    second benefit, 210
    third benefit, 210
San Francisco sound, 259
Sandoz, 261, 262, 263, 265, 271, 272, 275, 288, 292
sattvam, 182
Sazer, Eliot, 206
Schafer, Steve, 193
Scheer, Max, 48
Schevill, James, 173
Schnepf, Bob, 183, 197
Scully, Rock, 92, 93, 115, 121, 122, 224
Seidemann, Bob, 248
Shaivism, 41
Shankar, Ravi, 111, 119, 200
Shapiro, Ben, 89
Simon, Paul, 90, 92, 93, 97, 98
Sinclair, John, 178
Sleeping Where I Fall, 123
Slick, Darby, 242
Slick, Grace, 109, 209, 240, 242, 245, 348
    first performance, 240
    Monterey Pop, 119
Snyder, Gary, 34, 36, 39, 40, 45, 52, 59, 60, 61, 73, 74, 171, 181
    biography, 59–60
    Houseboat Summit, 66
Spence, Skip, 239, 257, 258
    drummer, 235
Stanley, Owsley ("Bear"), 44, 46, 93, 108, 116, 122, 202, 217, 222, 223, 229, 254, 271, 272, 273, 274, 275, 276
    biography, 271–77
    Kesey and, 276
    Leary and, 276
Steve Miller Band, 105

Stewart, Zack, 215
Sunday Ramparts, 150, 155
Swami Prabhupada, 254, 255
Syracuse, Russ ("the Moose"), 214

T

Take a Cop to Dinner, 132
Tao Te Ching, 186
Taylor, Derek, 90, 91, 92
Technical Services Staff, 264
The 13th Floor Elevators, 251
The Association, 96
The Ballad of You and Me and Pooneil, 109
The Beard, 168
The Berry Feast, 59
The Blues Project, 112
The Brotherhood of Light, 177
The Brothers Karamazov, 145
The Buddha Mind, 188
The Butterfly Kid, 151
The Byrds, 106, 107
The Circle of Sex, 37
The Cup of Socrates, 248
The Death of Money, 140, 141
The Death of the Mind, 171
The Dharma Bums, 60
The Electric Flag, 105
The Family Dog, 212
  collaborations, 219
  name, 212
The Frame of Reference, 135
The God I Worship Is a Lyon, 176
The Grateful Dead
  710 Ashbury, 224
  concerts, 225
  contracts, 228
  debut album, 229
  drug bust, 231
  drugs, 224
  HALO, 230
  Hell's Angels, 229
  improvisation, 222
  members, 221
  Monterey Pop, 97, 115, 121
  name, 222
The Ideology of Failure, 134
The Jabberwock, 256
The Jimi Hendrix Experience
  Monterey Pop, 116
The Last Mafioso, 203
The League for Spiritual Discovery, 43, 297
The Love Book, 42, 43
The Mamas and the Papas
  Monterey Pop, 117, 118
The Matrix, 206
  bands, 207
  live albums recorded, 206
The Monkees, 116
The Paper, 157
The Print Mint, 35, 36, 131
The Psychedelic Experience, 56, 186, 294
The Psychedelic Shop, 143, 173
The Resurrection of Pigboy Crabshaw, 104
The San Francisco Oracle
  editors, 163
  issue number eight, 182
  issue number eleven, 193
  issue number five, 174
  issue number four, 171
  issue number nine, 185
  issue number one, 167
  issue number seven, 181
  issue number six, 177
  issue number ten, 189
  issue number three, 170
  issue number twelve, 195
  issue number two, 169
  name, 167
  Ron Thelin and, 164
  symbol of the Aquarian age, 177
The Seven Tongues of God, 61
The Trips Festival, 215, 306
The Who, 113, 114
Thelin, Jay, 164
Thelin, Ron, 164

Index

Thomas, William ("Superspade"), 187
Thompson, Hunter S.
   San Francisco, 238
Thornton, Big Mama, 99
Tibetan Book of the Dead, 186
Time to Forget, 130
Tomorrow Never Knows, 186
Tork, Peter, 116
Toulouse-Lautrec, Henri de, 324, 325
Towle, Jack, 213
Townshend, Peter, 113
Treaty of Guadalupe Hidalgo, 19
Tribute to Dr. Strange, 214, 215
Trip Without a Ticket, 143
Tsongas, George, 188
Turtle Island, 60

U

Uncle Tim'$ Children, 160
Underground Press Syndicate, 157

V

Vadim, Roger, 32
Valenti, Dino, 104, 312
Vishnu, 40

W

Waldman, Anne, 59
Walker, Cummings, 328
Wall, Rosalind ("Gayla"), 177
Watson, James, 25
Watts, Alan, 52, 61, 64, 181, 198, 305
   biography, 52–55
   Food is God, 194
   The Basic Myth, 179
Weir, Bob, 115, 221, 223, 224
   LSD, 225
   Monterey Pop, 97
Welles, Orson, 51
Wenner, Jann, 150
White, George Hunter, 264
Who Wants Haight Street, 156
Whole Earth Catalog, 69
Wild in the Streets, 270
Williams, Alex S., 78
Wilner, Phyllis, 140
Wilson, Brian, 91
Wilson, Wes, 36, 217, 302, 303, 304, 305, 307, 308, 309, 310, 311, 323, 324, 327, 330, 331, 332
Winstanley, Gerrard, 125
Wolf, Leonard, 173

Z

Zap Comix, 321, 327, 330
Zappa, Frank, 209
Zedong, Mao, 65, 103

Made in the USA
Middletown, DE
12 June 2021